Media Law

Media Law

A USER'S GUIDE FOR FILM AND PROGRAMME MAKERS

Rhonda Baker
S.J. Berwin & Co.
London
UK

A BLUEPRINT book
published by Routledge
London and New York

First published by Blueprint 1995
Reprinted 1997
By Routledge
11 New Fetter Lane, London EC4P 4EE
29 West 35th Street, New York, NY 10001

Typeset in 10/12pt Times by Falcon Graphic Art Limited, Surrey

Printed in Great Britain by T.J. International Ltd, Cornwall

∞ Printed on permanent acid-free text paper, manufactured in accordance with the proposed ANSI/NISO Z39.48-1992 (Permanence of Paper).

British Library Cataloguing in Publication Data
A catalogue record for this book is available from the British Library

Library of Congress Cataloguing in Publication Data
A catalogue record for this book is available from the Library of Congress

ISBN 0–415–13670–9

Contents

Introduction

This book's main title is *Media Law*. However, it does not cover all the subjects which that title might conceivably refer to, because it is aimed primarily at those who are involved in the process of film or television/ radio programme making. Other books on media law may cover topics which are relevant to the media as a whole, or to certain other sections of what is known as 'the Media', such as newspapers and magazines, journalists or broadcasters. However, although this book is restricted in one sense, it covers a wide range of legal topics, because film and programme makers are likely to encounter these topics more or less regularly in the process of developing audio-visual projects and bringing them to completion – topics such as:

- copyright;
- moral rights;
- performers' rights;
- the law relating to the making of contracts;
- basic employment law;
- tax law relevant to employment/engagement;
- defamation (libel and slander);
- trade marks;
- passing-off;
- obscenity and indecency laws;
- contempt of court;
- Official Secrets Act.

There are lengthy legal text books on many of these subjects. This book can therefore give only a broad view of them; its main purpose is not to explain the law in detail, but to explain it in **context**. In doing so, the logical approach was felt to be to start with the first legal problems and issues likely to confront an intending film or programme maker – setting up and running a company – and continue through the process of acquiring rights in literary and other material: developing and adapting that material to a point where it can be produced; raising finance for development and production and concluding agreements with financiers; contracting cast and crew; securing locations; obtaining insurance; and finally, exploiting the finished production. This approach means that the book often covers, in relation to one part of the process, a legal topic which is relevant to another part. To avoid the suggestion that any particular topic can safely be forgotten when dealing with other aspects of producing and exploiting film and television productions, cross references appear with relative frequency. If this is irritating to the reader, apologies are given in advance, but the aim is to make the book useful as a work of reference on isolated topics, as well as one which might repay full reading.

Two things need to be said about the book (the second following naturally on from the first). In the first place, since it covers such a relatively wide area, as well as trying to place its subject matter in the wider commercial context, it can be only a relatively superficial guide to the areas of law covered. Anyone involved in a particular legal problem and needing further detail on any particular aspect of the law must consult either the lengthy text books already referred to, or a lawyer. This leads on to the second point, which is that the book is no permanent substitute for a good, suitably experienced lawyer. Lawyers are expensive, and this expense is something a producer would rather spend on what he or she regards as positive steps towards the production and/or development of the project.

The point to be made is that money spent on taking legal advice **can** be a positive step – film and television production is a business and a business needs both legal and accounting advice to prosper. Legal bills are, however, a waste of money to the extent that they are for advice on topics which the client ought to have known about already. The purpose of this book is to cover as many of those topics as possible, in the sort of detail which it is hoped will enable producers and others involved in production to get an informed overview of the law as it relates to the business of producing entertainment. This may help to avoid the need to ask basic questions of lawyers and running up unnecessary bills; but ideally, it will also help to identify when it is essential to take legal advice.

Some comments should be made about the style of the book. First, while it will be a potential source of information to anyone involved in the production process (such as directors, writers, actors, etc.), it is written primarily for, and from the viewpoint of, a film or programme maker. This expression can cover individuals or companies, major film studios, broad-casting companies which make the programmes they broadcast, or independent producers of audio-visual or simply audio material. In this book, the word 'Producer' is used to describe all these possible varieties of film or programme maker, and the word begins with a capital letter to distinguish this use of it from the individual producer(s), namely the individuals who, as part of the production team, do what is necessary to see that the production is made. Additionally, because 'the Producer' will usually be a company, the neuter gender is given to it in the book. In references to individuals, the writer has attempted to use both masculine and feminine words on an equal number of occasions – although there is a rule in legal writing that references to 'he' include, where the context permits it, both 'she' or 'it', readers of the book who are not lawyers might be annoyed by consistent references to the masculine gender. If the aim of avoiding sexism has led to a certain inelegance of language, the author apologizes. There are sections of the book which focus on the position of the so-called independent producer in the UK, because independent production companies are often small entities, with fewer corporate resources than, for instance, producer/broadcasters, and so might find particularly welcome a basic guide to the laws which affect what they do. Thus, this book does not cover the legal requirements to which, for instance, broadcasters are subject (such as restrictions placed by the Broadcasting Act 1990 on cross-media ownership) unless those restrictions also affect broadcasters in the process of **producing** programmes (such as the obligation to comply with standards and codes on programme content which are laid down from time to time by the Independent Television Commission). However, some consideration is given to the position of those who finance production, if only to help the Producer to negotiate from a position of understanding. As with film and programme makers, financiers come from various different sources – they can be film studios, distributors, broadcasters, or government-financed bodies such as British Screen Finance. Once again, for the sake of convenience, they will be referred to in this book by the word 'Financier'.

The book, as it is written by an English lawyer, concentrates only on English law, and the business of producing films and television programmes in the UK, although this does involve the European perspective. When doing business abroad, other laws may become relevant and local advice will have to be taken as necessary, but this book does mention in passing when foreign laws may have to be taken into account. Incidentally, at the time of writing it has now become more usual to refer to what was the European Community ('the EC') as the European Union ('the EU'). This book uses the term EC because this term has been used for so long, that it should be immediately recognizable to anyone picking up the book and looking through it at random.

One feature of this book is that it contains examples or case studies of the principles which have been described, with a view to setting them in context. However, it must be stressed that these examples are strictly fictional. As in the wording used on so many films and programmes, 'any similarity to any real persons, events and situations is entirely unintentional and coincidental'!

Finally, the law, as well as the comments of the author on commercial practice in the production industry, reflect the position as at June 1994.

2	# The business

This chapter covers the basic areas of law which a Producer needs to know in:

- setting up and running a company;
- employing individuals.

SETTING UP A FILM OR TELEVISION PRODUCTION COMPANY

Setting up a limited company is a step that many sole traders or partners take when their business grows or when they want a self-contained business vehicle for a particular project or venture. There are a number of benefits which arise from forming a company. These stem from the concept that, in the eyes of the law, a company is a 'person', distinct from its shareholders and directors. The main benefits are **tax benefits** and **limited liability**.

Tax benefits

A company is taxed differently from a sole trader or a partnership. A sole trader pays income tax on profits and capital gains tax on capital gains. A partnership pays tax similarly, but profits and gains are amalgamated together. A company, however, pays only one tax on both profit and gains. This tax is known as corporation tax.

The rates of income tax and capital gains tax are different from corporation tax rates. They are also assessed and payable at different times. This usually means that a profitable company is likely to pay less tax than if the same business was being run by a sole trader or as a partnership and was subject to the income tax and capital gains tax rules.

Limited liability

The benefit of limited liability is especially relevant in cases where a company is established for a particular project or kind of work which carries some degree of risk. As a company has separate legal personality, it is not only the owner of the business, but it is legally responsible for the debts and liabilities of the business.

Its shareholders, the people who provide the company with capital by buying its shares, are only liable for the debts of the company to the amount outstanding (if any) on the shares they own. Normally, in a private company, shares are fully paid for and therefore no further money is payable by the shareholders to the company. This means, then, that the most a shareholder can lose is the value of its shareholding. The company, on the other hand, has unlimited liability for its debts and, if it is unable to pay them, it could become insolvent.

Sole traders and partners also have unlimited liability for the debts of their business. The difference here, of course, is that the liability is **personal**. In the case of a partnership, the liability of each partner is 'joint and several' so one partner could end up having to pay the debts of the whole partnership if the other partners do not have enough money to pay their due share or are not available to be sued.

Investment benefits

A further benefit is the increased likelihood of attracting investors. If investors wish to participate in a company by buying its shares, they restrict their financial risk to the amount of their investment. For this reason, it is usually easier for a company to raise money than a partnership. A person is much more likely to put a finite sum into a business than to risk the potential nightmare of joint and several liability involved in becoming a partner.

A further advantage in this respect is that people tend to assume that a company is more 'reputable' than a business run by a sole trader or partnership. Because of this perceived higher status, a company is often viewed as being more 'established' and likely to be able to pay its debts. There is some truth in this view. Often, companies are formed when a business starts becoming more profitable. Also the burden of complying with accounting and administrative formalities is greater than that imposed on a sole trader or partnership and the financial results of a company are open to public inspection.

One further investment benefit is that banks are often more willing to lend money to a company. Unlike sole traders or partnerships, companies can create a 'floating charge' over their assets, which is a special type of charge over their property as security for their borrowings. (Chapter 6, pages 99–100, describes how charges operate.)

Despite these benefits, however, banks commonly also ask for personal guarantees from the directors of the company to protect their loans to the company (in addition to a charge over the company's property). This is more likely if a large amount is borrowed or the company has few assets or no trading history. Such personal guarantees make the director **personally liable** to the extent of the guarantee. The amount covered by the guarantee should be the maximum personal contribution which the director will have to make towards the company's debts, unless he has acted fraudulently or otherwise improperly in breach of certain provisions of the various Companies Acts.

Other consequences of forming a company

There are a number of other advantages in forming a company. These include the separation of **ultimate control** of the company, which is done through its shareholders, and the **day-to-day running of the business** which is done by the directors. Often, the directors are the main shareholders, but they are treated as separate people in law. This allows passive investors to exercise control of the business through the composition of the board of directors, yet enables them not to become involved with the actual business management of the company if they so desire.

Finally, further benefits include name protection for a business (as no company name may be registered if the same name is already on the register of companies) and additional tax incentives, especially in relation to pensions and business related benefits, such as company cars.

There are some **disadvantages** in forming a company. There is the need for registration. Additionally, there are continuing formalities relating to accounting and other administration, all of which are open to public scrutiny. Also, the business being carried on belongs to the company and not the individuals themselves. This sometimes causes a problem for directors who are also shareholders. In this case, it is very important for them always to be aware of the capacity in which they are acting. The duties which a director owes to a company are different and much more onerous than those of a shareholder. Depending on which 'hat' is being worn dictates the formalities to be complied with and the procedures to be followed.

Formation and 'off the shelf' purchases

Once the decision to operate a business as a company has been taken, the next step is to actually form one or buy one. A company is **formed** by filing certain registration documents and a fee with Companies House. The main registries are in Cardiff, Belfast and Edinburgh although there are also branches of these registries around the country (for example in London). When the Registrar of Companies issues a Certificate of Incorporation, the company comes into existence and can commence trading. The 'new born' company is given a registration number which remains constant throughout its existence, even if it changes its name.

A company can be formed in a few weeks (or even days). It is an exercise probably best left to a solicitor or a company formations agent such as Jordan & Sons Limited. The cost of incorporation, if carried out by a company formations agent is, at the time of writing, in the region of £150–£200. They will deal with the initial administration and send a pack which will include the company books (a set of registers each company must have), a seal and several copies of the Memorandum and Articles of Association (the constitutional documents of the company). It is possible to incorporate a company in a day, but Companies House charge a higher fee and the total cost is more likely to be in the region of £400.

As an alternative to formation, one can buy a 'ready-made' or 'off the shelf' company. These are companies which have already been incorporated, but which have never traded. They can be bought from a solicitor or accountant (who sometimes keep stocks) or from a company formations agent. The cost will be the same, except that it will probably be necessary to change the name of the company to something more suitable (as 'ready-made' companies tend to have very uninspiring names!). Currently, a fee of £50 is levied by Companies House to register a change of name.

A 'ready-made' company is a good option if the company is needed urgently. It can commence trading immediately and any changes to the Memorandum and Articles or any administrative matters can be carried out as and when required (as described below). However, it is important to check when buying such a company that the company has not traded previously. If it has, the person buying the company will be taking on any existing liabilities that the company may have.

What's in a name?

There are a number of rules relating to the choice of names for a company. A company's name (which does not have to be the same as the name under which the company trades) has to contain the word 'Limited' or 'Ltd'. Furthermore, it cannot be the same as any name which appears on the index of companies' names at Companies House, it cannot be offensive and its use must not be a crime.

There are also some 'sensitive' words, such as 'international', which can only be used if the company meets certain criteria.

There is another potential problem with names which may arise if a name is similar to a name which already appears on the companies index. The new name will not be refused registration, but an existing company may object to the Secretary of State for Trade and Industry within 12 months of the name appearing on the index. The grounds of the complaint will be that the new name is 'too like' its own and the Secretary of State can, if he agrees, order the other company to change its name. Alternatively, the company could bring a legal action for 'passing-off'. (Chapter

14, pages 239–41). Whether or not the objection or the legal action will succeed will depend on a number of factors including:

- how similar the names are;
- whether the companies operate in the same field of business and area;
- whether the public are or could be confused.

The Memorandum and Articles of Association

The **constitution** of a company is known as the Memorandum and Articles of Association. Every company must have these documents. The Memorandum sets out certain information relating to the company itself and it must contain five clauses.

The **first** clause states the name of the company, and the **second** a statement of where the registered office of the company is to be located (either England and Wales, Scotland or Northern Ireland).

The **third** clause is a statement of the company's objects. These are the purposes and activities for which the company was incorporated and the company cannot do anything which is not permitted by this clause. For this reason, the objects clause is usually very widely drafted and split into many paragraphs. The clause generally begins with a statement of the 'main' objects of the company (for example, the usual activities carried out by a film production company) and then lists many ancillary activities which a company may need to undertake in order to carry out its business. These include such things as the power to lend or borrow money, buy land and invest company money.

The **fourth** clause of the memorandum states that the liability of the shareholders is limited, and the **fifth** and final clause sets out the authorized share capital of the company.

The authorized share capital represents the amount of money that can be raised by the company through the issue and sale of shares. Shares have a nominal (or par) value (often £1) and they may not be sold for less than the nominal value. They may, however, be sold for more. Most 'ready-made' companies have an initial authorized share capital of £1000. This can be altered, if necessary, if more money is to be raised by way of share issue. The minimum number of shares which need to be issued by a private company is two. Many companies do actually trade with only two issued shares and capital is then raised by other means, such as loans.

The **Articles of Association** are the rules and regulations of the company. They set out the way the directors and the shareholders should act and cover such matters as the appointment and removal of directors, the issue and transfer of shares and the procedure for calling and holding meetings.

Directors and secretary

On incorporation, a company will need at least one director and a company secretary. A director can also be the secretary unless he or she is the sole director. Directors are the persons who look after the affairs of the company on a day-to-day basis and generally manage its business. Ultimately, the shareholders of the company decide the identity of the directors. Directors owe certain duties to the company and are responsible to it. The Companies Acts lay down rules to regulate the behaviour of directors (in addition to the restrictions imposed by the Articles) to prevent directors from abusing their position of trust.

Normally, the board of directors can appoint other directors (although not dismiss them). The shareholders can both appoint and dismiss.

Often, in small companies, the directors and shareholders are the same people. The company is just another structure through which a business is carried out. However, as companies get bigger or director/shareholders disagree or fall out, directors who hold less than 50% of the issued shares could find themselves removed from office and hence from the management of the company. If there are a number of co-investors who take shares and also wish to be (and remain) directors, it is worth addressing this issue early on. It is possible for directors to protect their position by having a clause in the Articles giving them weighted voting rights if a resolution to dismiss them (or to appoint a number of additional directors to 'swamp' the board) is proposed.

The company secretary has a much less onerous task. The secretary is basically the administrative officer of the company, whose job it is to comply with the Companies Acts' provisions relating to the keeping of registers and keeping the company's affairs open to the public. Usually, the company secretary is responsible for the filing of documents with Companies House. In a private company there are no special qualifications required to be a company secretary.

In a 'ready-made' company, the first director and secretary are often the employees (or nominee companies) of the company formation agents. When the company is taken 'off the shelf', these officers resign and new director(s) and secretary must then be appointed.

Registered office

Each company must have a registered office. It does not have to be a trading address. It is required for the service of legal documents and Companies House correspondence and some of the company's registers must be kept there for inspection by the public. Often, the address of the company's solicitors or auditors is given as the registered office, and this address must appear on the writing paper and any order forms of the company.

A registered office cannot be a post office box number, although it can be a residential address, such as the home of a director, the secretary or a shareholder. However, a word of warning: there may be legal constraints on a person using his/her home for business purposes, such as a restrictive covenant in the title deeds, restrictions in the mortgage on business use, or planning restrictions. It could be argued that no business activity is actually carried on from that address, but legal advice should be taken to clarify this point before adoption of a residential address as the registered office.

First board meeting

Once a company has been established and it is ready to start trading, it is usual to hold a board meeting to deal with various administrative matters. The company will probably want to open a bank account and appoint auditors. Also, new directors may be appointed, the registered office changed or shares issued. At this time, it is also usual to hold a shareholders' meeting in order to make any amendments to the Memorandum or Articles of Association to make sure that everything is in order prior to the first steps of the new company into trading.

EMPLOYMENT

Once a business is established and begins to trade, it will need to employ workers and employment law issues will undoubtedly arise. A great deal of legislation governs the relationship between employer and employee. This area of law is complex and is constantly being updated. If employment problems become apparent, it is always advisable to obtain professional advice from an employment expert.

Employee status

When workers are taken on by a business, the first thing to ascertain is whether they actually are working as employees of the business (under an employment contract), or working as independent or freelance contractors (under a consultancy agreement). The distinction is important for several reasons. First, an employee will pay income tax under the PAYE scheme, where tax is deducted at source by the employer who is responsible for its payment to the Inland Revenue. In contrast, an independent contractor will be responsible for his own tax returns. Second, any employment protection provided by statute (including unfair dismissal, redundancy and health and safety legislation) is only available to an employee. A third reason is the risk to the employer of being 'vicariously liable' for his employees. Under this rule, an employer can be liable for loss and damage caused by his employees to other persons if caused during the course of their employment.

Whether a worker is an employee or an independent contractor is a question of law. One approach taken by the courts is to consider whether the work done by the worker is an integral part of the business. If the business could not survive without him, he is obviously likely to be considered an employee rather than an independent contractor.

The courts also consider the amount of control the employer has over the worker, to provide an indication as to the worker's status. The greater the degree of control that the employer exercises over the way in which the worker carries out his or her tasks, the more likely it is that the worker will be an employee.

The modern approach which the courts use to decide the status of a worker is known as the 'multiple test'. Using this test involves taking a number of factors into consideration. The most important of these factors are set out below.

- **Remuneration** – an employee is likely to receive 'wages' or 'salary' as opposed to a 'fee' for his work.
- **Premises** – an employee is more likely to perform his services on the employer's premises than his own.
- **'Distinct calling'** – if the worker is holding himself out to be in a 'business of his own' he is likely to be classed as an independent contractor.
- **Provision of equipment** – an independent contractor would be reasonably expected to bring his own tools required for the job.
- **Hours of work** – the independent contractor would often be in a better position than the employee to choose his own hours of work.
- **Duration** – the typical independent contractor is hired for a specific task. Once this is completed, he is no longer engaged. The employee, however, is usually contracted for an indefinite period, to accomplish several consecutive and often concurrent tasks.
- **Express terms** – the express terms of the contract itself are a relevant factor to consider, and weight is given to them. They are not, however, conclusive. It is common in the entertainment industries to give 'short-term contracts', and a declaration in the contract that the worker is 'self-employed' is in no way conclusive (Chapter 8, page 128).
- **National Insurance and income tax** – the employer must deduct National Insurance for all employees as well as income tax under the PAYE scheme. Thus, whether or not the employer pays tax and National Insurance contributions on behalf of his workers will be a relevant factor.

If an employee is wrongly regarded by the employer as an independent contractor, the employer may find himself liable for back-payment of a large income tax bill and accumulated National Insurance contributions. The Inland Revenue like to be sure of a taxpayer's status. This can be seen from a recent case [*Hall (Inspector of Taxes)* v *Lorimer* (Simons Tax Cases [1993] 23) (November 1993)] decided in the Court of Appeal, where a freelance vision mixer was held to be an independent contractor. This view was taken despite the fact that he worked at the production company's studios, had no control over working hours or engagement length, ran no financial risk, provided no equipment and hired no staff.

The Court of Appeal held that there is no single path to obtaining a 'correct' decision. Furthermore, an approach which was appropriate in one case, may not be helpful in another. In this particular case, the question as to whether the individual was in business on his own account was considered to be of little assistance. More important factors were the duration of the engagement and the number of other people by whom the individual was engaged. A more traditional approach was followed here, under which the significant factor was the extent to which the individual was dependent on or independent of a particular paymaster.

Following this approach, a cameraman who is employed full-time and works consistently for the same employer on different 'shoots' may well be considered an employee. Conversely, a person engaged to provide casual labour on a daily basis, and who may work for other 'employers' on those days when his services are not requested, is more likely to be treated as an independent contractor. Clearly, this is a grey area and any decision of either the Inland Revenue or the Courts will depend on the specific facts of each particular case.

The employment contract

A contract of employment does not necessarily have to be in writing although, as with any contract, this is a good idea, especially for senior employees. In any event, all employees working eight hours a week or more are entitled to receive a **written** statement of the **main** terms of employment from their employer within the first two months of their employment.

The statement of terms, known as a 'Section 1 statement' (as it was first required by Section 1 of the Employment Protection (Consolidation) Act 1978), must contain certain information. The information required is now listed in the Trade Union Reform and Employment Rights Act 1993. Any employee who has a statement provided under previous legislation may request a written statement in the new form at any time until three months after his employment ends. Written statement forms are available at legal stationers. The details now required in the statement include:

- the names of the employer and employee;

- the date of the commencement of the employment and the date on which the employee's period of 'continuous employment' began (the period of 'continuous employment' is important in determining whether the employee has certain statutory rights and **may** include employment with a previous employer);
- the rate of remuneration (or method of its calculation) and the frequency of payment;
- all terms and conditions relating to the hours worked, holiday entitlement and holiday pay, and incapacity for work due to sickness and/or injury including any provisions for sick pay;
- details of pensions and pension schemes (if any) together with a statement as to whether a contracting-out certificate is in force;
- the respective lengths of notice to be given/received in order to terminate the contract of employment;
- the job title (or a brief description of the work);
- the place(s) of work and details relating to working abroad if the employee will have to work outside the United Kingdom for more than a month;
- where the employment is not intended to be permanent, the period for which it is expected to continue, or if it is for a fixed term, the date when it is to end;
- details of any collective agreements which directly affect the terms and conditions of the employment (including the relevant parties to them);
- details of disciplinary and grievance procedures.

It is also possible to refer to and/or incorporate other documents into the statement for terms relating to sickness, sick pay, pensions and disciplinary procedure. These must be reasonably accessible to the employee or he must have a reasonable opportunity to read such documents. As a matter of practice, it is preferable to give all employees a brief letter or contract setting out their main terms and conditions of employment. This ensures certainty and clarity. Employers of more than a few people should also prepare a standardized staff handbook and incorporate it into the employment contract. The staff handbook could deal with most employment issues in greater detail and also have sections on pensions, sickness, sick pay, disciplinary and grievance procedures, etc.

For more senior employees and certainly for senior executives, a written service agreement is usually prepared. This will go much further than the simple statement of terms and conditions. It is usually to the employer's advantage to have a written Service Agreement which should be drafted to allow maximum flexibility as well as encompassing matters such as confidentiality, restrictive covenants, deductions from salary and 'garden leave' provisions (namely, remaining away from work on paid leave pending investigation of disputes). The executive in question should, for example, be required to travel on business if this is required, to change job location if the company should move its offices (within reason) and to work such hours as may be necessary to fulfil his/her duties without additional remuneration.

Other considerations

There are a number of other considerations about which an employer must be aware. These include the following.

Health and safety at work

There is a considerable amount of legislation which applies to employers to protect the health and safety of employees at work premises. This covers a vast range of work scenarios and the requirements for a particular business will depend on the nature of the business carried on. Basically, an employer is required to take reasonable care to ensure the safety of all its employees and ensure that the staff it employs are competent. It must also make sure that the premises and the machinery, materials and plant provided are adequate, that there are proper work systems in place and employees are suitably supervised.

Social security contributions

An employer must pay social security contributions on its own behalf and also on behalf of its employees.

Insurance

Every employer carrying on business in Great Britain is obliged to maintain insurance against liability for any bodily injury or disease sustained by employees and arising out of and in the course of their employment. An employer should also consider various other kinds of insurance such as fire and theft, public liability, motor and business travel. The range of insurance required will vary according to the type of business carried on by the employer.

Rights of employees

There is extensive legislation to protect employees from discrimination. There are four main forms of prohibited discrimination – direct, indirect, victimization and segregation. Discrimination could be on grounds of **sex** or **marital status**, **race**, **nationality**, **colour** or **ethnic origins** and **trade union membership**. The scope of unlawful discrimination is very wide and covers every stage of employment including recruitment. Therefore, an employer must be careful not to discriminate when advertising for new employees, or when interviewing them, or when promoting existing employees.

It is also important for the employer to be aware of employees' rights relating to pregnancy and maternity leave, sickness, holidays and the legislation protecting employees from unfair dismissal and redundancy.

Dismissal

An employment contract may be terminated in several ways. For example, by mutual agreement, by expiry of a fixed term, by resignation of the employee or by dismissal by the employer.

An employee who has been employed for a fixed term would normally be entitled to claim unfair dismissal or redundancy pay on its expiry without being renewed, since that is included within the statutory definition of dismissal. This right is, however, excluded if, before the term expires, the employee has agreed in writing to exclude any right to redundancy payment or unfair dismissal on expiry. The fixed term contract has to be for a minimum period of two years to be able to contract out of any right to redundancy payment and for a minimum of one year to be able to contract out of the right to an unfair dismissal claim. The contracting out of the employee's right only applies where dismissal is on the 'expiry of the term' not if it occurs beforehand or for some other reason.

Dismissal can be actual or constructive. Mutual trust and confidence is an extremely important aspect of the employment relationship. A breakdown of mutual trust and confidence may allow the employee to argue that the employment relationship has come to an end. This may be obvious from statements made by the employer or by the employer's conduct. Such an act of or statement by the employer which breaches the implied term of mutual trust and confidence enables the employee to resign and treat himself as constructively dismissed and claim unfair and wrongful dismissal. Additionally, any other **fundamental** breach by the employer of an employment contract term, whether an express or implied term, would also entitle the employee to resign and claim that he was constructively dismissed. As circumstances of constructive dismissal are usually not planned by the employer, the dismissal will almost always be procedurally unfair and result in a finding of unfair dismissal.

Claims available to a dismissed employee

Generally, the three claims available to an employee who has been dismissed by his employer are:

- wrongful dismissal;
- unfair dismissal;
- redundancy.

As mentioned above, only an employee (and not an independent contractor) is entitled to the statutory protection offered by the unfair dismissal and redundancy legislation (and only then if certain conditions are met). An independent contractor will only have a claim for damages for breach of contract.

Wrongful dismissal

This is a contractual claim where the employee claims damages to compensate for the loss suffered as a result of the employer's breach of the employment contract. Clearly, the employee must show that the employer was in fact in breach of the contract. This will involve careful consideration of the terms of the contract, and the reasons for, and manner of, the dismissal. Where the contract still has a substantial period to run, the amount of damages awarded may be quite large. On the other hand though, the employee has a duty to 'mitigate' his loss (for instance, by taking reasonable steps to find other employment).

Where the employee is not able to show that the employer was in breach of the employment contract, he may still be able to exercise his statutory rights and obtain some form of compensation. For example, he may be entitled to relief in the form of a redundancy payment, or to compensation for unfair dismissal provided he has (amongst other things) more than two years' continuous employment service.

Wrongful dismissal claims are brought in the County Courts or, if for sums more than £50 000, in the High Court. Proceedings may be commenced at any time within six years after the breach, in contrast to statutory claims for unfair dismissal which must be brought three months after the dismissal, or redundancy pay which must be brought within six months. Generally, statutory claims, although usually for a smaller amount, are heard sooner than wrongful dismissal claims. In addition, Industrial Tribunals are usually more relaxed about the nature and form of the evidence that they will agree to hear.

Statutory claims

In addition or as an alternative to a claim for damages for wrongful dismissal, an employee may have a statutory claim for **redundancy** pay and/or **unfair dismissal**. These claims are brought before an Industrial Tribunal (as opposed to a court). An unfair dismissal claim must be presented within three months of the employee's dismissal and a redundancy claim within six months. The employee is under no obligation to show a breach of contract on the part of the employer, but must satisfy the Tribunal that:

- he is an employee (rather than an independent contractor); **and**
- his continuous period of employment (as defined by law) is at least two years.

An employee will have no right to an award if he has attained the normal retiring age (maximum of 65 years).

Unfair dismissal

Once an employee has shown he has been dismissed, he will have a legitimate claim for unfair dismissal unless the employer can show that the dismissal was **not** unfair. The employer must show that:

- the dismissal was for a 'fair reason'; **and**
- it acted reasonably in dismissing the employee for that 'fair reason'.

There are five **fair** reasons, namely:

- reasons relating to the capability or qualifications of the employee for performing work of the kind which he was employed to do (namely, the employee is physically or mentally incapable of doing the job);
- reasons relating to the conduct of the employee (namely theft, dishonesty, violence, etc.);
- redundancy (as defined below);
- that the employee could not **legally** continue to work in the position held (for example, a driver who has had his licence disqualified);
- some other substantial reason of a kind such as to justify the dismissal.

'Some other substantial reason' may include, for example, the reorganization of the business which may not necessarily lead to a redundancy situation but leads to the dismissal of certain employees.

If the employer can establish one of these five fair reasons, it must then go on to prove that it acted reasonably and that the dismissal was, in all the circumstances, fair. The employer should always follow a fair and detailed procedure. What amounts to a fair procedure will depend on the reason for the dismissal and the circumstances of each case. However, as a general rule, and particularly in cases involving conduct and capability, an employee should be:

- warned;
- consulted;
- allowed to present his point of view;

- given the opportunity to respond to any allegations;
- allowed an employee of his choice to be present at any hearing;
- allowed the right of appeal against the decision to discuss.

When an Industrial Tribunal finds that a complaint of unfair dismissal is well founded it may make an order for the reinstatement or re-engagement of the employee or (more usually) an order for compensation. In practice, a Tribunal will order compensation. Reinstatement or re-engagement is only ordered in 1–2% of cases.

When the Tribunal makes an award for compensation for unfair dismissal the award will consist of two parts, a 'basic award', calculated in the same way as a redundancy payment (described below), and a 'compensatory award'.

The compensatory award is an amount which the Industrial Tribunal considers 'just and equitable' in all the circumstances, having regard to the loss sustained by the employee and the consequences of dismissal, to the extent that this loss is attributable to action taken by the employer. It includes expenses reasonably incurred by the employee as a consequence of dismissal and the loss of any salary and benefits which the employee might reasonably have suffered but for the dismissal. A Tribunal also takes into account the likelihood of the employee finding alternative employment. The maximum amount of the compensatory award is currently £11 000.

If an order for reinstatement or re-engagement is made but the employer refuses to comply with it, unless the employer can satisfy the Tribunal that it was not practicable to comply with the order, the Tribunal will award the complainant additional compensation over and above the basic and compensatory awards to the extent necessary fully to reflect the sums which would have been payable under its original order.

Redundancy

The right to a redundancy payment is only given to an employee who has been continuously employed for a period of two years. At the date of termination, the employee must be aged 18 or over and be less than 65 or the normal retiring age in the business in which the employee works.

To be entitled to a redundancy payment, the employee must show that there has been a dismissal. In addition, the dismissal must have been made on the grounds of 'redundancy'. If the fact of dismissal is proved there is a presumption that the reason for dismissal is redundancy. Once the employee has shown that there was a dismissal, the employer is obliged, in order to avoid the redundancy payment, to show that the dismissal was for a reason other than redundancy.

Redundancy is a term defined by statute law, but is, in essence, a dismissal which is mainly attributable to one of three sets of circumstances.

- The employer has ceased (or intends to cease) to carry on the business **for the purposes** for which the employee was employed by it (for example, a manual job is computerized).
- The employer has ceased (or intends to cease) to carry on the business **in the place** where the employee was so employed (for example, the factory closes).
- The employer ceases to require the employee to carry on work **of a particular kind** (for example, diminishing orders or commissions).

If the employee is successful in his claim, the payment awarded to him will be calculated in accordance with a statutory formula, based on the number of years he has been working for that employer, his age and his weekly wage (subject to a maximum (currently) of £205).

The receipt of a redundancy payment will not prevent the employee from pursuing a claim in damages, nor affect the extent of those damages, for wrongful dismissal.

Where the employer proposes to dismiss 100 or more employees as redundant within 90 days or less, or 10 or more employees as redundant within 30 days or less, he must inform the Secretary of State for Employment of his intention at least 90 days or 30 days respectively before the first dismissal is to take effect. There is no need to notify the Secretary of State when it is proposed to make fewer than 10 employees redundant. Failure to notify can result in a conviction.

In addition, in circumstances where the employee proposes to make collective redundancies and recognized trade unions are involved, then the trade union(s) must be consulted as early as possible and where more than 10 **or** 100 employees are to be made redundant at any one place then such trade union(s) must be consulted at least 30 **or** 90 days (respectively) before such redundancies take effect. The consultations must be genuine and 'with a view to reaching agreement'.

3 The idea

PROTECTING AN IDEA WHEN PRESENTING IT TO OTHERS

Every film or television project begins with an idea. That idea may be to adapt some existing material, such as a novel or short story, or even to develop a story suggested by a popular song. In this case, the Producer will need to identify whether the existing material is protected by copyright. As a rough guide, it will be, if the person who wrote it is still alive or has been dead for less than fifty years (or seventy years – page 22). (However, the law of copyright is very complex and in using pre-existing material, it is often wiser to assume that it is protected by copyright until this has been definitively proved otherwise.) If the Producer's idea involves adapting another copyright work then Chapter 5, *Development*, gives a guide to acquiring the necessary rights in that work.

This chapter considers the protection of new and original ideas or 'formats'. Anyone in the film or television industries is familiar with the problems which Producers encounter almost as soon as they devise that brilliant new idea for a film or television series. In the case of a dramatic project, practically the only way to bring the idea to fruition is to write a script from which a film or television series can be made. However, scripts cost money and the average Producer with a new project does not generally have the spare cash to pay a writer. Even if cash is available, it is not a sensible investment to make, until the Producer has found out whether the idea or format will ultimately be of interest to anyone with enough money to finance production. If it is not going to attract that kind of interest, it will be a waste of money and the scriptwriter's time to proceed.

So the time-honoured practice of Producers with new ideas or formats is to go and sell them to potential Financiers (known as 'pitching an idea'). The hope is that the project so excites the audience that the Producer will receive a commitment to finance the writing of a treatment or script by the Producer's chosen writer (and/or to pay for the cost of the preparation of the budget, production schedule, the scouting of locations and all the other preparations which need to be made before production can commence). On the basis of the script and the budget, the potential Financier will eventually make a decision.

The Producer may therefore be 'pitching' to a variety of people – television broadcasters, other larger production companies (which have cash resources to finance developments), or even Hollywood Studios if the Producer is a sufficiently serious contender to be invited into those kinds of circles. But even in Hollywood, new and original ideas are not that common, as a brief survey of the output of Hollywood Studios at any one time will show. Lack of inspiration is not confined to Hollywood either. A Producer has to face the fact that whenever it is trying to sell an idea, there are three possible outcomes. The best is that the idea meets with approval and the Producer gets an agreement to pay to develop it all or part of the way to production stage; the usual result is that the audience regretfully passes on the idea. But the third is the worst: the idea is apparently rejected, but mysteriously something very like it is subsequently produced by or with the involvement of the person or persons to whom the Producer 'pitched' it. When the Producer protests, it may be told that the idea was similar to one already on the stocks or, even more galling, that 'there is no copyright in an idea'.

So how does the Producer protect itself and the idea when revealing it to others, as the Producer must do to get it financed?

The answer is to do everything possible to make sure that the idea is encapsulated or represented in some form which is **legally protectible** as property. For example, though a mere idea in an individual's mind will not be protectible by copyright law, the individual may be able to express it in some form which will in itself attract copyright protection (page 23). Alternatively (but less likely) the creator of the idea may be able to claim trade mark protection for a phrase, logo or design which is an integral part of the idea itself. (See Chapter 14, *Secondary exploitation*, in relation to merchandising and format sales.) If the idea or format cannot be expressed in a form which attracts copyright, the creator may still be able to protect it by an agreement with those to whom the material is revealed, requiring them to treat the subject of the presentation as confidential. Then if that confidentiality is not respected, the creator may be able to take legal action for breach of confidence. The law of copyright and breach of confidence, and how to establish these rights is discussed here. (See Chapter 15, *Legal proceedings*, for what is available to those whose rights are violated or infringed.) However, there is a practical point to be made about taking action when legal rights are infringed, and it is particularly relevant in the context of starting off with a new project – the fact that it is possible to sue someone when they have stolen an idea is no great consolation if there is no money to finance legal action. In those circumstances, the best protection that the law can give is to operate as a deterrent. By making it clear to others that the creator of a project has legally enforceable rights, the creator will be less likely to have any trouble. It is therefore up to those who devise and hope to develop production projects to know what their rights are and to make others aware of this.

COPYRIGHT AND HOW IT WORKS

The purpose of copyright law is to encourage and reward authors, composers, artists, designers and other creative people who take the risk of exposing their works to the public.

This is done by giving to the author of the copyright work certain exclusive rights to enjoy the benefit of it for a certain limited time, usually the life of the author plus fifty years. However, within the EC, the period of protection is, within the next few years, going to be increased to the life of the author plus **seventy** years as part of the EC's moves to harmonize copyright law throughout the Community. This increase may mean that some works, which had ceased to be protected by copyright, may come back into copyright when the EC Directive on the term of copyright protection is brought into force in the UK.

The word 'author' is used in the sense of the 'maker' of a creative work, and therefore it can apply to anyone who has created a work of copyright, of which there can be several different kinds.

When the term of copyright expires, the work is said to fall into the public domain, and then anyone can use it without permission.

Copyright is a right to **stop** others from doing something – it operates as a purely negative right.

Legislation

Copyright law in the United Kingdom derives from the Copyright, Designs and Patents Act 1988. However, the Copyright Act 1956, and some of the law before that, is relevant, as copyright can last a long time and the law in force at the time of creation of the copyright may be relevant to that copyright.

There are various types of material which are capable of copyright protection, and the legislation refers to them all collectively as 'copyright works'.

'Copyright works' consist of:

- **original** literary, dramatic, musical and artistic works;
- sound recordings, films, broadcasts and cable programmes;
- the typographical arrangement of published editions.

Anything not in these categories is not copyright. However, the categories are very wide, since, for example, 'literary works' will include telephone directories, statistics tables and computer programs. Artistic works are defined as 'graphic works', photographs, sculptures or collages (irrespective of artistic quality), and therefore this includes engineering drawings, photographs and buildings. Television programmes and video tapes are in the category of 'films', so in copyright terms the word 'film' will cover any audiovisual production regardless of the medium for which it was originally produced.

A mere idea (such as the basic story or plot for a film or television programme) is not within the protected categories. The idea must first be recorded in some kind of material form (in writing or otherwise), but as soon as it is, it *may* be protected as a literary work. However, copyright protection will be given as long as and to the extent that the record of the idea amounts to an **original** literary work in the copyright sense. (Of course, if the story is fully developed into a script, the script will be a dramatic work and therefore protected by copyright.)

The word 'original' and how it is used in copyright law is crucial, because as regards literary, dramatic, musical or artistic works, only those which are **original** are protected. The sense in which this word is used here is that the work must represent the end result of a **sufficiently substantial amount of skill, knowledge or creative labour** on the part of the author. The work can be derived from someone else's work (so not original in that sense), but if sufficient skill and labour have been put into making the new work – trivial alterations are not sufficient – it will be original for the purposes of copyright law and is capable of being protected.

In deciding whether a work is sufficiently substantial to deserve copyright protection, the courts have tended to take the practical view that what is worth copying is worth protecting. This is why, say, a title of a book or film is usually too trivial and insubstantial to count as original (although, for practical commercial reasons, it is obviously a good idea not to use a title which has already been used for a different work because this may lead to an action for 'passing-off' (Chapter 14, *Secondary exploitation*)). But it is important to note that, as a general rule, copyright does not protect ideas, but only the form of their expression. If someone devises a scheme to make money, and writes it down, the actual way it is expressed is protected from others copying it verbatim or even adapting it to produce their own version. But copyright law will not enable the person who devised the scheme to prevent others from simply taking the ideas which he or she has expressed, and putting them into practice.

Even where protection is given to a work, there are some exceptions, in that certain uses will be allowed without the need for the copyright owner's permission, because the public interest has to be served in certain cases. For example, 'fair dealing' (which has to be a very limited use of a small amount of a work, otherwise it would not be 'fair') with a literary, dramatic or musical work for the purposes of **research**, **private study** or (if there is an acknowledgement to the author) **criticism**, **review** or the **reporting of current events** will not be an infringement. Chapter 9, *Rights clearances I*, pages 141–4, explains how these exceptions operate.

What is copyright infringement?

Copyright is **not** a monopoly. A copyright owner who claims that his rights have been infringed must be prepared to prove that the supposedly infringing version was **derived from his own work**, as opposed to being created independently or derived from some other, independent work – there can be no infringement if there has been no copying. So someone who has never read, seen or heard of the contents of a particular work of copyright (such as a book), but who has produced something substantially similar by her own efforts, will not be infringing the copyright in the other work.

> For example W, a writer, writes a script about a little boy, living with his rich parents in Shanghai just before the Second World War, who is separated from his parents when the War breaks out and who is captured and put into a prisoner-of-war camp with other expatriates. The script describes his adventures and the relationships he strikes up with the other people in the camp. This plot may sound very familiar (as it is a summary of *Empire of the Sun* by J.G. Ballard, a book based on his own real-life experiences). However, for the sake of the example, assume that W wrote the script in 1958, before J.G. Ballard published the book, and that W had never met Ballard, or indeed anyone to whom Ballard might have told the story. The fact is that W wrote the story himself, possibly based on stories he heard of other people's experiences, but the script and the book are written independently. W has not shown the script to anyone, and kept it in a drawer for years (although he very prudently deposited a copy at his bank when it was originally written). The result of this is that:
>
> - W could not have objected to the publication of *Empire of the Sun*, since it was clearly written independently of W's script.
> - J.G. Ballard could not prevent the publication or use of W's script (assuming that anyone wanted to use it after *Empire of the Sun* had been published), because it was written independently of his book. It makes no difference that the events in question (being events very similar to those described in W's script) actually happened to him!

Copyright operates by prohibiting the doing of certain acts in relation to a copyright work without the consent of the proprietor of the copyright or, indeed, without the consent of the exclusive licensee of the copyright if such a person exists. These are known in copyright law as the 'restricted acts'.

The acts restricted by the copyright in a work are:

- **copying** (which in relation to a **literary, dramatic or musical** work means reproducing it in any material form);
- **issuing copies** of the work **to the public**;
- **performing** or playing the work **in public**;
- **broadcasting** the work or **including it in a cable programme service**;
- **making any adaptation** of the work;
- doing, in relation to any adaptation of the work, any of the acts specified above.

An adaptation includes translating the work or putting a story into pictures or changing a non-dramatic work into a dramatic work or vice versa. A fresh arrangement of a piece of music which involves more than a change of key or register is also an adaptation of it. Any such adaptation will attract its own copyright if sufficient skill, labour or knowledge has been put into it.

To copy (or perform or broadcast or adapt) the whole of a copyright work, is undoubtedly infringing the copyright, but even copying only a part of it may also be infringement, if a substantial part of the work has been copied. 'Substantial' here is not used as a measure of quantity but rather as a reference to the relative importance, within the framework of the work as a whole, of the part which has been taken.

The exploitation of films and sound recordings involves doing a number of 'restricted acts', because these works are essentially the result of collaboration. For example, to synchronize a record ('a sound recording') of a song ('a musical work') on to the soundtrack of a television programme, involves:

- making a fresh record of the sound recording and therefore reproducing it;
- reproducing the actual musical work in a material form;
- broadcasting the sound recording (by broadcasting the television programme including the recording);
- broadcasting the musical work.

It will therefore be necessary to obtain the consent of the person or persons controlling all these rights.

HOW TO USE COPYRIGHT TO PROTECT AN IDEA

How does one fit an idea or format into the framework of copyright protection? The answer depends upon the nature of the idea. If it is a drama or comedy subject (which will eventually, when it is in script form, be a 'dramatic work'), it is generally sufficient to write the idea down in treatment or outline form (namely, recording it in a material form, a vital prerequisite to copyright protection). It is important to express all the aspects of the idea in as much detail as possible, including a description of the characters, a full statement of the plot and any other information which will demonstrate the originality and distinctiveness of the idea. The treatment should announce who owns the copyright by bearing a copyright notice in a prominent position. The form of the notice should consist of the symbol © in a circle, followed by the owner's name (or the name of his or her copyright, if that is to be the owner of the project) and the year in which the idea was first put into a material form. On the treatment itself, it is normal practice to have the copyright notice on the title page, but there is no harm in including the © in a circle symbol and the owner's name at the foot of each page. Then, if anyone to whom the treatment is given or sent gives copies of the treatment to others, those others will have notice of the owner's rights as well.

To summarize:

- write it down in full detail;
- include a copyright notice in a prominent position.

HOW TO PROVE OWNERSHIP AND HOW TO PROVE WHEN THE IDEA ORIGINATED

Assuming the idea is capable of copyright protection when expressed in written or other form, and that it has duly been written down and plastered with copyright notices, what can a Producer do if someone to whom it may have been shown starts developing a similar project and claims he or she had the idea independently?

If someone else has quite genuinely come up with a similar idea and it was not **copied** from the Producer's, there is no breach of copyright and nothing can be done about it. But if that other person has seen the Producer's treatment or outline, if the matter ever got to court, the court would assume in the Producer's favour that there has been copying, unless the person accused can prove otherwise **and provided always that the Producer can show that the project was devised before that other person came up with his or her idea**.

In copyright disputes, when the person accused denies that they have copied, they will generally claim that they had already thought of the idea. It will, therefore, often be crucial to the Producer to prove when the work was first created.

The best means of dating an idea independently is to send a copy of the treatment or outline as soon as it has been written down, through the post, to someone else who can be trusted to keep the work and to produce it when the need arises to prove the date of creation. Producers can send it to their bank or to a lawyer with a covering letter asking them:

- to acknowledge receipt in writing;
- to keep the document and the envelope containing it (which should bear a legible post mark as useful extra corroboration of the date) until it is needed.

It will **not** be safe to tell the recipient to discard the treatment when the film or television programme has finally been produced. It may still come in useful if, as occasionally happens, someone comes forward with a claim that what the film or programme produced was copied from **their** work.

For example, if (using the same circumstances described on page 24) W had published his screenplay shortly after *Empire of the Sun* had been published, J.G. Ballard might have (quite justifiably) taken the view that the similarities between the script and his book were so striking that W **must** have copied it. However, because W deposited the script with his banker in 1958 and W's banker can prove the date of the deposit, this should absolve W from any suggestion of copying.

The other thing which someone who is claiming infringement of his or her copyright may have to prove, is that he or she **is** the owner of the copyright in the treatment or outline. This is simple enough if the Producer is also the author of it, but if someone else has devised and written it or contributed to it (possibly the Producer's partner in the project or someone who works for the Producer) the Producer needs to be sure that it has proper title to the copyright and can establish that. The formalities to bear in mind are more fully described in Chapter 5, *Development*.

WHEN COPYRIGHT WILL NOT HELP TO PROTECT AN IDEA

If the project has a storyline and characters, the Producer may be able to use the law of copyright to its advantage. But if, even when written down, there is little to the idea apart from a basic concept, the Producer may have trouble in claiming copyright protection for it, however original (in the sense of being novel) the idea is. This is because, as has been seen, there may not be enough there to attract copyright protection. A mere title does not get copyright protection – under copyright law, there must be enough skill, knowledge or creative labour put into devising something before it is deserving of copyright protection. And this may apply to ideas or formats of films or television programmes, to the extent that they consist of little more than concepts.

The word 'format' is used generally in the television industry to describe an idea which consists of a set of constant elements within which variable elements can be inserted. For example, in a soap opera like *EastEnders* the constants are Albert Square and the characters living in or around it. But each episode will also have new storylines and new and different characters – these are the variable elements. For this kind of format, if it can be expressed in writing in the form of a detailed treatment, the treatment will probably be protected under copyright as a literary work – there will be a degree of skill, labour and originality in the description of the setting, the characters and the suggested ways in which they will interract with each other. If a rival production company, having seen this kind of treatment, produces its own version of the programme, the Producer would have a fair chance of persuading a court that this was infringement of the literary work which was the original treatment.

However, some formats do not provide that kind of scope for creative expression.

The most obvious example is the format for a game or competition show. A description of the elements of the average light entertainment or game show will still usually consist only of a basic idea (or a collection of such ideas). For instance *Opportunity Knocks* could be described as follows.

> A television entertainment show with a compere, on which four or five different acts, who are unknown to the viewing public, have the opportunity to perform on television for the first time and in doing so, to compete against each other for the approval of the audience. The television viewers are invited to vote for their favourite act and the winner of this poll goes on to appear on the following week's show to compete against a whole set of new acts. By way of a preview of the viewers' reaction, the studio audience's reaction is tested at the end of the programme by recording the level of applause for each act in turn, on a device known as a 'clapometer'.

In copyright terms, in trying to protect that idea, one would not be much better off for writing it down. The description just given may just qualify as a literary work, but it is unlikely that the writer could claim any greater protection than the ability as the author to prevent others from copying it **verbatim**. If, however, someone took the idea expressed in the literary work (or any single element of it) and reproduced it in the form of a television programme, the law of copyright could probably not be used to prevent this.

The example given is particularly pertinent. Hughie Green, who originally devised *Opportunity Knocks*, sued the New Zealand Broadcasting Corporation for broadcasting, without his permission, a similar show under the same title in New Zealand. Mr Green lost his case. He claimed that copyright subsisted in the 'scripts and dramatic format' of the show. Unfortunately, as far as the scripts were concerned, he could not produce any, and in the absence of the actual scripts, the court felt that it would be difficult to imagine that such scripts as may have existed would be likely to express anything more than a general idea or concept for a talent quest. If that were the case, they could not be protected. 'The dramatic format' claimed by Hughie Green consisted of the characteristic features of the show which were repeated every week, such as his catchphrases and the 'clapometer' – but the court decided these lacked sufficient certainty, and did not have 'the necessary unity to be capable of performance as a dramatic work', as they were unrelated to each other, but were only accessories to the dramatic or musical performances of the contestants (who, naturally, were different every week).

This is not to say that one cannot protect the format of this or similar shows. In Chapter 14, *Secondary exploitation*, various ways that a Producer of such shows can hedge the format round with enough elements to make it a saleable property are discussed. But that is when the show has been produced and broadcast and established in the public mind. In the beginning, when the format is little more than a gleam in the eye of its creator, how can it be protected? At present, although there are moves afoot to try to expand the Copyright, Designs and Patents Act 1988 to protect programme formats, the only viable **legal** option is to try to take advantage of the law on breach of confidence.

BREACH OF CONFIDENCE

There are essentially two circumstances where obligations of confidentiality arise between people dealing with each other. First, in particular relationships, an obligation of confidence will often be treated as being owed as a matter of course by one party to another (for example, doctors and patients, lawyers and their clients, employers and employees).

But for those presenting ideas for film and television projects in the hope of getting them financed, this will rarely be relevant. The second and most effective way of imposing an obligation of confidentiality is to seek an agreement of non-disclosure with the person with whom you are dealing, if you are concerned that there is a real chance of the idea being taken.

Two points should be made here. The first is that there is a practical drawback when presenting an idea, if the presentation is not being made at the specific request of the broadcaster or other potential financier. The Producer may find in these circumstances that asking its audience to sign a confidentiality agreement does not go down well. Their attitude may even go beyond mere reluctance to sign (even if they do not go as far as most of the Hollywood Studios, which actually send back unsolicited material unopened with a polite letter recording the fact that the material has **not** been looked at and requesting the sender **not** to send anything else). If the

Producer's request to sign a confidentiality agreement is refused, there is little to be done. Of course, where the audience actually wishes to see the material and has asked the Producer to show it to them, the position is different. In those circumstances, they may be quite willing to sign an agreement in return for the privilege of seeing the idea.

The second point is that whether or not the Producer can get an agreement to maintain confidentiality, the idea should still be put into writing, or into the form of drawings, recording or any other suitable material form and the Producer should take steps to be able to prove when it was first created. This is because if there is no confidentiality agreement, the Producer may just be able to claim copyright protection if the worst happens and those to whom the idea has been shown seek to use it without consent. However, if the Producer **does** get an agreement, and that agreement is broken, it will still be necessary to prove exactly **what** it was that should have been kept confidential and, in certain cases, **when** the idea was created. This will be vital because confidentiality agreements generally exclude any obligations to keep confidential information which the recipient already had, so it will be open to the person to whom one sends an idea to say that he was already in possession of a similar idea.

Other factors which may make it impossible to enforce confidentiality are:

- that the material has already entered into the public domain;
- that it is not in the public interest to keep the material secret (and that there is a just and valid reason for disclosing it).

Only the first of these needs to be expanded on to any extent. Not only does it mean that one cannot claim confidentiality for anything which is publicly known, but it may also be fatal, even if the material in question is not known to the public as a whole, if it is still fairly widely known. So if a Producer has told a few too many people about its idea (other than in confidence), it may not be able to enforce a confidentiality agreement against any one person to whom the material is officially disclosed.

The contents of a confidentiality agreement

What is required (and particularly what formalities have to be observed) to make an agreement which is legally enforceable is considered in detail in Chapter 4, *The deal*. Those principles will apply to any kind of agreement. However, the actual provisions one might want to include (or is likely to see) in a confidentiality agreement are set out below.

What the Producer needs to include

- the obligation to maintain confidentiality (this should apply to employees, directors, or officers of a company to which the idea is sent or shown);
- a description of (or other means of identifying) what is to be treated as confidential;
- an exact description of for what purposes (if any) the other party may make use of the material (i.e. any copying of it should be restricted, as should any disclosure of it to anyone other than those who absolutely need to see it);
- a requirement to return the material within a certain time limit;
- an acknowledgement that the material is original as far as the recipient is concerned (or alternatively the Producer may wish to include a provision that it must be notified **at once** if the other party thinks the material is at all similar to any other projects of which the other is aware or which it owns, and that full details of the other project(s) will be supplied to the Producer).

What the other side may wish to include

If one presents a confidentiality agreement to someone, he or she may accept it at face value or may refuse to sign it. But the most likely response is that he or she will ask for changes to be made to it, to modify or qualify the obligation of confidentiality in some or all of the following ways.

- The restriction shall not prevent disclosure of the material to professional advisers or some other specific category of people (this is fair enough, but the Producer should ensure that the agreement makes it clear that any such disclosure must be reasonably necessary for the purposes which the other party is trying to achieve, i.e. the evaluation of the Producer's material to see if it is worth proceeding with).
- The restriction shall not apply to any part of the material disclosed which is:

  (a) already in the possession of the recipient **or** has already been made available to the public;
  (b) which infringes the rights of third parties.

As for how to avoid a claim that the recipient of the project has something like it already, the Producer should provide in the agreement that, if the recipient does not reveal details of the competing project to the Producer within a certain period, he or she shall not be entitled to make such a claim at a later date.

4	**The deal**

BINDING AGREEMENTS

Agreements are the basis of commercial life – they are the manifestation of people doing business with each other. When an agreement is working well, it forms a blueprint for the relationship between the parties to it, either on a short-time or on a long-term basis, who can then refer back to it to see what should be happening in a particular instance, or try to find a solution when the relationship is not working.

This book as a whole considers the essential elements of many different types of agreements, and seeks to demonstrate what type of agreement is required for each relationship which can arise in the film or television industries. So this chapter takes as its subject the basic elements common to all agreements, and shows:

- how to conclude a binding legal agreement;
- how to avoid creating a legally binding obligation, when discussions with another person are still at the negotiating stage.

This latter point is especially relevant, because it is quite common for one party discussing business with another to send a so-called 'letter of intent' or a 'comfort letter', giving the other party an idea of what is being offered, but not wishing to incur any obligation. Most deals in film or television are dependent on other elements being put in place; for instance, a Producer raising finance for a production is very unlikely to secure the whole of that finance from one source, and its ability to get any part of it from a particular Financier will usually depend on the Producer's ability to demonstrate that others have committed to provide the rest of the necessary finance.

To take an example:

A Producer approaches a potential Financier at the Cannes Film Festival with a project ready for production, and with a production budget of £3 000 000. The Financier says that he will not finance the

entire cost but expresses a willingness to provide £800 000. The Producer will have to raise the balance elsewhere, but it will certainly help
to persuade other Financiers to contribute, if they are shown evidence
that £800 000 worth of funding is already in place. It therefore makes
sense for the Producer to get something in writing from the first
Financier, recording the offer to provide £800 000.

The Financier's response will be to try to provide a letter which
does not actually commit him unconditionally to parting with
£800 000. He may do this by saying that he **will** provide £800 000 as
long as the balance of £2 200 000 is actually **committed** by other
financiers. This, if all the other factors necessary to create a binding
agreement are present, may be an obligation which is enforceable by
the Producer, as long as the **pre-condition** (namely, that others
commit to providing £2 200 000) is satisfied – a so-called 'conditional
contract'.

Or the Financier may (and this is more likely) try to keep his options
open, and word the letter so that, even when the rest of the money is
found, he will still be able to decide **at that point** if he wishes to part with
his own money. The letter will, in this case, only be a 'letter of intent' or
'comfort letter'.

In these examples, how does the Financier ensure that he is achieving his
real objective? How does the Producer tell the difference between one
kind of letter and another, and which amounts to a legally binding
contract?

To look at the situation from another angle, the **Producer** may not
want to be committed to taking that Financier's money, if a better offer
comes along, and if so, will not want the letter to be a binding
agreement obliging him to deal with that Financier once the rest of the
money is found.

In this case, how does the Producer avoid being committed?

The questions posed above can perhaps best be answered by answering
the question: what constitutes a binding agreement? When one knows that,
one should know, in theory anyway, how to **avoid** creating a binding
agreement unintentionally.

Does the contract have to be in writing?

It may or may not come as a surprise to learn that parties can commit to
each other legally, without recording what they have agreed on paper. Sam
Goldwyn is supposed to have said that a verbal contract 'is not worth the
paper it's written on'. That tells us not only that such contracts exist, but
also emphasizes that they are not an ideal way to do business. Earlier on in
this chapter, it was suggested that the ideal use of a contract is as a

reference work for a relationship – but quite obviously, if the agreement reached between the parties is not recorded in writing, there is nothing to refer to except the (possibly faulty) recollection of each party. Proving what was agreed can boil down to one person's word against another's in the witness box of a court. Hence the exhortation on the William Morris Agency's business stationery – 'Get it in writing'.

Some contracts, to be enforceable, have to be in writing (for example, a contract relating to an interest in land or other real property). But the kind of deals which Producers might negotiate do not have to be recorded in writing before they constitute a legally binding commitment – they simply **should** be.

One or more documents?

Again, since there are no rules about the **form** of a contract, it follows that it does not have to be one document, but can be contained in several, such as (and most typically) an exchange of letters.

When exchanging correspondence about a potential deal, if any or all of the writers want to avoid a contract being created, each letter should indicate that what is being said is not to be regarded as legally binding, unless set out in a single written document, signed by all the parties. The simplest way of doing this is to write 'subject to contract' somewhere in the letter, preferably at the beginning. This is **not**, however, an absolutely foolproof way of avoiding the creation of a contract – there have been court cases where the judge took the view that the parties **had** created a contract, because the circumstances showed that they really intended to be bound by what they had agreed with each other. But this has not often happened, and should not happen so long as any one of the parties to correspondence is fairly unequivocal about not committing to anything until it is all recorded in a formal contract which has been signed by everyone.

Ingredients of a binding contract

So, what would make a contract of, for example, an exchange of letters, if the words 'subject to contract' were not firmly set out at some stage in the correspondence?

The necessary ingredients of a binding contract are:

- an offer;
- an acceptance of that offer;
- 'consideration';
- certainty of the essential terms or provisions;
- an intention to create a legal relationship.

It may assist to consider each of these things in turn (although it makes sense to treat offer and acceptance as one subject).

OFFER AND ACCEPTANCE

The concept of 'offer' does not need much explaining: one party must offer to do or give something for the other (or perhaps even for someone else whom the other party, to whom the offer is made, would like to benefit). To take our example above, the Producer may offer the Financier certain distribution rights in the proposed film.

To create a contract, that offer must be accepted in the form in which it is made, i.e. the Financier must unequivocally indicate that he accepts the rights actually being offered.

If the Financier comes back and says that he would like to pay a smaller price, or that for the same price he would like more rights, this will not amount to **acceptance** of the Producer's offer. It is what is known in legal terms (and rather unusually quite logically!) as a 'counter-offer'. The Producer can either accept this counter-offer or make a further counter-offer. While the parties are still offering each other different deals, there cannot be a contract – they are still negotiating. But once an offer is accepted (as long as the last three factors listed above are **also** present), there is a binding agreement.

It is useful to remember, though, that an offer can be withdrawn at any time **before** it is accepted. So, if one person rashly offers something which is later regretted, the very worst thing is to sit back believing it is too late to draw back – the thing to do is to contact the person to whom the offer is made and let him or her know that it no longer applies.

CONSIDERATION

'Consideration' is an example of a normal word being used, rather unhelpfully, in a legal way which does not bear much resemblance to the natural meaning. In this case, when a lawyer says that there must be 'consideration' for an agreement, it means that in return for the agreement made by one party to the other, the other party must provide some kind of benefit in return. The benefit can take almost any form, but in film and programme production it will almost always be money (or its equivalent), or rights in the production.

To take the example given already, the consideration for the Producer's promise to grant certain distribution rights to the Financier will be the Financier's promise to pay the agreed amount, say £800 000. Or to reverse this scenario, the consideration for the Financier's providing £800 000 is the grant by the Producer of the agreed distribution rights.

However, and perhaps confusingly, the 'consideration' provided does not have to be worth the same as the promise in return for which it is given. Under English law, so-called 'nominal' consideration (such as an agreement to pay £1 or $1) will be enough. Not even that amount of consideration will be required to make a legally enforceable agreement, if a contract is signed by the parties with the intention that it should take effect as a **deed**.

To show how this works in action:

A writer, W, tells a Producer, P, that she is going to **give** P all rights in a script which W has written. This gift will be given in six months' time. If W changes her mind before the six months are up, or simply fails to make an assignment of the rights when that day arrives, P cannot enforce an assignment because the offer was purely gratuitous – P had provided no consideration for the promise to transfer the rights.

However, if W records her promise to give the rights to P in six months' time, in a document which records that P is paying W **now** the sum of £1 in return for (or 'in consideration of' her promise to transfer the rights), W will be legally bound to assign the rights when the six month period has expired.

Even more simply, if W records her promise in a document and in the document itself she states that it should take effect as a deed (**and** her signature is witnessed by a third party, which is a formality required for creating a 'deed'), once again it will be legally enforceable by P at the end of the six month period.

Incidentally, the second and third instances given above are further examples of a 'conditional contract'. In this case, the condition which has to be satisfied before W has to perform her obligation is that six months will have passed.

CERTAINTY

For an agreement to be legally binding, the provisions of it have to be **certain**, or capable of being precisely ascertained, and all the **essential** provisions needed to make the agreement work have to be agreed.

Taking our example once more, the Producer offers a Financier, in return for £800 000, unspecified distribution rights in the proposed film, the territory and nature of which is to be agreed by the parties at a later stage. Even if, as is very unlikely, the Financier says that he is happy with this, the Producer could not enforce the obligation to pay £800 000, because there is no certainty about what the Financier is to get in return – it still has to be agreed, and it is just as likely as not that the parties may not agree on the exact nature of the rights to be granted or the territory in which they should operate.

The position would be the same if the Producer offered theatrical exhibition rights, in return for an **amount** to be agreed. The description of the rights in question (whilst undesirably vague from a practical point of view) would probably be specific enough for the purposes of forming a contract, if the amount payable for them had been agreed, but certainly not if it had not. However, if the Financier has offered, say, 25% of the budgeted cost of the film, in return for the same rights, this would be an enforceable obligation, even if the budget figure had not actually been fixed at the time when he made his offer. This is because, once the amount of the budget has been fixed, it will then be easy enough to calculate the amount equal to 25% of the budgeted cost. Since the fixing of the production budget is not within the Financier's control, he was committed, without an exit route, when he made the original offer and it was accepted by the Producer.

As said before, the need for certainty not only requires that the obligations of each party be exactly defined (or capable of being exactly defined by reference to extraneous factors, as in the example of the offer to pay 25% of the budget), but that **all** the obligations necessary to make the contract work are provided for as well. Sometimes, if a vital element (without which the contract does not make sense) is left out, a judge (if the contract was taken to court by one of the parties seeking to rely on it) **might** imply the inclusion of that provision to give the contract 'business efficacy', but it is more likely that a court would simply find that there was no agreement, because one of the essential elements necessary to make the contract work had been left out. This is such a complicated area of law that it would take a book of its own to explain it in full detail. In most cases, experienced people doing business with each other should be able to tell whether they have covered in letters or other documents sufficient aspects of their relationship in sufficient detail to make the parameters of the relationship certain in all material respects (although at that stage it is probably wise to check with a lawyer experienced in that type of deal). And it is quite acceptable to leave certain aspects of the relationship 'to be agreed' at a later date if failure to reach agreement would not obstruct the working of the essential parts of the relationship.

As an example, if our Producer and our Financier have agreed on exactly what is being paid and the exact nature of the rights to be granted, they may also specify that the Financier will receive a credit on the film in a form to be agreed. If they do not agree, when the time comes to discuss it, the exact nature of the credit (for instance, the Financier wants a front-end credit on a single card in a type size which is 85% of the size of the title, and the Producer wants to give the Financier a 'with thanks to' credit in the end titles), it would not affect the integral part of the deal – the exchange of money for a specific exploitation right. However, in all similar circumstances, it might well be sensible to provide that someone – either of the parties, or an independent third party – will have the final say on any aspect left to be agreed, if agreement cannot actually be reached by the parties.

In this context, it is worth commenting at some length on the use of so-called 'heads of agreement' (otherwise known as 'deal memoranda').

Heads of agreement

When parties are contemplating doing business, they find it convenient and quick to record the essential terms of their relationship in a brief memorandum or heads of agreement. In view of what has been said above, it is quite likely that this will be a legally enforceable agreement, and the parties will intend it to be so (unless they specifically state otherwise, when the necessary **intention** to create a legal relationship will be absent). However, it will not have dealt with (because space would not have permitted it) a variety of subjects which one or other of the parties, had they thought about it, might have wanted to provide for.

For example, our Financier is a UK distributor ('D') who has been granted by the Producer ('P') theatrical exhibition rights in the UK. The parties sign a deal memorandum which states clearly how much D is supposed to pay and when (say, 70% of the income received by D from exploiting the distribution rights to be payable by D to P, at six monthly intervals), but the memorandum does not state that P can terminate D's distribution rights as soon as there is any suggestion that D might be insolvent (the most obvious manifestation of which, if D is a company, is if the company is put into liquidation). The memorandum might not even state specifically that P can terminate the rights granted to D if D fails to pay what has been agreed (but a court will usually apply a right to terminate if one party commits what is regarded as a **material** breach of an agreement). So what can P do if D goes into liquidation three months after he last accounted to P? Unless and until P terminates D's rights, D will continue to be entitled to collect the income derived from the exploitation of the rights. D will **owe** 70% of that income to P, but, as anyone who has ever been a creditor of an insolvent person or company will know, P cannot insist on being paid in full, because D may not have enough assets left to pay the full amount once those of D's creditors who have priority over the others have been paid, such as the Inland Revenue or any 'secured' creditor (Chapter 6, *Financing*, page 99). Once his turn comes to be paid, P may find that he gets less than 10% of what he should have received, if he is lucky.

It is therefore vital, in a situation where one party has authorized another to collect income which both parties have agreed to share, that the first party has the ability to withdraw that authority when the second party becomes insolvent, **and** the ability to notify all third parties who would otherwise have paid the second party, to pay all money to the first party instead.

But in our example, P does not have the right to terminate simply because D is insolvent – P does not even have an **expressly stated** right to terminate if D fails to account at the next date when he is due to do so. Since it is more than likely that D would not be able to pay what P is owed when the next accounting date falls due, P **could** argue that he is entitled to terminate the agreement for anticipated breach. But because there were no express provisions in the deal memorandum dealing with this situation, it would certainly be open to D's liquidator to dispute P's right to terminate (and the liquidator may have an incentive to do this if the benefit of the contract with P is an asset which the liquidator could sell to someone else) – and while this dispute is being sorted out, the income-earning value of the film to P might well be seriously diminished.

This example demonstrates one of the key dangers of not drawing up a full agreement, but merely relying on heads of agreement. Of course, it is not always possible in a fast-moving world to negotiate and agree on every possible aspect of a deal before entering into it. But if it is possible, it is better for all concerned to do it, and not to resort to heads of agreement simply to avoid expense or from a misplaced desire not to appear to be too difficult or demanding.

INTENTION TO CREATE BINDING LEGAL RELATIONS

The last requirement, before a binding agreement can be created, is that the parties must clearly intend that there should be some form of legal relationship between them. This will not have to be spelled out, however, where the parties are business people or entities – on the contrary, if all other factors necessary to a contract are present, the parties will have to go out of their way to show that a binding contract was **not** intended. The best way to achieve this has already been covered, namely by making it obvious that the discussions or correspondence are subject to the conclusion of a separate written agreement signed by all parties.

Another way of avoiding obligation is to express the relevant act or benefit as an intention rather than a definite promise.

> For example, A says to B 'I will give you £100 in return for a full list of all your business contacts'. This would be a legally binding commitment – if B supplies the list, he can enforce payment of £100 from A.
>
> **But** if A says 'I intend to give you £100 if you show me your list of contacts and they look useful to me', it would not be advisable for B to disclose the list without getting the £100 in his hand – A could argue that he had changed his mind about the money, or that the list was not useful for A's purpose.

This is a demonstration of the fact that an expression of **intent** is not legally binding under the law of contract.

However, where one party or the other is keen to avoid any commitment, there are other pitfalls to be avoided, even if a binding contract has **not** been created by the communications between the parties. If A writes a letter to B, which contains statements which purport to be fact and there is (or at least ought to be, in A's mind) some question that B might rely on any of those statements, A could be rendering himself liable to action by B for 'tortious misrepresentation'. This is because the law of tort provides a legal claim (and remedies) to anyone who has been damaged by another's wrongful act. There does not have to be a contract between the person claiming and the wrongdoer – all the claimant has to show is that it was reasonable that he or she (or anyone in the same position) would be damaged by the wrongdoer's act.

Thus, in our example, where A either deliberately or carelessly makes a misstatement of the truth, A may be liable to B in the tort of misrepresentation, if B could reasonably have been expected to rely on that statement and has actually done so, to B's detriment.

> For example, A may tell B that A will be able to present B to very important people, if B will come to the Cannes Film Festival with A. B spends a considerable amount of money on air travel and hotels, to find out that A knows no-one of importance. This level of loss might not be worth suing – but if B had incurred much greater expense in reliance on what A told him, he may well find it worthwhile to sue A for misrepresentation.

These then are the basic elements necessary to create binding agreements. In addition, it is appropriate to consider some other topics which affect the making and performance of contracts:

- the damages payable when a contract is broken and how indemnities work;
- the meaning of the expressions 'best endeavours' and 'reasonable endeavours';
- UK and European Community competition law.

WHEN A CONTRACT IS BROKEN

If one party to a contract breaches its obligations, the other party will be able to sue, if a more convenient way of resolving the problem cannot be found. In a legal action for breach of contract, the injured party ('the plaintiff' to the action) can claim:

- **damages** for breach of contract;
- an **injunction**.

Injunctions are considered in more detail in Chapter 15, *Legal proceedings*. **Damages** are an award by a court of monetary compensation. The amount is assessed on the basis of putting the plaintiff in the position he would have been in, had the contract been properly performed. Naturally the plaintiff will be compensated for loss suffered by him in consequence of the contract not being performed. Unfortunately, this does not necessarily cover all the loss which the plaintiff might suffer, but only loss which was a **reasonably foreseeable** consequence of the contract being broken, in the light of the circumstances known to the defendant.

It is perfectly possible for the plaintiff to have suffered loss which was not reasonably foreseeable.

For example, A has a contract with B under which he is due to pay B the sum of £500. B, in turn, owes C £500 under a separate contract. B does not have the money to pay C unless he is paid by A. If A does not pay to B £500 when he is due to do so, B will be in breach of his contract with C.

In that example, if B sued A for breach of contract, he could expect to recover £500, plus interest, plus a part (but not always all) of his legal costs in suing A. However, if he has also been sued by C, B may well not be able to recover the legal costs he incurs as a result of having to defend the action.

INDEMNITIES

It is therefore prudent for each party to an agreement to require the other party to agree to give an **indemnity** against all losses which might arise as a result of the other party's breach of contract. What this means is that the

indemnifying party is agreeing, if he is in breach of contract, to pay damages which will cover **all** the loss and damages which the injured party suffers as a result of that breach. In the example above, that means that if A agreed to indemnify B, B can recover from A all the loss he suffers as a result of not being able to pay C.

Indemnities in practice

If one enters into a contract, it is always sensible to require the other party to a contract to indemnify one against the consequences of that party's failure to perform. However, indemnities are particularly important to Producers when agreeing terms with Production Financiers, or with distributors. Under agreements with either Financiers or distributors, the Producer will often be assigning the **benefit** of contracts entered into by the Producer for the purposes of production or exploitation of a film or television programmes.

Under English law, it is possible for a party to a contract ('A') to transfer the **benefit** of the contract, but he cannot transfer his obligations. Although he can require the person to whom he transferred the benefit ('B') to perform those obligations, A has to be careful, because if B does **not** perform them, A is still liable to be sued by the person with whom A originally contracted ('C'). This is because B and C have no direct connection with each other. C made the contract with A, and whatever private arrangements A might make with B, C is still entitled to look to A to perform the contract. An example of a Producer assigning the benefit of contracts is if the Financier takes over production (because something has gone badly wrong), and therefore needs to be able to administer and control cast and crew who were originally taken on by the Producer (Chapter 7, page 112). Another example is where the distributor needs to be able to exercise the rights which the Producer was originally granted by contributors to the production, which authorize the Producer to exploit the contractor's contribution in the production itself. The Producer transfers those rights to the distributor but still remains liable to the contributor to pay an extra fee if those rights are exploited.

In either case, the Producer will have originally undertaken obligations to the other party to the contract (such as to pay fees, accord credits, or to pay a share of the proceeds of exploitation). Having assigned the contract, the Producer no longer has the power to perform these obligations because (in a take-over situation) control over the budget has reverted to the Financier, so that the Producer will no longer have the cash to pay the fees it has agreed to pay to cast and crew; or because (in distribution) the distributor is collecting the income realized from exploiting rights in the production, out of which the contributor is entitled to be paid his share.

It is therefore usually a condition of the Producer assigning the benefit of these agreements that the Financier or (as the case may be) distributor will **perform the Producer's obligations**.

If these obligations are not performed, the person with whom the Producer originally contracted (for example, an actor) will sue **the Producer** – the actor cannot sue the Financier or the Distributor because he has no contractual relationship with those persons. This is the effect of what is referred to as 'the doctrine of privity of contract'; only the direct parties to a contract can sue or be sued on the contract.

In these circumstances, the Producer must require the Financier or Distributor to **indemnify** the Producer from **all** loss suffered by the Producer if its obligations to other persons are not observed.

'BEST ENDEAVOURS' AND 'REASONABLE ENDEAVOURS'

Those familiar with contracts are aware of the practice of substituting an obligation to use 'best' or 'reasonable endeavours' to do something, for an absolute and unqualified obligation to do it.

It is wise to do this if the obligation in question is one that a party to a contract cannot absolutely **guarantee** to be able to perform.

An example of this would be something which needed the agreement of a third party.

For example, P, a Producer, acquires the right from a Foreign Producer, F, to make a British television series based on a series format which F owns. P is going to produce the British series for the BBC. F wants the right to be able to distribute P's series in the rest of the world outside the UK. However, the copyright in the series will almost certainly belong to the BBC, and it will be up to the BBC whether F can distribute the series. For this reason, P cannot agree that F will be appointed as distributor. P can only agree to use best or reasonable endeavours to get the BBC to agree to appoint F.

What is the difference between 'best' and 'reasonable'?

The standard of obligation on someone who has agreed to use best endeavours is very high. It does not require the impossible to be done, but if **anything** can be done which could possibly achieve the desired result, it is likely that someone who has agreed to use 'best endeavours' will be required to do it.

For example P, a Producer, agrees with a Financier to use 'best endeavours' to engage the services of a particular director for a film. The director says he will only do the film for a fee of $5 million. P's budget only allows for a fee of $4.5 million. The Financier could probably require P to make up the difference out of the fees which would otherwise be payable to P out of the budget. Otherwise, P would not be using **best** endeavours to secure the director's services.

It would be different if P had stated that it would use 'best endeavours' within the confines and restrictions of the agreed budget to get the director on board.

'Reasonable' endeavours is a lower standard of obligation, although still quite exacting. In assuming what is required of a person who has agreed to use reasonable endeavours, a court takes into account what is **commercially feasible**. Again, however, if the performance of the obligation could be brought about by paying a particular sum of money, it is likely that the person who agreed to use reasonable endeavours will have to pay up.

The message is clear – when undertaking a best or reasonable endeavours obligation, one must exclude any question of doing something which one is not actually prepared to do.

For example P, a Producer, agrees that A, an Actor, will receive a credit in respect of his performance in P's film in all major paid advertising relating to the film. However, the advertising of the film will be carried out by the Distributor, D. P will require D, in the distribution agreement, to make sure that A gets his agreed credit in paid advertising.

However, A will usually ask that, if there is any occasion in which his credit is not given, P will correct this. P **should** restrict its obligation to using **reasonable endeavours** to correct the credit, **prospectively only**. However, the use of reasonable endeavours might imply that P would have to sue D, if D refuses to make the correction in future advertising. Or P might have to pay for the cost of replacing all the film posters which have been printed up, omitting A's credit. So P should specifically state that its obligation to use reasonable endeavours to correct wrong credits does not oblige P to incur expenditure (other than minor expenditure, such as the cost of writing to the distributor asking for the correction to be made) or to commence or carry on legal proceedings against any person.

COMPETITION LAW

Here, very briefly, is the effect of UK and EC competition law on the making and performance of contracts.

United Kingdom competition law

The Restrictive Trade Practices Act 1976

Consideration must always be given as to whether the Restrictive Trade Practices Act 1976 applies. Without going into excessive detail, it will apply where there is an agreement or series of connected agreements between two or more parties carrying on business in the UK in the supply of goods or services, where there are certain specified restrictions on at least two parties. In practice, it rarely does apply to film and programme production and distribution contracts, because it is rare for **both** parties to be placed under restrictions as to the way in which they can perform or enjoy the benefit of the contract.

If the Act applies, the agreement or agreements have to be sent to the Office of Fair Trading ('OFT'). If the restrictions are thought to be significant, they will be referred to the Restrictive Trade Practices Court and may be found to be unenforceable. If they are not referred to the Court the OFT recommends that particulars are placed on the Restrictive Practices Register (which is open to the public, although there is a procedure for applying to have particulars placed on a special secret section of the Register, but only where they relate to secret processes of manufacture and similar matters). Where a registrable agreement is not registered in time, it will be void and unenforceable.

The provisions of the Restrictive Trade Practices Act are extremely complex and where it is likely that the Act will apply, it is advisable to consult a competition lawyer. However, the following are guidelines as to when the Restrictive Trade Practices Act might be relevant in agreements and what to do if it is.

When the Act is likely to apply

The Agreement has to be between two parties or more and at least two parties accept relevant restrictions. These could be:

- tie-ins – an obligation on the one party to purchase products or services only from the other party (such as an obligation on a Producer to use the studios or facilities of a financing broadcaster);
- exclusive grants of rights (it is common for rights to be granted exclusively in film and programme distribution contracts, but as said above, restrictions have to be placed on both parties to the contract);
- any restrictions on the parties' ability to compete in the market (such as, for example, when granting rights to a video distributor, prohibiting the distributor from selling the video to certain retailers).

What to do in case the Act does apply

First, the relevant agreement should contain a provision suspending the effect of any relevant restrictions until particulars of the agreement have been filed at the OFT. Otherwise, it will be too late to register and the parties (as well as possibly facing penalties for non-registration) will, if they wish to enforce the agreement, have to terminate it and enter into it again after particulars have been furnished.

If the restrictions are suspended, the parties then have up to three months to furnish particulars.

This can be done on the basis that the submission to the OFT is not an admission that the agreement is registrable, so if there is any doubt of registrability, it is always safer to furnish particulars.

There may be no way of avoiding the need for registration under the Restrictive Trade Practices Act if the parties to an agreement are determined upon imposing relevant restrictions on each other but good advice before the agreement is entered into can prevent later unexpected problems.

European Community competition law

The Treaty of Rome (which is a part of English law) has direct relevance to contracts entered into in the UK. The two most important provisions of the Treaty are Articles 85 and 86.

Article 85

This prohibits anti-competitive agreements or practices which may affect trade between member states of the EC and which restrict or distort competition in the EC in some way. Notable examples are:

- direct or indirect fixing of the purchase or sale price of goods or services, or other trading conditions (such as requiring a video distributor to sell videos at a certain price);
- limiting or controlling production, markets, development or investment (such as prohibiting a distributor from selling a film or programme into particular territories);
- sharing markets or sources of supply (for example, if particular distributors agreed with a cinema chain that their films and no others would be shown in those cinemas);
- applying dissimilar conditions to similar transactions (such as where a broadcaster in commissioning two independent Producers to produce similar productions gives much more favourable terms to one of them);
- making the conclusion of an agreement subject to supplementary

obligations not connected with the subject of the contract (for example, if a broadcaster refused to commission an independent Producer unless the Producer used the broadcaster's studios in making the programme).

Some restrictions may be permitted if they improve production, distribution or technical or economic progress and are for the benefit of the consumer generally. The parties to an agreement can, accordingly, if they feel that the agreement is ultimately beneficial (even though it contravenes Article 85 in certain aspects), refer it to the Commission for exemption. The Commission may exempt it, either as written, or subject to certain modifications. In any given case, the European Commission will look at the actual **effect** which the agreement or practice has on trade. (This procedure will only be necessary if the agreement cannot be brought within one of the relevant 'block exemptions' described below.)

Contravention of Article 85 is very serious as it may involve the payment of massive fines. It is therefore important for any business which has more than a minimal share of a particular market within the EC to give detailed consideration to Article 85 when negotiating and drawing up agreements.

Certain types of agreements (particularly exclusive film and programme distribution agreements or exclusive copyright licences or development agreements) are likely to offend against Article 85 as they are inherently anti-competitive. However, specially recognizing the need to allow intellectual property owners to impose certain restrictions when entering into agreements, the European Commission has issued block exemption Regulations relating respectively to Patent Licences, Franchise Agreements, Know-How Agreements and Distribution Agreements. These state which clauses will be permitted and those which will not and, if the relevant agreement complies with the applicable block exemption, it will be treated as not contravening Article 85.

Article 86

This Article is intended to prevent persons within the EC abusing a dominant position, so it may take effect to prevent the exercise (or more usually non-exercise) of a copyright owner's rights if that owner has a dominant position in a relevant market and is using its rights in a manner which abuses that position. The most obvious examples of persons in a dominant position in the UK film and programme industry are the BBC and the ITV network, because the television broadcast market is still so small. They must therefore be careful not to abuse the power which the lack of competition in that market gives them.

For example, recent case law shows that the Commission will actually force a rights owner to exercise his rights, if the non-exercise means that a consumer demand for an ancillary product will not be met. An example of this is the Magill case, where the would-be publishers of a complete television listings guide, to whom the UK and Irish network broadcasters had refused to supply a licence of television listings information (in which the broadcasters had copyright protection), successfully obtained a ruling that they were entitled to a licence on reasonable terms, because the refusal to grant a licence meant that the public were not able to obtain, from one source and in advance, complete information about television programmes on all channels.

CONCLUSION

This chapter has attempted to encapsulate a subject which in a legal textbook might easily amount to a hundred or so pages of small print. The intention is to help the reader identify the main points and pitfalls to bear in mind when doing deals. But if the deal is worth more than he or she can afford to lose, it is always worth consulting a competent lawyer to check whether:

- there **is** an enforceable deal;
- all the essential areas have been covered.

Clients who have to watch their finances are naturally anxious to keep legal bills down to a minimum and sometimes think that if they draft contracts for themselves and then ask their lawyers to vet them, this will always be cheaper than asking the lawyer to draw up a contract. This is not a safe assumption to make – whether or not it is true will depend upon the contract and will depend on the lawyer (and, of course, on the client's competence at drafting!). If, for instance, the deal is one for which the lawyer has a standard agreement which can be used as a precedent and will only need the names and addresses of the parties inserting and the figures of any relevant payments, it is bound to be cheaper for the lawyer to provide a contract, because this will take less time than if the lawyer had to read an unfamiliar document drafted by someone else and then have to add whatever extra provisions are required to get that document into proper legal shape.

| Development | 5 |

DEVELOPMENT ISSUES

The 'development stage' of a film or a television project involves many activities after the initial idea has been formulated. During this stage, the Producer will be doing and arranging everything necessary to put the project into shape to start production.

Development issues include:

- the raising of development finance and contracting with a Financier;
- the preparation of a draft production budget, cash flow schedule and production schedule;
- the selection of a writer or writers and contracting them to write treatments and scripts;
- the engagement of other personnel required at development stage (for example, a location scouter to reconnoitre potential locations, or a production accountant to help with budget preparation, or a supervising director);
- the acquisition of the necessary rights in underlying material on which the project is to be based.

This chapter will concentrate on the business and legal aspects of all these activities.

DEVELOPMENT FINANCE

The purpose of development

The idea may be enough to persuade a Financier to pay for the development of a project. However, a Financier (whether a distributor or a television broadcaster or anyone else) will not commit to the financing of the **production** of a project without knowing exactly what it would entail. The hopeful Producer therefore needs to present the Financier with:

- a production budget and projected cash flow schedule;
- (where relevant) a draft script at least to first draft stage, if not in a final polished state;
- a production schedule;
- details of proposed locations;
- if possible, details of proposed main production personnel;
- (where relevant) details of proposed main artists or performers;
- documentary evidence that the rights in any underlying material have been or can be secured.

This is the sort of package which is put together as part of the development process. It requires expenditure of time and effort by more than one person, so a relatively substantial amount of money will be needed to finance development, even if the Producer does the absolute minimum required to enable a decision as to production financing to be made.

Sources of development finance

The first step in getting a project off the ground is to find someone who is prepared to provide development finance. This will not always be someone who will ultimately go on to finance the production of the project. There **are** specialist organizations, such as the European Script Fund or the National Film Development Fund, which exist solely to select ideas for development and to fund development. However, companies which are interested in acquiring the rights to exploit films or television programmes are often in the business of funding development as well, such as the BBC, ITV companies and, of course, Channel Four. These broadcasters have all, at times, also participated in the initial funding of **feature film** projects.

Whoever finances the development of a project, similar business and legal issues will arise as part of the relationship between Producer and development Financier. The agreement governing the relationship between these parties, is usually referred to as a 'development agreement'.

Set out below are the main areas which most development agreements should cover, with some commentary on the issues which might arise between the parties to the agreement.

Development contracts – general issues

People who work in the media industries are notoriously reluctant to record the arrangements they make with each other in contract form in any kind of detail. This reluctance is particularly marked at the development stage. There are a variety of reasons, some good, some less so. Cost is a major factor – using an experienced lawyer to draw up contracts can be expensive. But it is not wise to assume that the shorter the contract the cheaper it will be. Lawyers' standard documents may not be all that long, but if they deal with all major issues, they will generally be longer than the one page which most Producers prefer! If a Producer insists on having a one-page agreement, the lawyer has to spend **more** time in considering exactly what can be discarded from the standard document to make it shorter, without significantly increasing the risks to the client of something important having been left to chance.

Another reason why Producers prefer no contracts or very short ones, is that getting things done in the film and television world depends very much on personal relationships. Producers hate to give the impression that they do not trust the people they do business with. However, the reason for having a proper contract is only, in the last resort, to have proof of what the parties have agreed, in case there is a dispute, or one of the parties wishes to get out of its obligations. A contract concentrates the parties' minds on what **should** happen in the numerous circumstances which can arise during the course of their relationship, and it can ensure that both parties actually want the same thing to happen (misunderstandings about what was intended are very common). English contract law operates in such a way that, sometimes, if a contract does not provide specifically what should happen in a particular instance, the law may imply certain consequences. These consequences may be something which none of the parties would have wanted, had they thought about them beforehand.

The development agreement

There follows a discussion of the areas which will be dealt with in most development agreements. Each topic is preceded by a specimen clause from a development agreement, with explanatory comments. The agreement is in letter form.

Description of the project

FROM: FINANCIER ('we' or 'us')
TO: PRODUCER ('you')

                                        Dated   19

Dear Sirs
['   ']
This letter is formally to confirm the arrangements agreed between us for the development of a [feature length film ('the Film')], [series of [length] television programmes ('the Series')], [a television programme of [length] ('the Programme'] based upon [   ] ('the Work') written by [Writer] [published in the UK by   and in the USA by   ].

The project under development must be properly defined. For example, the agreement should state what kind of production it is intended to be – feature film, television series, one-off documentary, etc.; the overall finished running time of the production; what underlying works it will be based on and so on.

When referring to the title of the project, it is sensible to state that the title is provisional. However much the Producer and Financier love it, there is no guarantee that using the title will remain a good idea. Although there is no copyright in a title, there can be other problems in using a title, as described in Chapter 12. It will help to avoid arguments later if it is made clear at development stage that there is no question of there being some kind of contractual commitment to use the original title.

Development work

> With a view to your developing the Film/Series/Programme for production we have agreed to finance and you have agreed to undertake the following development work ('the Development Work'):
>
> (a) to engage [   ] ('the Writer') to write a [script and/or storylines] ['the Script'] for the Film/Series/Programme under the terms of an agreement which we shall have the right to approve in advance;
>
> (b) to engage [   ] (during the period of the preparation and delivery of the Development Work) to act as an Individual Producer to generally oversee the preparation and production of the Development Work under the terms of an agreement which we shall have the right to approve in advance; and
>
> (c) to prepare a production budget for [the first programme in the] Film/Series/Programme ('the Production Budget').

The agreement should state with precision what the Producer is required to do. Typical obligations are:

- engaging a writer to write a treatment or script;
- engaging a named person to act as individual producer to oversee development work and sometimes also engaging a supervising director;
- acquiring an option over the rights in any underlying material;
- acquiring an option over the services of a director and even principal performers.

The mechanics of the contracts which the Producer should be entering into to achieve these ends will be considered in more detail below.

The Producer will almost certainly also be required to produce a full-scale production budget, and perhaps even a production schedule and cash flow schedule.

Development budget

> The agreed budget for the Development Work is [£   ] excluding VAT ('the Development Budget') a copy of which is attached as an appendix to this letter. This sum represents our maximum financial commitment to the Development Work, you will endeavour to keep your commitments to a minimum and any sums not expended will be returned to us within 30 days of delivery of the Development Work. In the event that we commission/finance the Film/Series/Programme, the Development Budget shall form part of the agreed production budget for the Film/Series/Programme.

The agreement should include a budget, setting out under itemized headings of expenditure, exactly what is required to finance the preparation and delivery to the development financier of **all** items of development work.

It is the usual practice to attach a copy of the development budget itself as a schedule or appendix at the end of the development agreement. If this approach is adopted, one should not forget to mention in the agreement itself that the schedule/appendix attached forms part of the agreement, and the parties may also wish to date and initial the schedule/appendix to identify it in case it becomes detached. This is good practice whenever a separate document is attached to an agreement where the parties intend the contents of the document to have a bearing on their obligations.

Accounting

> You will open a separate bank account for the project into which all payments by us shall be made, and shall be used solely for the purpose of defraying the cost of the Development Work.
> We shall be entitled to copies of all bank statements.
> You will retain all receipts and vouchers for all expenditure incurred for inspection by us.
> We shall be entitled to audit your books of account relating to the Development Work.

The Financier will want to ensure that, even if a relatively small amount is involved, proper financial controls are exercised as part of development spending.

It is sensible to require the Producer to open up a separate bank account for the project and to pay the development finance into it, and **no other money** (unless the Producer itself is providing part of the development finance). It is then easier for the Financier to trace its money and to check on expenditure (either through being provided with statements of the bank account or, more usually, through specific accounting reports to be provided by the Producer at regular intervals during the development).

If the development is either lengthy or expensive, the obligations on the Producer (as with production financing) should be to provide financial reports a reasonable amount of time before the Financier is due to pay another instalment of development finance. That way, the Financier can control and limit risk by withholding the next instalment if things are going badly wrong.

It is also normal for the Producer to be required to keep all receipts and invoices relating to its expenditure on the project, and, of course, to keep proper accounts and to make these available for inspection by the Financier at any reasonable time. These kinds of obligations are not unique to development agreements.

Ownership of rights

> As Beneficial Owner you **HEREBY ASSIGN** to us by way of assignment of existing and future copyright the entire copyright and goodwill and all other rights of a like nature throughout the universe in the Development Work **TO HOLD** the same unto us absolutely for the full period during which such rights subsist including all renewals, reversions and extensions thereof whether the right to such renewals or extensions now exist or is thereafter created throughout the universe and thereafter in perpetuity.
>
> The ownership of all materials prepared and/or delivered to us pursuant to this Agreement shall vest in us absolutely including all material written or prepared in connection with the Development Work.

This is a vexed question in any development or production situation. Certainly in the UK broadcasting field, Financiers who provide 100% of the finance for the production of a project have historically required to own all rights, which are rarely passed back to the Producer at any stage. Independent Producers, on the other hand, can point to this attitude as one of the reasons why many of them cannot escape the rut of living from project to project, since it is a steady cash flow which enables the building and development of a business, not the receipt of fees of unpredictable amounts at unpredictable intervals. Production fees and development fees are not enough – Producers need the steady income which comes in from the ownership of distribution rights, if they are to develop into other fields and take the necessary risks involved. Broadcasters who are also Producers would testify to the truth of this statement.

However, the eventual ownership of rights in projects which proceed to production is an issue which only arises marginally at development stage. This is because the development Financier will usually either ask to own outright, or will take a 'charge' over, the rights to the project and the benefit of all contracts which the Producer enters into as part of the project. This includes all rights of the Producer in the format or underlying work on which the project is based. At production stage, however, if the project is commissioned, the format/underlying rights will usually be re-assigned to the Producer (Chapter 7), although some ITV broadcasters try to resist this. However, if the development Financier is one who may well also finance production (for example, a UK broadcaster), the Financier will probably try to keep all remaining rights. If the Producer is interested in retaining some distribution rights, it might be wise to make it clear at development stage that the assignment of all rights to the Financier at this time must not lead to an automatic assumption that all rights in the finished production will also be assigned.

The reason why the development Financier takes ownership of (or, with a charge, the ultimate right to own) the project, is simple. In this instance, the Financier is acting like a bank or a mortgage company – it is lending money to the Producer on the tacit or explicit understanding that the money will be repaid in certain circumstances. It is good business practice for a lender to take **security** over an asset in order to reinforce its ability to get its money back should the borrower become insolvent or deliberately try to avoid its obligations to repay. In this case, the only available security (or rather the only security which it is reasonable for a development Financier to require) is the rights in the particular project, and not any other assets of the Producer.

The Financier may take an outright assignment (namely, a legal transfer) of all rights in the project. This is more common where the Financier may agree to finance production (for example, a broadcaster). Alternatively, the Financier may take a charge (which a body like the NFDF would normally be expected to take, although the European Script Fund does not, at least at the time of writing). A charge (or a mortgage) over an asset gives the beneficiary of the charge the right to seize ownership of the asset in certain circumstances. Since there are various legal complexities involved, which it is not appropriate to go into here, anyone taking or giving charges should get specialist legal advice to make sure that their rights are fully protected. However, the mechanics of a charge are discussed in more detail in Chapter 6, *Financing*.

It is more usually the case in development agreements (not least because it is simpler) for the development Financier to have all rights **assigned** to it. The Financier is looking to get its money back – in the case of a body such as the NFDF that will be its only concern since it is not looking to finance the production; but the obligation to repay is **not** absolute – it will usually only arise if a film is made and based on the project. The Financier will then agree to release its interest in the project when all sums lent by it for development (plus interest, unless there are commercial reasons why interest should not be payable, as explained below) have been repaid, and this is generally expressed to be required to happen on or before the start of **principal photography** of the project. 'Principal photography' is a feature film industry expression used to describe shooting involving the participation of the principals (namely, the main cast). The Producer, although it might put in hand some second unit shooting, should never start principal photography unless and until the production finance is committed. The Producer, in raising production finance, includes the repayable development amount in the budget, and that is why the money should be available on the first day of principal photography.

Obligation to repay and 'turnaround'

If we do not within [twelve] months following delivery of the Development Work agree to commission/finance the Film/Series/Programme you shall thereafter have the sole and exclusive right to re-acquire all the rights in the Development Work on the following terms:

(a) you shall have the right to try to arrange for the finance for the making of the Film/Series/Programme;

(b) you shall be entitled to continue to develop the Development Work and to have written and/or to offer scripts and synopses to third parties with a view to obtaining their interest for the financing thereof;

(c) if you are successful in arranging for alternative funding for the Film/Series/Programme you shall repay to us on the first day of taping or principal photography or on the date when any third party commitment to finance the production becomes unconditional (whichever is the sooner) of the first or only film/programme made and based upon the Development Work a sum equal to the Development Budget. Upon repayment as aforesaid we shall assign free of any lien charge or other encumbrance to you (or as you may direct) all the rights acquired by us pursuant to this Agreement;

(d) until such repayment as aforesaid you will not except with our prior written consent (which will not be unreasonably withheld after you have become entitled to repurchase the rights in the Development Work) enter into any agreement with any third party for the production of the Film/Series/Programme or any similar television programmes or enter into any agreement or make any arrangements for the publication of any printed matter based on or related to or containing any of the material in the Development Work.

The obligation to repay, as described above, applies in the case of bodies such as the NFDF. However, other kinds of development financier may want an interest in the production of the project, and may take more extensive rights. For instance, a broadcaster will generally finance development with a view to commissioning the production of the project. In this case, it is normal to specify in the development agreement that the Financier must make a decision as to whether or not it wants to participate in the production, within a certain time after delivery by the Producer of the development work. How much time the Financier should be allowed will vary according to the particular circumstances. The usual range for 'decision time' is six months to eighteen months. Eighteen months is a long time, and if the broadcaster insists on this sort of time period, the Producer should at the very least ask for the agreement to state that the broadcaster will make a reasonable effort to give an earlier decision.

If a broadcaster turns down the opportunity to commission or participate in the project or has not made a decision within the time limit, the Producer is normally given the right in the development agreement to approach others to finance the production and will agree to repay a certain amount of money to the broadcaster either on the first day of principal photography or (if the broadcaster is quite demanding) on the date that any third party commits to finance the production of the project (if that happens sooner than the start of principal photography). At the time of repayment, the broadcaster should be under an obligation to reassign all rights to the Producer or to anyone the Producer may nominate. This is what is known as a '**turnaround**' provision.

A cautious Financier may also specify that, until repayment, the Producer cannot actually conclude any agreement with a third party for the production of the project (or any other kind of exploitation of the project) without the prior consent of the Financier. This may not be entirely necessary – if the Financier owns the rights and is under no obligation to return them without being repaid, there is very little that the Producer can effectively do to progress the project.

What amount will be repayable? This depends on the deal with the Financier. It may be **all** of the amount invested by the Financier (it may not include interest as well where the development Financier is a broadcaster, although some ITV broadcasters **do** require interest), or only a proportion. The Producer may argue that the whole should not be paid (or at least not interest) because the Financier has had an exclusive period to decide whether it wishes to commission production. Payments made to acquire that exclusivity (which is effectively an option), by common industry practice, are not repayable if the option is not exercised. This argument may or may not be accepted by the broadcaster.

One final point – in commissioning an original script, the Producer may have to agree to the writer having turnaround rights namely, if a production based on the script does not proceed within two years of delivery of the script, the writer can re-acquire all rights on repayment of a certain sum of money. For further comment on the problems this can cause, see page 83.

Warranties

You warrant and undertake that:

(a) you are entitled to enter into this Agreement;

(b) the Development Work will be delivered to us free of all liens, claims and encumbrances;

(c) for the duration of this Agreement and in the production of the Development Work you will comply with all relevant industry agreements and all statutory obligations;

(d) subject to any limitations approved by us you will obtain the entire copyright in all material commissioned by you for the Development Work and obtain all necessary consents to permit the Development Work and/or the Film/Series/Programme based on the Development Work to be produced and exploited throughout the universe;

(e) you will at our expense execute such further documents and do such other things as we may reasonably require to vest or perfect the rights and benefits granted or assigned to us hereunder;

(f) unless we otherwise expressly agree in writing, all material incorporated in the Development Work will be original except insofar as it may be in the public domain;

(g) nothing in the Development Work will be defamatory of any person, firm or corporation and nothing therein will, if broadcast, infringe the copyright or other personal or proprietary right of any person, firm or corporation or infringe any statutory obligation.

As with any agreement when ownership of rights is an issue, the Producer may be required to give certain assurances (or 'warranties') in the development agreement. Typical examples are set out above.

If there **is** some problem in any of these areas, the Financier might find that its development finance has been wasted, because the project is not able to proceed to production in any event. If these warranties turned out to be untrue, the Producer would therefore be in breach of contract, and the development Financier would have the right to sue for damages (the most obvious damage being the loss of the amount paid to finance the development).

Termination

If you commit a material breach of this Agreement or shall fail to remedy any breach capable of remedy within fourteen days of us drawing the same to your attention, or should you suffer the making of an administration order or have a receiver (including an administration receiver) or manager appointed of the whole or any part of your assets or if any order is made or a resolution passed for your winding up (except for the purpose of amalgamation or reconstruction) or if you enter into any composition or arrangement with your creditors or if you cease to carry on business, we shall have the right to terminate this Agreement.

Termination provisions are not necessary in every contract. However, any contractual relationship which provides for the performance of a series of actions over a period of time in return for the payment of money over the same period (like a development agreement) should contain a termination clause. If the other party fails to meet its obligations at any particular time, no one wants to have to go on performing their part of an agreement. Depending on the type of breach of contract, it is quite common practice to qualify termination rights by stating that the party at fault will have a certain period to remedy any default before the agreement can be terminated, unless the default is, quite objectively, one which is incapable of being remedied.

For example, a warranty, that the project is original, not based on any other copyright work and does not infringe any rights, will be broken if it turns out that the project is based on a short story which is still in copyright, and there is no agreement with the copyright owner of the story for its use. This is evidently a breach which cannot be remedied.

The Producer may also wish to ask for a provision allowing it to terminate (and for the rights to go into 'turnaround') if the development financier becomes insolvent. This is **essential** where the Financier is anyone other than bodies like the NFDF or the major broadcasters. There is actually no reason why broadcasters should be immune from insolvency either but they have, at least historically, been fairly secure until now and most broadcasters are very hostile to any suggestion to the contrary.

UNDERLYING RIGHTS

Assuming that development finance is forthcoming, the first issue on the agenda for the Producer, if it has not already been done, is to secure the exclusive rights to any underlying material which is going to be used in the project, or on which the project will be based.

This usually involves acquiring film and/or television rights to a copyright book, story or play (or even another film). However, it is not an issue confined to fictional productions. If the project is one that revolves around or is based on true events, it may be wise (although not always possible, except in so-called 'docu-dramas') to tie up agreements with the individuals who originally participated in those events. Some consideration of what such an agreement should contain appears later in Chapter 9, and a specimen agreement appears in Appendix D. The remainder of this chapter reviews the basic principles involved in acquiring the right to produce a film or television series based on a pre-existing copyright work.

Option agreements

Copyright searches

There is no need to take rights in a work which is out of copyright (or, in other words, in the public domain). This could explain the popularity of certain authors when it comes to film adaptations. The Producer should also be certain that it is acquiring the necessary rights from **all** the persons who may own them. When buying a house, one does not just take the vendor's word on questions of ownership and the nature of the property being purchased, but carries out searches to check these aspects.

In this country, copyright material exists without having to be recorded on a register (unfortunately for Producers acquiring rights). In the case of any widely-published work, however, there is a relatively (but not completely) reliable way of finding out more information about it. A search at the United States Copyright Office at the Library of Congress in Washington DC will reveal the information entered at that Office in respect of the work in question. Registration of a copyright work at the US Copyright Office used to be a prerequisite of copyright protection in the United States. This is no longer the case, but anyone who is exploiting or might possibly wish to exploit a copyright work in the United States would be well-advised to register the work. This is because US law provides for certain advantages in copyright infringement actions to copyright owners who have registered their work. So, while not **all** works will have been recorded at the US Copyright Office, **all US works** and most foreign works which are exploited in the US will be. The register contains details of transactions in relation to the recorded work such as transfers or licences of film and television rights in the work. Thus, while a search at the US Copyright Office is not a surefire way of ensuring the truth of everything which a Producer has been told about a work, it will often show if anything is wrong. A search might show that the copyright has been recorded in the name of someone other than the person claiming to be the owner, or that the film rights have been granted elsewhere. If a Producer finds out discrepancies of this nature, it may be that they can be sorted out, but either way, it is better to know about these things before any money changes hands.

These searches can be carried out at varying levels of expense, but they usually cost a few hundred dollars. Since one of the key motivating factors in development is to try and keep costs to a minimum, many Producers hesitate to commission copyright searches at a very early stage. However, it is imperative to do it before the Producer is actually committed to buy (and to pay a substantial sum for) the rights in a work, because after that it may be too late to re-negotiate. Also, a copyright search is normally required by Errors and Omissions insurers at the production stage (Chapter 11 contains a description of Errors and Omissions insurance and why it is necessary).

Mechanics of 'options'

The time-honoured way of acquiring underlying rights is to take an option to purchase them at some stage in the future rather than to buy the rights outright early on. The price for an option for whatever option period is negotiated (one, two or perhaps three years) will be considerably less than the full purchase price of the rights. In fact, it is often about one-tenth of the eventual price (although possibly less, where the developing Producer is really operating on a shoestring, and the owner of the underlying work is prepared to be accommodating). It should never be 'free' – the Producer must agree to pay at least a nominal amount (£1 or $1) for the option; otherwise it may not be enforceable under English or US contract law. (Chapter 4, *The deal*, discusses the topic of 'consideration'.)

An option will give the Producer the exclusive right to buy the rights during the option period. If the option is not exercised, the Producer is left with nothing and the underlying rights owner keeps the option price – this is **always** non-returnable, and expressed to be so in the option agreement (although from a legal point of view, there is an argument that the Producer would be able to get the money back by legal action, if it turned out that the rights owner actually did not own the rights at all).

The Terms which will apply if the option is exercised – acquisition agreements

If the option is exercised (usually by the Producer sending a notice to that effect to the owner, accompanied by the agreed purchase price), the Producer will then acquire the rights. **But** it must be stressed that one thing the Producer **cannot** avoid at the time of taking the option is some degree of negotiation and agreement on exactly what rights the Producer will be acquiring if the option is exercised and, in particular, what purchase price is to be paid. The money paid for the option is potentially a complete waste if the two parties have not actually agreed what each will be getting. This is because, in law, an agreement to be negotiated at a later date is not legally enforceable – after all, there is nothing to enforce, in the absence of specifically agreed terms.

Historically it has been the practice that an agreement to grant an option has attached to it a full and complete record of the agreement which the parties will enter into (if the option is exercised) for the acquisition of the rights. This is referred to in this section as 'the acquisition agreement'.

Wishing to keep expenditure of time and effort down to a minimum at this development stage, Producers often prefer to leave the terms of the acquisition to negotiation – for the reasons given above, this is extremely inadvisable. The very least which must be done is to agree the main terms – what each party will get, when and how, and for how long the rights will be granted. The less which is agreed at the option stage, the greater the risk to either party. If something one party considers important has not actually been agreed at the initial stage, it may not be conceded by the other party when the option is exercised.

> For example, if the Producer simply agrees to acquire 'film and television rights' without further elaboration, this will not automatically include character merchandising rights, the right to publish a 'book of the film' or even to publish the screenplay. The producer who has assumed that these rights could be taken as read, may be very disappointed.

For this reason, it can be a false economy not to have a fully negotiated and detailed acquisition agreement at the option stage.

Set out below is a review of the more important provisions in option and acquisition agreements with some explanatory comment.

Option agreement

How long is an option?

1 **Option**
   In consideration of the sum of (   ) (£   ) paid by the Purchaser to the Owner (receipt of which the Owner hereby acknowledges) the Owner grants to the Purchaser the exclusive option to acquire the rights in the Work specified in the Acquisition Agreement for the consideration and upon the terms specified in the Acquisition Agreement.

2 **Exercise of Option**
   At any time before the end of [twelve (12) calendar months] from the date hereof the Purchaser may either:

   (a) exercise this option by notice in writing to the Owner accompanied by payment of the consideration specified in Clause 2(a) of the Acquisition Agreement; or
   (b) extend the option for a further period of [twelve (12) calendar

months] by notice in writing to the Owner accompanied by payment of a further sum of [   ] and if the Purchaser so extends the option it may exercise the same by notice in writing to the Owner at any time before the end of the said further period of [   ].

3 **Payments**

The sum or sums paid to the Owner pursuant to Clauses 1 [and 2] will be in advance and on account of the consideration specified in Clause 2(a) of the Acquisition Agreement but shall not be returnable in any event.

The usual structure of options over underlying rights is that they are granted for an initial period of one year. During that year, the intending purchaser can either exercise the option or renew it for a further period of up to a year. Some agreements allow the automatic right to renew for a third period, but this is not common – if the rights are worth anything, the rights owner will not want to tie them up that long without some substantial payment. The agreement will provide that all renewals cost extra (quite often more than the original option payment). The first option payment is always treated as having been paid on account of the eventual purchase price (if the option is exercised). The purchaser of rights will also prefer that payments for **renewal** of the option should also be treated as an advance against the purchase price. But it is fairly common practice that payments to **extend** the option will be additional and not on account of the purchase price (and the agents for rights owners will usually require this).

Documents required if the option is exercised

4 **Execution of the Acquisition Agreement**

Within fourteen (14) days of the exercise of this option the Owner will at the Owner's expense:

(a) execute and deliver to the Purchaser an engrossment of the Acquisition Agreement;

(b) if so requested by the Purchaser execute in the presence of and have authenticated by a duly authorized Consular Officer or Secretary of Legation of the USA and deliver to the Purchaser a short form assignment in [the form annexed hereto as Exhibit B or such [other] form as the Purchaser may reasonably require];

(c) procure the execution of and delivery to the Purchaser of quitclaim in [the form annexed hereto as Exhibit C or such [other] form as the Purchaser may approve] by all English language publisher of the Work.

As evidence of the terms on which it has been agreed the rights will be acquired, if the option is exercised, it is convenient to attach to the option agreement the form of acquisition agreement, which when the option is exercised can be prepared as a separate document for signature. Sometimes, a short form assignment/licence will also be attached (effectively a summary of the acquisition agreement) and the option agreement will provide for this to be signed at the same time as the main acquisition agreement – this document can then be deposited at the US Copyright Office as evidence of the grant/assignment of rights. Sometimes, there will also be a publishers' quitclaim (if the work being acquired is a published book) in which the main publishers of the book confirm that they have no financial interest in the rights being acquired by the Producer. This is less important than it used to be, as it is now comparatively rare for publishers to acquire any interest in the film or television rights (either as licensee or as exclusive agent for the sale of these rights) in the books they publish. Exceptionally, publishers of non-fiction or children's books do take an interest in film, television or radio rights. If the publisher **does** own or control the rights, then the option and acquisition agreements should be with the publisher. What this means, of course, is that enquiries as to the publisher's rights should be made by the Producer at the time of entering into the option, rather than waiting until the option is exercised, and then finding out that the agreement was with the wrong party. To satisfy itself that no film/television rights have been granted to the publisher, the purchaser may ask for the right to see the main publishing agreements in respect of the book. The owner should not object to this if he is permitted to delete all financial and other confidential details from the copies of the publishing agreements before they are shown to the Producer.

Consent to adapting the work during the option

> During the subsistence of this option and any extension thereof the Purchaser will be entitled to make adaptations of the Work in the form of film [or television] treatments and scripts and to show the same to third parties who may be interested in the production and/or exploitation of a film [or television programme or series] based on the Work.

It is good practice for a Producer acquiring an option to obtain the right, set out in the option agreement, to commission the writing of treatments or scripts based on the work during the option period. An option does not of itself permit the Producer to adapt the Work without the owner's consent (and in this case, writing a treatment/script is making an adaptation (Chapter 3, page 25) and therefore an act restricted by the copyright).

Buy-back rights

> (a) If this option expires without being exercised the Owner will have the exclusive option to purchase all the Purchaser's rights in any

treatments or scripts based on the Work subject to the terms upon which the Purchaser may hold such rights.

(b) The Owner's option under sub-clause (a) above may be exercised by written notice at any time before the expiration of [   ] from the date of this Agreement.

(c) The price payable by the Owner upon exercise of the said option will be a sum equal to all sums paid by the Purchaser in connection with the acquisition of the relevant rights together with interest thereon at two per cent (2%) over the base rate from time to time offered by [Bank plc] and the Owner will indemnify the Purchaser against liability for any future payments that may become due in respect of such rights.

Sometimes, the rights owner/his agent will want the right to purchase treatments or scripts made during the option period if the option expires without being exercised. From the Producer's point of view, such a request is not unreasonable, because once the option has lapsed without being exercised the treatment/script can only be of value either to the rights owner or to a third party to whom the rights owner has granted rights in the Work. Even though the copyright in the treatment/script belongs to the Producer, it cannot be used without the underlying rights owner's consent.

Authority to pay the agent

The Owner hereby authorizes and requests the Purchaser to pay all moneys due to the Owner hereunder to the Agent whose receipt of such moneys will be a valid discharge to the Owner therefor.

Where the rights owner is represented by an agent, the owner should specifically authorize the Producer to pay the option fee to the agent, so that there can be no later argument that it has not performed its obligation to pay the owner.

Publishing agreements

It was common practice in the past, by way of investigating the owner's claim to own the rights title, to require details (if not copies) of any prior signed publishing agreements (the details to be specified in a Schedule attached to the acquisition agreement). As it is now relatively uncommon for authors either to grant film rights to their publishers or to grant them rights in income from such rights, it is not essential to ask for details of publishing agreements when dealing with recent works (roughly, for present purposes, post-1975) or works written by established authors, as long as the Producer has the right to call for a publisher's quitclaim from the main publishers of the work.

Documents to show the owner's title

If the rights owner is not the original author of the work (which will evidently be the case if the rights owner is a company or if the original author is dead), the rights owner should be asked to produce the documents by which he claims title (for example, an assignment by the original author, or the author's will) which should be listed in a Schedule attached to the acquisition agreement.

Has the work been published in the US?

It is worth checking with the US Copyright Office to see if the work has been previously published in the US. If it has, a search at the US Copyright Office is advisable.

Acquisition agreement

Grant

In consideration of the agreement by the Purchaser to pay to the Owner on or before the date specified in Clause 2(a) hereof the sum therein specified and of the further agreement by the Purchaser to pay to the Owner the further sums specified in Clause 2(b) hereof the Owner as beneficial owner hereby [assigns/grants by way of irrevocable licence] to the Purchaser [the whole of the film [television] and allied rights in the Work throughout the World including but not by way of limitation the sole and exclusive right] [the following sole and exclusive rights]:

(a) to adapt the Work for the purpose of and to reproduce the same in the form of [films] [the Film] (including the writing of film treatments and scripts or screenplays in all languages and for this purpose the making of changes or additions to the Work notwithstanding any moral right or 'droit moral' or similar right to which the Owner or any other person may be entitled under the Copyright, Designs and Patents Act 1988 or under the Laws of any other country) and trailers of [such films] [the Film];

(b) to perform the Work in public by exhibition of [such films] [the Film] by all methods now known or hereafter to be invented including but not by way of limitation:

(i) exhibiting [such films] [the Film] before live audiences in cinemas and theatres and non-theatrically;

(ii) broadcasting and transmitting [such films] [the Film] by television and radio (including so called 'free' and 'pay' television);

(iii) including [such films] [the Film] in a cable programme service (including pay cable) and broadcasting such films directly by satellite);

(iv) distributing or transmitting electronic, magnetic or other recordings or reproductions of [such films] [the Film] whether in the form of video cassettes, video discs, video tapes or any other audio visual devices whether now known or hereafter to be invented;

(c) to make adaptations of the Work or any part thereof and to use the same for the production distribution and exploitation by all means and in all media [other than exhibition before live audiences in cinemas and theatres] of [one [or more] television programme(s)] [the Television Film] based upon the Work and recorded on film, tape or otherwise;

(d) for advertising and publicity purposes only to broadcast and transmit by television of all kinds (whether now known or, hereafter to be invented) and radio (whether live or on film or tape) excerpts of the Work or any adaptations thereof (with such alteration as the Purchaser may think fit) [not exceeding fifteen (15) minutes in duration];

(e) to adapt the Work into dramatized form and to broadcast by radio performances of such dramatizations (but not including performances by readings of a single voice of the original text of the Work);

(f) to adapt the Work into a dramatic work (including musical versions) and to perform such dramatic works in public;

(g) to write print publish and [subject to the proviso to this sub-clause)] sell or to permit the writing printing publication and [(subject as aforesaid)] sale of synopses and resumes of the Work not exceeding [seven thousand five hundred (7500)] words in length for the purpose of publicity and exploitation of [such films] [the Film] [television programmes] [the Television Film] [provided that such synopses and resumes shall not be sold except usual sales of any publications in which such synopses or resumes may appear such as (but not so as to limit the generality of the foregoing) periodicals newspapers magazines or souvenir programmes];

(h) to make and sell sound recordings on disc, tape or otherwise [of the Work or any adaptation thereof] [from the sound track of [such films] [the Film] [television programmes] [the Television Film]] whereby the same may be separately performed and to perform such sound recordings in public to broadcast and transmit them by television of all kinds (whether now known or hereafter to be invented) and radio;

(i) to secure in the name of the Purchaser copyright registration and protection in any or all countries of [such films] [and television programmes] [the Film/Television Film] [and sound recordings];

(j) to exercise all so-called 'merchandising rights' (as that expression is understood in the film industries of the United Kingdom and the United States of America) including but not by way of limitation the manufacture and sale of goods (including comic strips and printed matter of all kinds [other than books]) reproducing depicting or decorated with the characters scenes and incidents of or articles appearing in the Work or in [such films] [television programmes] [the Film/Television Film] and to protect such manufacture and sale by registration in its own name or otherwise as it may think fit of patents trade marks or designs or otherwise as may be available in each state or country of the World [provided that nothing in this Clause shall confer any right to publication in book form or (except as a comic strip) in any newspaper or periodical but without prejudice to any synopses or 'book of the film' rights specifically granted by this Agreement];

(k) to write or cause to be written and to print, publish and sell [adaptations in book form based on] the screenplay of [such films] [or television programmes] [the Film/Programme/Series] [(customarily known as 'a book of the film/series/programme')];

(l) to use the [Author]'s name likeness and biography in connection with the exploitation of the rights hereby assigned;

(m) to do all other acts customarily comprised in grants of full film [and television] rights;

(n) to assign or license to any third party the rights specified above;

[TO HOLD the same unto the Purchaser absolutely in all parts of the World in which copyright (or rights analogous thereto) in the Work subsists or may be acquired during [the full term of copyright (or such other rights) and all renewals, reversions and extensions thereof] OR [the period of (   )] calendar years commencing on the date of this Agreement Provided That the expiry of the Licence hereby granted shall not affect the Purchaser's right to continue to exploit by all means and in all media permitted hereunder [any films] [the Film] [any television programme] [the Television Film] [if] produced prior to the date of expiry of the licence hereby granted for the full period of copyright subsisting therein and thereafter in perpetuity] [Provided That the Reserved Rights are hereby expressly reserved to the Owner and are excluded from the [grant] [assignment] of rights made or intended to be made hereunder].

The rights to be acquired

The Producer may often only obtain limited rights (i.e. to produce only **one** theatrical feature film, or only **one** television series or programme) as opposed to the right to make an unlimited number of films and/or television programmes (the more limited grant has become the norm). If the Producer is only entitled to make one feature film for the purchase price, the Producer may still want to acquire the right to produce remakes or sequels (rather than leaving these rights with the owner, who can then grant them to third parties who wish to cash in on the success of the original production). Then the agreement should enable and require the Producer to make further payments on production of remakes or sequels. A very hard-nosed rights owner may only agree to grant **first offer and matching rights** over additional rights not included in the purchase price. First offer (or refusal) and matching rights operate as follows.

- If a Producer is granted the right of **first offer or refusal** by a rights owner, that means the rights owner cannot transfer those rights to a third party without first offering them to the Producer who, if it wants the rights, then has a specific period to negotiate to acquire them. If at the end of that period, the parties cannot agree, the rights owner can sell the rights to someone else, but a wise Producer, in this instance, should get the owner to agree not to do so on terms which are actually worse than the Producer was prepared to offer (and which were rejected by the owner).
- To have **matching rights** means that the rights owner will have agreed with the Producer that, before selling the rights to anyone else, the owner will offer the rights to the Producer on the terms on which he was willing to sell them to the other person and, if the Producer can 'match' those terms within a certain time period, the owner must sell to the Producer.

Definition of 'film'

The agreement should include wording which defines what is meant by 'a film', where the grant of rights is for a theatrical feature film production only. This is because otherwise there is a risk that the expression 'film' may be given the meaning it has in the Copyright, Designs and Patents Act 1988, where the word embraces both theatrical feature films and television programmes.

Assignment or licence?

It is becoming more common for rights owners to prefer to **grant** a licence for the full period of copyright (or for a shorter period), rather than

assigning rights by way of partial assignment of copyright. When this is so, remember the following points.

- A licence, unlike an assignment, can theoretically be brought to an end. So the Producer should require the licence to be **incapable** of being terminated (i.e. **irrevocable**) during the period for which the licence is granted. There should also be a clause limiting the owner's rights, in the case of breach by the Producer of the agreement, to the recovery of damages only (Chapter 8, page 133 gives an example).
- If the licence is for a period less than the full period of copyright (and the Producer will prefer at least 15 or 20 years, although 10 year licences are not unheard-of) remember that one of the rights granted by the owner will be the right to **exploit** films or programmes made after the licence is granted. The Producer must therefore preserve its right to continue to exploit them while they remain in copyright, even after expiry of the licence. In that case, the only thing which the Producer will lose, when the licence period ends, is the right to make **more** films.

Moral rights

There should be a specific waiver of the moral rights of the owner (Chapter 9, pages 144–8).

Ancillary rights

A grant of film or television rights will not automatically be taken to include ancillary or secondary rights such as merchandising. or publishing rights. So if the Producer wants them, they should be specifically listed in the agreement.

Rights to publicize the film

The Producer must also specifically acquire so-called 'publicity rights' (namely, the right to broadcast on radio and television extracts of the work; the right to publish (but not to sell) synopses to promote the film). Synopses are usually restricted to a specific number of words to prevent publication of anything which would compete with the work itself but the top limit of 7500–10 000 words applies in the case of a full-length novel. In the case of a novella or short story, this may drop to 2500 or 3000.

When to pay?

Sometimes the Producer will want the right to pay the cash purchase price in more than one instalment. If this is the case, it is usual for the second payment to be made by no later than on 'the first day of principal photography' of the relevant production.

Escalators

> In consideration of the foregoing licence and of the agreement made by the Owner pursuant to this Agreement the Company will pay to the Owner:
>
> (a) a sum equal to two and one half per cent (2.5%) of the Budget of the Film and subject always to a minimum payment of [   ] Pounds [£   ] and a maximum payment of [   ] Pounds [£   ]; and
> (b) sums from time to time equal to five per cent (5%) of one hundred per cent (100%) of Net Profits.
>
> the Budget   in relation to any feature film contemplated to be made under this Agreement an amount equal to the final agreed budgeted cost of production less any contingency provision, less any fee payable in respect of a completion guarantee and less any part of such cost (if any) which is budgeted to be paid to the Owner under this Agreement.

When a feature film is intended, the full purchase price is commonly expressed as a percentage of the budget, or even the final cost of production (which may well be different), so that the Producer pays:

- a minimum sum (a 'floor') of a specified amount;
- an 'escalator' of the excess over the minimum amount up to, for example, two per cent (2%) of the budget or the final cost of production.

The escalator is usually capped (or in other words subject to a 'ceiling') of a specified amount, so that if the film's production costs do increase, the Producer's ultimate financial liability to the rights owner is limited. The definition of the budget or production cost should exclude what is being paid to the owner (otherwise the owner gets a percentage of that **as well**), and sometimes it will exclude the fee payable to the completion guarantor and the contingency amount (Chapter 7, *Production and financing agreements*, page 113) and any costs of financing (including interest payable to a Financier).

Deferments and net profits

> [The Purchaser will also pay the Owner] sums from time to time equal to [   ] per cent (%) of [the share of] net profits (as defined in Schedule [C] for which purpose references to 'the Payee' shall be

construed as references to the Owner) from the [first or only [film/ television film] that may be made pursuant to rights hereby granted] [to which the Purchaser shall remain entitled after deduction of any shares of such net profits payable to or retainable by any distributor or payable to any third party in connection with the provision of any services rights finance or facilities in connection with the production of [such film]/[the Film/Television Film] which would be recognized as part of the production cost if such shares had been quantified and paid out of finances provided for the said production].

The payment provisions may include a 'deferment' (Chapter 6, *Financing*, pages 95 and 98) or a share of net profits. Either way, the agreement needs to make it clear how 'deferment' or 'net profits' should be defined. A written net profit definition (which will normally include a definition of 'deferment' because deferments have to be taken into account in calculating net profits) may be attached to the acquisition agreement in the form of a Schedule. Alternatively, the Producer may prefer not to attach a definition at this stage because the definition which will eventually apply is likely to be imposed on the Producer by the Financiers and/or distributors of the production at a later date and may well differ. In this case, the following wording will usually be used.

'Net profits' and 'deferment' shall be defined, computed [and payable] in accordance with the principal production, finance and distribution agreements relating to the first or only film to be produced under this Agreement

A well-advised rights owner will ask for, but may not always get:

- the Producer to agree to procure **direct payment** to the owner by the distributor or other person receiving exploitation income and paying out income shares. Certainly direct payment should occur where the owner is entitled to a share of gross receipts (**very** unusual) or a deferment. If the owner is receiving a share of 'Producer's Net Profits' (Chapter 6, *Financing*, page 98) or the Producer is unwilling or unable to agree to procure direct payment, the Producer should agree to pay the owner his share within a fixed period (say 30 days) after receipt by the Producer of relevant income;
- 'favoured nations' treatment with all other profit participants as to the definition which is used (namely, that the owner's share of net profits will be calculated under a definition not less favourable than that applicable to any other net profit participant).

Payments for television rights

If the Purchaser in exercise of the rights granted by Clause 1(c) broadcasts or transmits or causes to be broadcast or transmitted [any television programme or series of programmes (not being a film)] [the

Television Film] the Purchaser will pay to the Owner [not later than twenty-eight (28) days after the date of such broadcast or transmission] a fee of £   for each [hour] of running time (including so-called 'commercial breaks') PROVIDED THAT the fee will be reduced or (as the case may be) increased on a pro rata basis if the running time of [each such programme] [the Television Film] is less or (as the case may be) greater than [one (1) hour] (including so-called 'commercial breaks'). Payment of such fee shall permit an unlimited number of further broadcasts or transmissions of [such programme]/[the Television Film].

As implied by the example above, where television rights are being purchased, it is becoming more usual these days to have a purchase price which permits the production of a specified number of hours of television, but which is payable in full and up-front, even if fewer screen hours are eventually produced. When the Producer is taking a grant of full film and television rights with a view to making a particular production, it is normal to provide for further payment (again based on the number of hours produced) to the owner if a television programme or series is **also** produced **subsequently**. This payment will become due either when the programmes are being made or (less usually) when they are transmitted. The payment may cover all kinds of subsequent exploitation after the first transmission (as in the example above). However, the rights owner may insist that the initial payment covers **only** the initial broadcast and that other exploitation will trigger further payment in the nature of residuals or use fees, as under the PACT/WGGB Agreement (page 80 below and Chapter 9, *Rights clearances I*, page 153), as if the initial payment were a script writing fee.

How long is an 'hour' on television?

Television 'hours' usually include commercial breaks (which is why people refer to so many 'commercial hours' of television). A commercial hour, throughout the television industry, is therefore about 50 minutes. Another way of doing this is to refer to a 'slot length' of an hour.

Payment for ancillary rights

If the Producer is granted secondary rights (such as character merchandising or certain publishing rights) the rights owner will usually require additional payment for these rights. This additional payment is generally expressed as a share of the net income received by the Producer from the exploitation of these rights. Chapter 14, *Secondary exploitation*, contains further detail. Alternatively, the Producer could take the view that the owner should simply receive a share of net profits, if the calculation of net profits includes income from these sources. Where the work has great merchandising potential, the owner will not accept this and may ask for up to 50% of the net income derived from character merchandising. However, the Producer might also remember that, where the work has been previously published, there is an argument that the Producer should receive a share of the income of future editions of the work, in circumstances where the sales can be largely attributed to the film or television production. It really depends on the circumstances, and while this kind of deal is not unheard-of, it is not that usual for a Producer to be able to obtain it.

> For example, P, a producer, requires the right to make a television series based on a series of children's books. The books were very popular in the 1950s, but have since gone out of fashion. However, P's television series updates the storylines and characters and re-introduces the books to the public. They start to sell so well that the publisher is able to create new editions which reflect the changes made to the originals by the television series. In those circumstances, it would be reasonable for P to get a share of the increase in income to the publisher since the television series increased the book's popularity.

Owner's warranties

The agreement should contain a number of warranties from the owner: that he owns the rights, that the work qualifies for copyright protection throughout the world, that the owner has not previously granted the rights to anyone else, etc.

Litigation

If the owner is not the author and cannot show a clean and complete chain of title to the copyright, it is also essential to have specific confirmation in the agreement that there is no present or prospective litigation regarding ownership of any of the rights being granted to the Producer. Note, however, that this kind of confirmation will not deflect problems in getting Errors and Omissions insurance. If there **is** a gap in the chain of title, insurance cover may not be given at all; or the insurer may just not give coverage against claims arising as a result of the incompleteness of title to the underlying rights.

Reserved rights – 'holdbacks'

The following points all arise where the owner has retained certain rights in which the Producer might potentially be interested, or the exploitation of which might have an effect on the production contemplated by the

Producer (e.g. live stage rights, television rights if the Producer has only feature film rights (or vice versa), etc.).

- The agreement may contain 'holdbacks'. A 'holdback' is an agreement **not** to exercise rights which the owner has retained but which might, if exercised, have an adverse effect on the value of the rights granted to the Producer. The only essential holdback is that of the television rights where feature film rights only have been granted.
- The 'holdbacks' of course do not last for ever, and are normally restricted to a maximum of seven years from the date on which the rights were acquired or (if sooner) five years from the start date of production of the Producer's film/programme based on the work.

Holdbacks

The Owner hereby warrants to and undertakes and agrees with the Purchaser that the Owner has not granted and will not grant any assignment or licence of or permit the exercise in any part of the World of the rights severally specified in the first column below for the periods commencing on the date hereof and expiring on the dates respectively set against such several rights in the second column below.

Column one	Column two
[(a) Broadcasting and/or transmitting live and recorded performances by television (including pay television, cable and satellite)	7 years from the date hereof or 5 years from the date ('the Start Date') of the start of principal photography of the first or only film to be made pursuant to the rights hereby granted or transferred (whichever is the earlier)]
[(b) Broadcasting by radio dramatized versions or straight readings of the Work by live or recorded performances	7 years from the date hereof or 5 years from [the date ('] the Start Date['] of the start of principal photography of the first or only [film/television film] to be made pursuant to the rights hereby granted or transferred (whichever is the earlier)]
[(c) Performing the Work on the Stage	7 years from the date hereof or 5 years from the Start Date (whichever is the earlier)]

- The Producer should also take a right of first refusal and matching rights in relation to certain rights retained by the owner (e.g. theatrical feature film rights if the original agreement was for television only,) or sequel or remake rights if the owner has not granted these). As previously mentioned, the Producer will have a set number of days in which to negotiate after it has been offered first refusal, or in which to match an existing offer (in the case of matching rights). The number of days are open to negotiation but the Producer will normally require at least 45 for first offer, and 15 days for matching rights).

If the Purchaser wishes to make and exploit a feature film based on the Work primarily for exhibition in cinemas theatres and other places to which the public is admitted or to exercise the live stage rights in the Work it must give notice of such wish to the Owner and the parties will negotiate with a view to reaching agreement on the terms on which such film will be made and exploited or such live stage rights exercised.

In the course of such negotiations (and not later than 90 days after receiving the notice referred to in sub-clause (a)) the Owner will submit to the Purchaser in writing the terms on which it is prepared to grant such film rights or live stage rights and if such negotiations are unsuccessful or if there having been no negotiations the Owner wishes to grant such film rights or live stage rights to any person other than the Purchaser it shall not do so without first offering them to the Purchaser on the same terms as they have been offered to the other person and the Purchaser shall have [   ] days in which to accept or reject them and if the Owner subsequently alters the financial terms offered to that person (except by way of minor alteration of no substantial importance) it shall be obliged to offer such altered terms to the Purchaser and this sub-clause shall apply to those terms.

Owner's credit

The following points apply to the **credit** to be given to the owner in relation to the finished production (or the author if he or she is not the owner).

- There will of course be provision for on-screen credit (on all copies of the finished film) and sometimes the owner will also be credited in major paid advertising, but either way the Producer should restrict the obligation to give credit only to copies of the film/advertising which are issued by the Producer or under the Producer's control (by third parties with whom the Producer has a contract).
- The form of credit will usually be 'Based on the book by . . . . . . ' or, where the film has a different name, 'Based on the book entitled [   ] by . . . . . . '. The owner may ask for further refinements as to position, size of type and prominence of the screen or advertising credit, and that the credit be on a separate card. It is not unusual to provide that the author will be accorded credit in advertising wherever the screenwriter is mentioned and sometimes (if the author is very

famous) wherever the director is mentioned. Producers tend to try to avoid these specific obligations, unless the author is really famous (and therefore has so-called 'marquee value'), as with Stephen King or James Herbert. The ultimate distributor will be responsible for carrying out these obligations and may find them irksome.

- The obligation to give credit is always subject to a set of exclusions which are nearly always the same in any agreement. This is why they are often referred to as 'standard industry exclusions'. To refer to them as such in the agreement, to save listing them, can be dangerous, because the ultimate distributor/broadcaster of the production may have refined its own exclusions to include extra situations where credit will not be given. The Producer may thus simply state that the credit obligation is subject to the standard credit exclusions of the distributor and/or broadcaster of the production. Chapter 13, page 231 contains a list of the usual exclusions.
- The owner may ask for credit on by-products, and especially on packaging of videogram copies of the production – this is not an unreasonable request for a famous author.

Chapter 13, *Distribution agreements*, contains further comments on credits and how a Producer's obligation to accord them should be limited in certain circumstances.

Whether the Producer can assign the agreement

As a matter of English law, if an agreement says nothing about whether or not a party can transfer (or assign) its rights under the agreement to someone else, that party will be able to do so without needing the other party's consent. It will generally be absolutely imperative for a Producer to be able to transfer its rights under an acquisition agreement. The Financiers of the proposed production will often require it, and certainly any **lender** of finance will want to take security (such as a charge or mortgage) over the rights to be able to enforce repayment. Such a charge will be meaningless if the underlying rights are not capable of being transferred to the lender (Chapter 6, *Financing*, pages 99–100 contains an explanation of how charges work).

Note that this applies only to **rights** or **benefits** given by an agreement – neither party can effectively transfer its **obligations** to someone else without the other party's consent, because the other party would have to consent to letting the person who originally promised to perform those obligations 'off the hook' and accept that it will look to someone else to perform them. Chapter 4, *The deal*, pages 42–3 considers this.

However, a rights owner may want to control when a Producer can assign its rights under the agreement, to stop the rights going to some fly-by-night who will never make anything of the project or, even worse, may do something disreputable with it. If the owner has the bargaining power, he may like to include a clause that the Producer cannot transfer its rights under the agreement without the owner's consent, except to a US 'major' or to a reputable production company of demonstrably similar standing to the Producer, or to a bank or other recognized lending institution for the purpose of raising the cost of production.

The owner may also ask for a share of the purchaser's profit if the assignment is made at a profit (the figure requested is generally 50% of the profit made by the Producer), on an outright sale to a third party.

Authority to pay the agent

Where the owner has an agent, the Producer should not agree to pay the purchase price to the agent without specific authority from the owner.

Value Added Tax

VAT is always payable on sums agreed to be paid for the transfer of rights of this kind, and from the payee's point of view, it is vital to provide that the sums agreed to be paid are exclusive of VAT which will be paid on top. In the absence of this, the law states that sums agreed to be paid for VAT-able goods or services will be treated as including VAT, and the owner would then end up having to account for 17.5% (at current rates) to HM Customs and Excise.

Governing law

Where the parties are not both situated or resident in the same territory, so that they are each subject to different laws and legal systems, the agreement should state what law will be applied in interpreting the agreement (if a dispute arises). It will generally be the law of the country where the Producer is based; if either party is based in another legal jurisdiction, that party would be well-advised, before signing the contract, to get the advice of a lawyer qualified in the law which is stated to apply to the contract.

Using a lawyer

As a note of caution, although the comments above may prove a useful guide to anyone trying to make sense of one of these agreements, this is one area where it is quite inadvisable to try to draw up an agreement without the aid or advice of an experienced media lawyer. The underlying rights are absolutely vital, and if the project does proceed to production, any error or omission made at the time of acquiring these rights may not be capable of being corrected. If not, this could (at worst) bring a halt to the production for good, or at the very least, prove to be extremely expensive to put right.

Formats – acquiring changed format rights

Sometimes the underlying work will be the format of a television series which has been successful in another country. 'Format' is the short term used to describe the characters, situations and other identifying elements of a television series. It is those elements which remain the same from programme to programme, whereas the plot changes around them. An example of an imported format is the sitcom *The Upper Hand*, based on the US sitcom *She's The Boss*. In acquiring the format of *She's The Boss*, the Producers of *The Upper Hand* will have bought the right to devise their own plot-lines around the underlying situation/characters/relationships.

The principles of acquiring rights in an existing format will be very much the same as for a book or a play. However, since the Producer will usually be acquiring the rights to make another television series based upon the format (but adapted for the Producer's country – hence the expression 'changed format rights'), the sums of money payable up-front will usually be considerably smaller than for drama production or a feature film. So the option agreement does not usually need to go into the same kind of protective detail.

What does the format owner get paid?

The usual financial structure is that the format owner will receive:

- a lump sum (or royalty) payable for each programme in the new series which the Producer makes based on the format;
- a share of income derived by the Producer from ancillary exploitation of the new series, such as merchandising and publishing;
- if the new series is sold overseas, a share of the income made from such sales which the Producer is entitled to keep for its own benefit.

What rights are granted?

The structure described above assumes that the format owner grants to the Producer ancillary rights and/or the right to sell the new series overseas. Quite often a licence of format rights **only** allows a Producer to make a programme/ series based on the format and show it in the Producer's territory.

The deal might also provide for the Producer to be able to use the scripts from the original series (instead of just the basic characters and situations of which the format itself could be said to subsist). This will usually involve an additional payment per script, and the owner will often require that the scripts are adapted, rather than used verbatim.

The acquiring Producer, if dealing with the Producer of the original series and that original Producer was not also the broadcaster of the series, should also make sure that the original **broadcaster** does not have an interest in the rights. If that broadcaster does, the Producer should ask for written evidence of the agreement of the broadcaster to the terms of the deal.

Further comments on formats are to be found in Chapter 14, *Secondary exploitation*.

COMMISSIONING A TREATMENT OR SCRIPT

For a non-factual production, the central part of development will be the writing of a script or, at the very least, a treatment.

Once the writer has been selected, he or she will be required to do one of two things: either to write material based on someone else's idea, format or work; or to write material based on his original idea.

The basic structure of the deal with the writer will be the same in either case, but if the project is the writer's own brainchild, there will usually be additional commercial terms. The additional terms will concern future and 'spin-off' exploitation of the project such as sequels, or changed format sales. As the foundation of the success of the project will have been the writer's own idea, he/she will wish to share in the proceeds.

WRITERS' AGREEMENTS

The basic terms

The structure and contents of the agreement will be based on the relevant collective bargaining agreements which the writers' union (the Writers' Guild of Great Britain ('WGGB')) has concluded on behalf of its members, either with the broadcasters (where the broadcaster is producing in-house) or with the body which represents independent producers (the Producers' Alliance for Cinema and Television ('PACT')). This book will consider only the terms agreed with PACT (referred to as the PACT/WGGB Agreement).

PACT/WGGB Agreement

Structure

The agreement operates by setting out general terms which apply to any kind of production for which the writer may be commissioned to write. The essentials of a writer's agreement are very similar to any other agreement for the services of a creative individual and such agreements are considered in more detail in Chapter 8, *Hiring and firing*.

As well as covering these general aspects, the PACT/WGGB Agreement contains separate provisions (largely relating to payment) for different types of production, currently classified as:

- feature films budgeted at £2 million and over;
- feature films budgeted from £250 000 up to £2 million;
- one-off television films budgeted at £750 000 and above;
- television series and serials with format provided by the Producer.

The second and third categories are currently treated in the same way and attract the same scale of fees.

Fees

In all cases, the agreement requires a certain minimum fee to be paid for the writing of a script. The writing process is split up into separate stages (e.g. treatment, first draft, second draft). The agreement provides for the copyright in the script to be transferred to the Producer in relation to each stage when it has been written, **but not until** payment for that stage has been made.

The basic fees set out in the PACT/WGGB Agreement are minimum amounts. A writer's agent will often require the writing fee to be greater than the minimum amount in the PACT/WGGB Agreement. Payment of the fee pays for the writer's work on the script **plus** the basic exploitation rights for the type of production for which the script is required. For instance, in the case of a script which has been commissioned for production as part of a television series, the basic fee buys the right to make one UK network transmission of the programme based on the script. For a script for a feature film, payment buys the right to show the film theatrically.

Then, any further uses will attract a further payment (usually expressed as a percentage of the basic fee) known as 'residuals' or 'use fees'.

Where the project was the writer's idea

The writer's share in 'spin-off' exploitation

Where the project is an original idea devised by the writer, he or she will generally want additional benefits other than the script fee plus residuals. Typically, the writer will ask for:

- a share of ancillary income (publishing, merchandising, etc.);

- the first refusal to write sequels or books based on the script;
- a share of income derived from licensing 'spin-offs' (such as a television series based on the original feature film based on the writer's script; or if the script was for a television series, a share of the income from selling changed format rights).

Rights reserved (i.e. not granted by) the writer

The usual situation where a writer is commissioned to write a script is that the writer **assigns all** rights to the Producer. However, if the writer is in a very powerful position, he or she may only **license** the basic film or television rights in the script to the Producer, and retain all other rights. But in this case, the Producer may wish to negotiate a share of income from exploitation by the writer of those other rights. The justification for the Producer is that the success of exploiting those other rights will have been founded on the Producer's film or television series. For example, the writer may have retained the right to write and publish a book based on the film or series. The sales of such a book are likely to be enhanced by the publicity given it by the film/series. Of course, this argument might not be so convincing if the writer is already a best-selling novelist, and could have expected extensive book sales anyway.

Writer's option to write sequels

Where the project is a television series, with the potential for continuing beyond the first series, the writer will often ask for the guaranteed right to write a certain number of the scripts for each series. In fact, this also happens with feature films when a writer has written an original script, and the subject matter is one which has potential for a sequel. The Producer, if agreeing to this, should make it subject to the writer being **available** when required, and should also try to make the extent of the commitment to the writer (if not the commitment itself) subject to the approval of the broadcaster of the future series, or Financier(s) of the sequel. Since the terms of the writer's engagement for these further scripts will have to be agreed at the time, the Producer should also state that if the parties cannot reach agreement within a **specific** time period on the terms of the writer's engagement, the Producer can engage someone else.

The writer may also try to reserve certain ancillary rights of exploitation (such as publishing or merchandising, or most importantly, changed format rights). However, it is more usual for the Producer to acquire control over these rights from the writer in return for an agreement to pay the writer a share of the income derived from exploiting them. This share can be up to 50%, depending on the stature and bargaining power of the writer.

Format royalty

The writer who has devised an original television series will in any event also have negotiated for a format fee or royalty, namely a fee for each programme made which is based on the writer's idea. The writer will ask for this fee for **all** episodes, but the Producer may only agree to pay it for episodes where the script has not been written by the format devising writer (on the basis that he or she will be getting a script fee for any other episode, for having written the script). The format fee is usually calculated as a percentage of the actual script fee paid for that episode.

Further details of the structuring of deals with writers in relation to secondary rights are contained in Chapter 14, *Secondary exploitation*.

Writer's turnaround

One last issue, in relation to ideas which the writer has created, is that the PACT/WGGB Agreement states that the writer will be able to re-acquire all rights in an original script, if principal photography of a production based on that script has not commenced within two years after the date of delivery to the Producer of the last material which the writer was commissioned to write. The writer, in return for the re-assignment of rights, has to repay 50% of the fees paid to the writer. However, if the Producer, in financing the development of the project, agreed in the development financing agreement that it would repay the entire amount of finance provided by the development Financier if a production based on the project ever proceeds, the Producer may have a problem: there is bound to be a difference, usually a substantial one, between the sums repaid by the writer and the sum which the Producer has to repay to the Financier. One solution is to get the writer to agree that he/she has to take on the Producer's obligations to the Financier, therefore the rights can be reassigned to the Writer. Another would be to try and get the Financier to acknowledge that the Producer's obligations to repay anything will come to an end if the writer becomes entitled to re-acquire the rights.

Credits

The same principles apply to the giving of credit to writers as are described more fully above (relating to the terms of option and acquisition agreements). However, there is a negotiated agreement between the predecessors of PACT and the WGGB (concluded in 1974) known as 'the Screenwriting Credits Agreement'. This sets out the terms on which credit is to be accorded and what credits a writer may be entitled to in different circumstances (such as where the final script has been written by more than one person or where the writer is also responsible for originating the idea). It is therefore often convenient (and shorter) to state in writer's contracts that credit will be accorded to the writer in accordance with the Screenwriting Credits Agreement. This Agreement also sets out relevant exclusions to the obligation to give credit. Credit is naturally extremely important for writers, particularly those who still have a reputation to establish. It is therefore one of the principal potential sources of dispute between the Producer and the writer, particularly where the Producer may have started with a script written by one writer and retained one or two others to work on the same script. It can then be difficult to value each writer's contribution to the final script. To save problems, it is common to state in a writer's contract that any dispute over credits will be referred to the President for the time being of the WGGB (or another person appointed by the President), who will make a decision based on the facts. Both the writer and the Producer will then agree to abide by that decision (whatever it may turn out to be).

Cut-offs

Payment in instalments – payment on 'delivery' or 'acceptance'?

As the script will be delivered in separate stages, a Producer normally agrees to pay the script fee in instalments, each instalment payable as to half on commencement of writing and the other half either on **delivery** to or **acceptance** by the Producer of that stage. The Producer will prefer not to have to pay the second half until the material delivered is **accepted**, as the writer will then have an incentive to carry out the extra work required by the Producer to put the material into an acceptable state. On the other hand, the writer would prefer to be paid on delivery. The fear here is that the Producer may have changed its mind about what was required between the date of commissioning and delivery of the script. The writer could in theory be forced to do considerable further work for no further payment, after having delivered what the Producer **originally** wanted, in re-writing the script to reflect the Producer's **new** requirements. This is obviously a matter for negotiation. It may not even be worth discussing when the parties have worked together before and know what to expect of each other.

However, the most important principle of the stage payments is that a Producer can call a halt at any stage if the writer's work is not what was wanted. This cuts the Producer's liability to a minimum, because the agreement should state that the Producer has no further liability to the writer, leaving the Producer free to bring in another writer and start from scratch.

Apportioning writer's fees if a writer is replaced but his work is used

Unfortunately, the situation can become more complicated if the Producer, having brought in another writer, wishes to use some part of the first writer's work. This is the kind of situation which can lead to the disputes over credits referred to earlier, if the second writer does not start from scratch but is given the first writer's material to work on. Established writers may actually require that if a Producer wants to proceed with the first draft at all, no other person may be engaged to work on the second draft (i.e. the Producer must use that writer alone, unless it decides to scrap the first draft completely and adopt an entirely new approach).

Naturally the biggest danger which the Producer runs, in using part of the first writer's book, is a financial one. The remuneration to a writer will usually be based on the writer receiving a certain fee for doing the work, plus another fee (paid, say, at the start of principal photography if a film or programme is made based on his/her work). Even where another writer has been brought in, if the first writer's work is used to any extent, the Producer will not be able to claim that it has no further liability to that writer. Furthermore, if the writer's agreement is not properly drafted the Producer may find that, having used some small element of the first writer's work, the **full** amount agreed to be paid, as if the production was made based on that writer's work alone, will become due to the first writer. It is therefore vital that the agreement should enable a reduction of the writer's ultimate financial settlement if only a fraction of his or her work finds its way into the final screenplay or script. Again, it is sensible to agree that the matter will be referred to a third party for 'arbitration' if the parties are unable to agree on what the writer's final entitlement should be.

Moral rights

Lastly, the issue of moral rights needs to be considered. These rights, who is entitled to them (apart from writers), and how they should be treated in film and programme production is considered in more detail in Chapter 9, pages 144–8.

<table>
<tr><td>**6**</td><td>

Financing

</td></tr>
</table>

FINANCING OPTIONS

This chapter concentrates primarily on production finance, since to some extent development finance and the issues that arise out of it have already been covered in Chapter 5, *Development*.

To finance a production, a Producer has various options, some of which it is more likely to achieve than others. These are:

- to raise finance for the **production company** on an investment basis (venture capital, business expansion schemes, etc.);
- to raise finance for the **production** on an investment basis – here, as in the above option, 'investment' means advancing money in return for a share of the profits; but in this instance, the investor will also wish to get the investment back from the proceeds of exploitation of the production;
- to **pre-sell** exploitation rights in the production either in part, or by agreeing a 'negative pick-up' deal with the studio (essentially, an outright sale of all rights to the studio for a sum which will cover the cost of production); or to sell all rights to a commissioning broadcaster;
- to obtain governmental, regional or EC grants (which may or may not involve securing official co-production status under one or other international co-production treaties);
- to use so-called 'tax shelter' schemes (which again may involve applying for co-production status under a co-production treaty);
- to secure a sponsorship deal for the production;
- to do a barter deal (namely, selling rights for broadcasting air-time so that the rights owner can raise finance from advertisers who wish to use the air-time to put out their adverts). This form of financing is not prevalent in the UK, so no further comment will be made on it;
- (for television programmes) to obtain a fully financed commission from a broadcaster.

It is unlikely, in the current climate of UK and European film and television production, that any single one of these options will provide the full finance needed by the producer to meet the budgeted cost of the production. An exception to this is where a broadcaster agrees to finance 100% of the budget of a television production, but this will usually only happen where the production is not significantly expensive. Even for television productions, where the budget is very large, the broadcaster or Producer will be looking for another (overseas) broadcaster to foot some of the financing costs by concluding co-production arrangements.

Some of the financing options are considered in more detail below.

INVESTING IN A PRODUCTION COMPANY

If a Producer has a moderately successful track record, it may be able to find backers to finance the running costs of the production company. These backers may be:

- a broadcaster;
- another production company;
- a venture capital house;
- private investors, either through an Enterprise Investment Scheme ('EIS') or otherwise.

In all cases, the investors in a **company** will usually be taking shares in it. However, the following points should be kept in mind.

- **If a broadcaster invests**, the production company may need to retain independent status under the Broadcasting Act 1990 (so that its programmes will qualify as part of the 25% quota of independent productions which broadcasters are required to transmit each year). If so, the Producer must ensure that no single broadcaster has a greater than 15% shareholding in the company, nor must a production company itself have a shareholding of more than 15% in any broadcaster.

  (The rules setting out what qualifies as 'an independent production' appear in the Broadcasting (Independent Productions) Order 1991, which has been made under the Broadcasting Act 1990. A summary of this Order can be found in Appendix F.
- **If another production company invests**, again, to preserve 'independent' status, the investee company must ensure that the investor is not 'connected with' a broadcaster, within the meaning given to those expressions in the Broadcasting Act 1990. Put simply, this means that the investor should not be 'controlled' by a broadcaster, or an 'associate' of a broadcaster. Again, these expressions are explained in Appendix F.
- **If a venture capitalist invests**, when investment is made by way of venture capital in a business (unless a new or 'start-up' company is formed using

'seed capital'), the investors are looking for a profitable company with a proven track record. Therefore, investors tend to target established companies with potential for maintaining and increasing profits. It is unusual for venture capital investment to be made into a film or television company because of the high financial risks involved in the business.

If, however, such investment were to be made, it would probably be made by the venture capitalist taking some of the shares, or partly by taking shares and partly by making a loan. The nature of the shareholding varies from deal to deal, but invariably the venture capitalist's shares will provide a preferential dividend return. If the investment is partly by loan, sometimes the loan or part of the loan is convertible into shares at the option of the investors. Sometimes there is a 'ratchet' (namely, a sliding scale of shares which the management will be entitled to be allocated if the company performs well) as an incentive to the managers.

Venture capital investors will usually want the right to appoint a director, with the right for that director to attend board meetings. They will also want:

- veto rights over decisions on certain issues which they anticipate might affect their position;
- regular financial reports (either monthly or quarterly);
- details of the financial budget.

They may also require that board meetings be held regularly and 'key man insurance' taken out to cover against the death or disability of people who are seen as essential to the future of the business.

- **If the investment is by private investors**, the expression 'private investors' simply means that the investment in the company is not 'public'. If the company is not a public one (i.e. floated on the Stock Exchange) the shares cannot be offered to the general public. There are very strict controls on offering shares in private companies, under the Financial Services Act 1986 ('FSA'). The requirements of this legislation, designed to protect would-be investors, are so 'user-unfriendly' and complex that they can really only be safely navigated with the assistance of an accountant or solicitor who specializes in this area of law.

Put simply, if the investee company is offering or distributing any kind of document containing information about the company which is aimed at attracting investment, it must be approved by a person authorized under the FSA for this purpose.

Even before the FSA came into force, it was necessary for investee companies to be very cautious about making statements (in any form) to attract, persuade or inform potential investors. If such statements were wrong or exaggerated, the investor who, on the strength of them, put his or her money into a company might well have had a legal action against the persons responsible for the publishing or making of the statements (the company itself and/or its directors). Under the FSA, the potential liability for misleading investors, or misrepresenting any material information is quite severe. Whilst this liability can be avoided by engaging professional advisers, as mentioned above, this makes the process of seeking private investment both lengthy and very expensive. It is therefore not a route which independent producers could often take, unless they could be entirely sure of getting the required amount of investment at the end of the day, both to meet their working capital requirements, as well as to cover the cost of the offer. The uncertainties of the production industry being what they are (or, sometimes unfairly, what those who are not in the industry **think** they are), independent producers who can be sure of attracting investment will be very rare indeed.

BES/EIS schemes

BES schemes ('Business Expansion Schemes') were one way of attracting investment. They were not historically of much interest for production companies, partly because the amount of investment allowed into production companies (before the scheme could qualify under the BES rules) was quite severely limited. (There is another reason, which is explained below.) In 1993, the BES scheme was replaced by the 'Enterprise Investment Scheme', or 'EIS'.

An EIS investment works in the following way: if the investment scheme qualifies under the EIS rules, the total investment which a company operating an EIS scheme can raise from all investors is £1 million per year during which the scheme operates. Each individual investor can invest up to £100 000 (as compared to only £40 000 under a BES scheme) in return for shares in the company, on condition that he or she does not withdraw the investment for five years. Then, at the end of the five year period, if the investor makes a profit on the sale of the shares, he or she will not have to pay capital gains tax on that profit. The benefit to the investor is that he receives tax relief on the amount of the investment, at a rate of 20%. For example, if an investor, 'A', invests £40 000, A will receive tax relief at 20% on £40 000 (being £8000). A therefore realizes £8000 in the first year (under the BES scheme, the rate of relief was 40%, so that the gain would have been £16 000). Averaged out over five years, and assuming that the value of the shares purchased does not fall over those five years, this does not constitute a particularly impressive investment (even with interest rates at the low level they have reached at the time of writing). Additionally, the value of the shares **can** fall and by the end of five years, A may not get all the original £40 000 back on selling them.

This risk is clearly seen as being much higher where production companies are concerned. Not many of these companies can show a five year period of continued growth and so, even with tax relief, production companies will rarely be seen as a good choice for an EIS investment. However, it might be suitable for a single project company such as, for example, one which intends to produce a television series for children based on an idea which has shown successful returns already (such as a series of children's books) and which has spin-off potential (such as character merchandising). This kind of project, if it succeeds, is likely to have a life-span of about five years. (That being said, certain children's programmes such as *Thomas the Tank Engine and Friends* are still going strong after a much longer period.)

INVESTMENT IN THE PRODUCTION

This section considers actual investment in and to the **production budget** of a film or television programme. This is distinct from **corporate** investment in the **production company**, which is rarely made for the purpose of financing individual productions, but rather to provide working capital to finance all the business activities of that company.

Investment in the **cost of production** is generally made on the basis that the investor will be repaid (or to use the usual expression, the investor will 'recoup' its money, plus interest, from the first receipts of the film). At the point where all investments are recouped, income after that will be what is generally referred to as 'net profits'. The investor may also be entitled to be paid a continuing share of the net profits, as a reward for risking its money in the first place.

This kind of investment – known as 'equity investment' – is relatively rare in this country, although it is the basis on which British Screen Finance Limited ('British Screen') invest in films and, sometimes, entities such as the broadcaster Channel Four. However, if a broadcaster invests in the film or programme, some or all of the money advanced by it will be a pre-payment for the purchase of rights of exploitation (such as UK Television Rights). To that extent, what the broadcaster pays should not be recoupable.

Pages 94–100 below contain a working example of how this kind of investment is made, in what order and on what basis investors will recoup and consequently how 'net profits' are calculated.

PRE-SALE OF RIGHTS

Mechanics of a pre-sale

By far the most common way (in this country at least) of raising money for a feature film and for large budget television productions is to sell some or all of the rights of exploitation in advance, before the film or television production is actually made. To sell all of the rights to one entity is what is known as a 'negative pick-up' deal.

The buyer will generally be a distributor who agrees to pay a particular price (known as a 'distribution advance') for the rights in question (say, theatrical feature film rights). The distributor's decision to buy will be made on the basis of the material which then exists: usually a script in final or very nearly final form, together with major actors and a director who has been attached to the project. If the budget of a film is about £3 million, the producer will be looking to procure pre-sales which will pay a sufficient amount to cover this budget. Sometimes this will not be possible and the producer must then look to other sources of finance.

Options over talent – 'pay or play'

At this stage, the Producer will generally have contracted the actors and the director on a **conditional** basis, to avoid having to pay these individuals if the film cannot be financed. This is one of the two basic choices which the Producer has – the other is to agree to pay the individual on a 'pay or play' basis. This means that the individual agrees to be available at an agreed time and, even if his or her services are not required, he or she will still be paid the agreed fee. It is evidently commercially preferable for the Producer to take an **option** over the services of the individual if that individual's agent is willing to agree it. In this case, the Producer will have the opportunity to contract the individual at an agreed time and for an agreed fee, but conditional upon the Producer giving notice by a particular date (usually accompanied by the first instalment of the agreed fee) that the individual's services are required. If no notice has been given, the individual will be free to take other engagements at the agreed time. On this basis the Producer will not have to pay very much to ensure that the director and actors it requires will be available, assuming that the film's finance can be raised.

Will the distributor pay money in advance?

If a pre-sale is agreed with a distributor, occasionally the distributor may agree to 'cash-flow' the agreed sum (i.e. pay it in agreed instalments over the period of production). However, this is not at all usual, as the distributor will only want to part with its money when it is **guaranteed to receive** the finished product. Otherwise, it is taking the following risks.

- If the distributor's advance is less than the entire budgeted cost, the rest of the finance will not be available and the Producer can only offer a partially completed film, having spent the distributor's money.
- The film as delivered is not what the distributor expected to get (and

agreed to pay for). For example, the stars may be different from those the Producer promised, or the script may have materially departed from the version which the distributor has seen and liked.

If the distributor **does** agree to cash-flow, the Producer's problems may not be solved anyway, if the distributor is not sufficiently 'cash-rich' for the Producer to be certain that the money will come in when it is needed.

Traditional film-financing – 'discounting' distribution advances

If the distributor will not cash-flow or the Producer does not feel confident that the distributor can do so, this leaves the Producer with a problem. There will not be enough money to finance the cost of production even though potential payments more than totalling the cost of production are payable (if and **only if** a film can be delivered). In these circumstances, certain banks will lend the Producer the money required to make the film (in other words the bank will 'discount the distribution advances') in return for the right to collect what the distributors have agreed to pay when the film is delivered. The bank will keep just enough of it to repay the bank its loan and to cover the bank's fees and costs, and pay over the surplus (if any) to the Producer. The amount which will be payable or repayable to the bank is the total of:

- the sum lent by the bank in the first place ('the principal amount');
- interest on the amount advanced (or, if it is being repaid in instalments, on any part of it still to be repaid) at an agreed rate;
- a commitment or arrangement fee (the amount of which may vary depending on the size of the loan);
- the costs incurred by the bank in relation to the transaction (most notably legal fees).

To make this a viable proposition, the distribution advances which the bank is agreeing to discount must add up to **at least** the total of what the bank needs to be paid or repaid.

The loan agreement

As part of the financing transaction, the Producer will enter into a loan agreement with the bank, under which:

- the bank will agree to advance the required amount (and the advance will usually **include** the commitment or arrangement fee so that, in essence, the bank lends the Producer the money to pay this fee);
- the Producer agrees to repay the bank on or before an outside repayment date;
- the Producer transfers to the bank all of its rights in the film by way of

security for the repayment of the loan.

This transfer of rights will of course be subject to any pre-existing distribution agreements, but the most important of the rights transferred to the bank will be the right to receive the income generated under those distribution agreements, until the time when the bank has received enough to meet the loan plus interest, costs and fees. At that stage when the Producer's liability to the bank has been extinguished, the bank releases its security or in other words re-transfers all the rights back to the Producer.

Collection agreements

Where there are a number of entities looking to receive a share of income from the exploitation of the production, either at the same time as or after the bank is paid, the Producer will often agree with the bank that the bank should set up a 'collection account'. Into this account all distribution advances will be paid, from which the bank makes payment to all interested parties according to their agreed shares. The operation of the account is generally regulated by a 'collection agreement', under which all the parties authorize the bank to collect distribution income, and the bank agrees to pay everyone their agreed share. Naturally the bank will charge for providing this service, which is why banks are willing to do this.

Protecting the bank's position

Since the bank will be providing the loan to cash-flow the production cost, paying the loan in agreed instalments during the period of production, the bank is running precisely the kind of risk which distributors find unpalatable. Therefore the bank (and the Producer, if it wants the bank's money) must do the utmost to ensure the following.

- The distribution agreements which are being discounted are absolutely watertight. This means that the distributor should be **unconditionally** obliged to pay the agreed distribution advance, so long as the film is delivered to the distributor in the form and condition which the distributor has contracted to receive.
- The film will be completed (even if the original budgeted cost of production is exceeded).
- The film will be delivered to the distributors in the condition and form which the distributor has contracted for.

To meet these two last requirements, it is essential for the bank to take out a completion guarantee for the film with a recognized completion guarantor. This is a form of insurance which will guarantee to provide the necessary money to complete the film if the Producer runs out of cash before completing production. However, in addition, the completion guarantor will also have the technical expertise necessary to take over production from the Producer if something untoward happens (such as, in a worst case scenario, the Producer becoming insolvent and being wound-up).

The mechanics and requirements of completion guarantees are explained in more detail in Chapter 11, *Completion guarantees and production insurances*, page 187.

CASE STUDY

Since it is so hard to raise production finance, a Producer generally has to resort to more than one of the sources of finance to raise the budgeted cost of production. To see how this works in practice (and before going on to consider the extra complexities introduced into the picture by governmental, regional or EC grants and the use of 'tax shelters'), there follows an example.

Freud's Little Secret

A Producer ('P') has developed a feature film project, which is based on the premise that Sigmund Freud was really a woman. The film is provisionally entitled *Freud's Little Secret*.

The script has been written and is ready to be shot. P has taken an option over the services of the main cast and director. The final production budget, cash-flow schedule and production schedule have all been completed, all locations have been found and pre-production is ready to start. The film will cost £2.5 million to make.

P has raised finance from:

- British Screen, £500 000;
- Channel Four, £500 000;
- a US distributor, £800 000;
- a German distributor, £300 000;
- a French distributor, £250 000;
- a Japanese distributor, £300 000.

(These figures are by no means a guide to what Producers can negotiate, but are purely imaginary examples and should be treated as such.)

This brings P to a total of £2 650 000. However, the reason why this film has attracted finance is because a Hollywood star comedian ('A') (a male) has agreed to play the lead role. This casting is hoped to attract a lot of publicity, on the assumption that US women's groups may make the obvious point that the character of Freud ought to be played by a woman.

A normally works at a fee of no less than £1.5 million per film. For this film, since he 'loves the script', he is willing to accept £1 million. However, the budget allowance for his salary is only £750 000 and P cannot raise the extra £250 000. A has therefore generously agreed to take a 'deferment'. This means that the payment of the £250 000 will be deferred until the film starts to make money. The other financiers have agreed to this, as they must if they are entitled to share in the net profits of the film, because deferments delay the time when the film goes into profit (page 99 below).

The various parties have agreed to pay the agreed amounts on the following basis.

British Screen is advancing the money as an 'equity' investment, namely on the basis that the investment will be repaid, with interest, from the distribution receipts of the film. In addition, British Screen will receive 10% of the 'net profits'. It is also agreeing to cash-flow its investment, so naturally requires that P arranges for a completion guarantee.

Channel Four is advancing £150 000 as an equity investment, and the balance of £350 000 as a licence fee in return for UK television rights. Thus Channel Four will take the right to **recoup** £150 000 plus interest from the proceeds of distributing the film and is in addition entitled to receive 5% of the net profits. However, the £350 000 licence fee will not be recoupable. Channel Four will also be interested, of course, to ensure that there is a completion guarantee to protect its investment.

The US distributor is taking all rights for the North and South American continents. The agreed sum is a distribution advance payable **on delivery** of the film and recoupable from P's share of the distribution income which is derived from exploitation in those territories. P's agreed share will be 40% of what is left after the distributor has deducted expenses (which will include any commission payable to third parties whom the distributor appoints to sell rights on its behalf), since the distributor is entitled to keep 60%. However, P will not start to receive any money until P's share of income has equalled £800 000, since the distribution advance is recoupable from that income first.

The German distributor is taking all rights for all German-speaking territories throughout the world for a straight commission of 40% of gross receipts from exploitation in these territories together with distribution expenses. This means that, out of all money earned by the German distributor, the distributor will deduct 40% followed by its expenses incurred as at that date and will then pay over the balance to P, but again P's share will be used to recoup the distribution advance of £300 000, so P will not receive any money until that figure has been reached.

The French and Japanese distributors are requiring, respectively, the rights for all French-speaking territories throughout the world and for Japan, and they are acquiring these rights on much the same terms as the German distributor.

(Where French-**speaking** and German-**speaking** rights are granted to different entities, P has to be careful to ensure that the rights do not overlap because, for instance, Switzerland could be claimed as a territory by both distributors, as German and French is spoken there, and unless P stipulates otherwise, P may find two different distributors seeking to sell the film to the same end user.)

For other territories of the world where the rights are not pre-sold, P has appointed a **sales agent** ('S') who will sell the film, before and after its completion, to distributors in those other territories. The sales will be made either on the basis that the distributor splits its own proceeds of exploitation with P (as in the case of the US distributor), or on the basis that the distributor takes an agreed rate of commission and pays over the balance to S. In either case S is entitled to a commission for its services as sales agent (usually 10–15% of what P is entitled to receive). Chapter 13, *Distribution agreements*, page 232, contains further details about sales agents.

To finance the balance (£1.5 million) of the budget which is **not** being cash-flowed, P has agreed with the film financing bank ('B&Co') to discount the distribution advances of the US, French, German and Japanese distributors. (This example assumes that these advances will together add up to an amount which will comfortably repay the bank loan plus interest, fees and costs. It also assumes that the distributors are agreeing to pay in Sterling and to take the risk of a fluctuation in the exchange rate. If these foreign distributors agree to pay in their own currency (which is much more normal), P will be taking the risk of exchange rate fluctuations. If P cannot make arrangements to meet this potential risk, B&Co will wish to ensure that the distribution advances add up to an amount which will comfortably cover any possible exchange rate losses.)

B&Co also require a **completion guarantee**. A completion guarantee will therefore be given in favour of B&Co, British Screen **and** Channel Four. These parties will be known as the 'beneficiaries' of the guarantee.

B&Co will take a **security interest (or charge)** over the rights which P owns in respect of the film, being:

- the **copyright**;
- the **physical material** embodying the film (negatives etc.);
- the benefit of all **agreements entered into for production** of the film (the main ones being those with the writer(s) of the screenplay, with the actors, with the producer and with the director);
- the benefit of all **agreements for distribution** of the film (particularly

those with the distributors and, of course, the licence agreement with Channel Four).

Each distributor will be sent a notice in writing from P that the benefit of its agreement with P has been transferred to B&Co, and all sums payable under that agreement should thus be paid to B&Co, until B&Co notifies the distributor otherwise.

As an extra safeguard over its rights in the film, B&Co will also require an agreement from the **laboratory** entrusted with the processing of the film materials, agreeing that all negatives and other materials in the possession of the laboratory will be held to the order of B&Co, and will not be released to P, but can only be used or duplicated to meet the specific print requirement of distributors nominated by B&Co. This is known as a **laboratory pledgeholder's agreement**. Naturally, B&Co will nominate the US, French, German and Japanese distributors as being authorized to order prints of the film from the laboratory. When other distributors are appointed, B&Co will also notify the laboratory that these distributors are entitled to have their processing and duplicating requirements fulfilled.

Assuming that all goes well with the production, the film is delivered to all of the distributors and they all pay up without demur. B&Co will then be paid all the sums by the distributors until it has been repaid its loan plus interest, costs and fees. At that point there may be some surplus. This is not payable to the Producer, but starts to be applied towards recouping the rest of the cost of production (£1 million plus A's deferment which is, essentially, a kind of investment).

At this point B&Co will release its interest in the film. However, B&Co may not be paid out in full when the film has been delivered. For instance, the US distributor may refuse to accept delivery of the film on the grounds that the film does not meet the requirements in the US distribution agreement. In this case, B&Co will retain its security interest and continue to be entitled to all proceeds of exploitation until it **has** been paid out.

When B&Co has been paid, both **Channel Four and British Screen** are entitled to be **repaid their investment**. They will have negotiated with P as to the order in which they should be paid. What is often agreed between two investors who have put their money in at the same time (so that one cannot really make a claim to be treated more favourably) is that they should each be paid at the same time as the other. However, the amounts they receive will be proportionate to the amount of their investment. This is what lawyers refer to as the parties being paid '*pari passu* and pro rata'. Remember that British Screen has contributed £500 000 and Channel Four £150 000. Thus for every £6.50 of distribution income which P receives, £5 will go to British Screen and £1.50 to

Channel Four, until they have each been repaid the amount of their investment (plus interest on any outstanding amount). This is assuming that all distribution commissions, sales agent's commissions and distribution expenses – which will be referred to, for convenience, as 'distribution deductions' – have already been deducted.

It is quite likely that both Channel Four and British Screen will have taken a charge or other security interest over the rights in the film to secure the right to be repaid their investment. There is nothing in law to prevent P granting more than one charge or mortgage over the same assets, but there has to be a 'pecking order' of priority (depending on the order in which the various charges have been created). Both these charges will have to rank second in priority to the charge taken by B&Co, because B&Co will insist on this. However, their charges will succeed to the position taken by B&Co when B&Co's charge has been released. As with the order of repayment, Channel Four and British Screen will have had to agree amongst themselves as to what order of priority their respective charges should take. However, in this instance, it is likely that they would have agreed that the charges taken by each of them would rank equally with the other, but that if the charges were enforced, British Screen and Channel Four would each be repaid '*pari passu* and pro rata' (as set out above) out of whatever money they can raise on the film.

At this stage, A's **deferment** begins to be payable, and all sums received by P (again after distribution deductions have been paid) will be paid to A until he has received his £250 000.

After this, all income which comes in (after the same deductions) will be **net profits** or what is known, rather less elegantly, as 'the back end'. P will use the net profits to encourage people to work on the film (by agreeing to pay them small profit shares), or will use it as an incentive to investors (such as British Screen and Channel Four). As a general rule of thumb, P should be prepared to allocate up to 60% of net profits to pay to investors. P will keep the rest either for its own benefit or to pay 'talent' (such as writers, actors, director) who require a share of net profits as part of their remuneration package. The balance retained by P is what is known as 'producer's net profits' and when P offers a share of 'net' to a writer or an actor, the agent of the writer or actor should enquire whether the percentage offered is of the entire net profits of the film or only of the producer's net profits. There is obviously a difference between 2.5% of 100% of net profits, and 2.5% of 40% of net profits.

'Net profits' and 'producer's net profits' are usually defined as follows.

Net profits will be all proceeds of exploitation of the film after deduction of (and in the following order):

- distribution commission(s);

- distribution expenses;
- sales agency commission(s);
- the cost of production;
- deferments.

Producer's net profits will be all proceeds of exploitation of the film after the above deductions **and** any share of net profits payable to a third party investor and not retainable by the Producer for its own benefit.

Charges/security interests

As already mentioned, banks and 'equity' investors will usually take a charge or other security interest. These different expressions crop up in film financing because a 'charge' is a creation of English law, whereas the US equivalent is known as a 'security interest'.

In this country or in the US the principle remains the same: to use our example once again, P will grant an interest to B&Co in the secured property (and in the case of the film, this will be the items listed on page 96 plus any other items which are incidental to them). Americans call this 'the collateral'. The interest granted to B&Co will be less (but not much less) than full normal ownership. It enables P to deal as owner with the film but subject to restrictions, which either the charge specifically imposes on P or which the law implies, by reason of a charge having been granted over the film. Put simply, P should not easily be able to dispose of any rights in the film without the consent of B&Co.

The charge operates by giving B&Co the right to take possession of the property charged and to sell it to realize a sum which will repay the sum which is due to B&Co. However, B&Co can only exercise this right **if** certain events occur. These are known as 'events of default', because they will usually consist of P not doing something it should have done (such as making repayments to B&Co by the due date) or getting into financial trouble (such as becoming insolvent).

The potential for P becoming insolvent is the main reason why charges/security interests are absolutely essential to a lender or equity investor. If B&Co lent money **without** security, P's promise to repay would have no priority over any other debts which P might owe. Once P has become insolvent, it follows that it will not have enough money to pay its debts as they fall due to be paid (since this is the technical definition of insolvency). It is thus self-evident that P will not have enough money to pay everything which it owes. Certain creditors will always have priority (i.e. the right to be paid before other creditors). The first in line will be the Inland Revenue and HM Customs and Excise (for Value Added Tax). At the point when they have been paid what they are owed in tax and VAT, whichever of P's creditors who has a security interest over P's property with any value can:

- take over that property;
- dispose of it in return for money;
- keep the proceeds derived from the disposal until that creditor has been repaid.

In our example, B&Co can take over the rights in the film and seek to dispose of these rights for a profit to try to realize enough money to repay itself. Only after secured creditors have been repaid do ordinary creditors get a chance of repayment out of the proceeds realized by selling off P's assets. More often than not, if they receive anything at all, it will be a 'dividend' (i.e. a share of what is left which is in proportion to that creditor's share of P's total debt).

TAX SHELTER SCHEMES AND GOVERNMENTAL GRANTS

It is not necessary, nor would it be very helpful, to go into great detail as to the usefulness of tax shelter schemes in film and television financing. This is because the tax law under which such a scheme would operate differs from one country to another. However, the basic principles are that certain countries have offered tax advantages to investors in feature films and/or television programmes.

Capital allowances

In this country, tax benefits have operated by allowing the investor 'write-offs' (namely, tax allowances in respect of the amount invested, which the investor can set against his liability to tax). At the time of writing, the tax benefits offered by the UK government to investors in film and television production are of limited use, because the circumstances in which they could be claimed are quite restricted. However, in the early 1980s, the government offered 100% capital allowances in respect of the cost of the **negative** of the film (which was treated in the same way as 'plant and machinery' in industry, the cost of purchasing which could be set off by industrial concerns against their tax bill). Quite a number of entities, which had precious little to do with the film and television industry, at this time went into the business of buying the negatives (and copyright) of films made in this country, simply to get the benefit of the tax write-off. People who read credits at the end of films might have noticed that some fairly unlikely names appear as the copyright owner of British films made up until 1984 (when the tax advantages were effectively abolished).

There are other countries in the world which give tax advantages to investors in films made in those countries. This means that Producers from other countries often take steps to ensure that the film they are making will qualify as a film made in a country which offers a so-called 'tax break'.

Producers are also given an incentive to do this by the availability of governmental or quasi-governmental grants or subsidies in certain countries. For instance in Canada, Telefilm operates funds to invest in films. Additionally, certain German states operate film financing funds. This makes it commercially advisable for UK Producers to try and set up **co-production deals** with Canadian or German co-producers when the nature of the project allows it.

Co-production treaties

How does a UK film Producer bring about the granting of funds or of tax advantages in another country, which are normally only given to films made in that country? The answer is that there are a number of **co-production treaties** in existence, which enable a film made under the treaties to claim the nationality of both or all of the countries which are a party to that particular treaty.

To take an example, P, a producer, wishes to get the benefits given to Canadian films in Canada. These benefits consist of government subsidies as well as 'tax breaks'. Telefilm (its full name being The Canadian Film Development Corporation) administers film financing funds which pay out annually well over 100 million Canadian dollars. In addition, there are other film financing agencies in the Canadian provinces (SOGIC in Quebec and the Ontario Film Development Corporation in Ontario, to name the most prominent) which provide loans or investments to certain films which are filmed in that province. Additionally, Canadian tax law provides a tax allowance of 30% (at the time of writing) to Canadian Producers against the cost to them of producing a film.

As there is a film co-production treaty between Canada and the UK, a Producer will be able to share in these benefits if it takes on a Canadian co-producer and the film meets the conditions under the co-production treaty.

In most co-production treaties these conditions usually take the following form.

- The co-producer must make an investment of no less than a specific percentage of the cost of production (often 20%).
- The copyright may have to be jointly owned by the co-producers in the same shares as the co-producers' contributions towards the cost of production.
- There may be a minimum number of actors, writers or crew who have to

be nationals of the co-producer's country.
- There may be requirements as to where the film (or most of it) must be shot.

The UK, like any country which has considered co-production treaties at all, is party to quite a number of them so as to enhance the opportunities for UK nationals to participate in production. The nature and conditions of the treaties will differ from one treaty to another even where the same country is a party. This is because it is a matter for negotiation between the two countries which agree each treaty as to its contents. However, they are normally very much along the lines described above. Some treaties are more specific than others as to the requirements to be met for a film to qualify – for instance Australia operates a 'points' system whereby the use of Australian personnel in key positions (such as director or composer) attracts points. If the film gets sufficient points, and other conditions are met (such as a sufficient amount of money being spent in Australia or on Australian elements in the budget), the film will qualify as an Australian film.

Where treaties are less specific, the Producer will have no choice but to liaise closely with the body which decides on co-production treaty status in the relevant country, to see that the treaty's minimum requirements are met.

In the UK, films and co-productions are under the auspices of the Department of National Heritage, which can provide further details of what co-production treaties have been made by the UK (and the contents of those treaties).

'Quotas'

Another reason (less compelling but quite useful) for qualifying under co-production treaties is that certain countries operate 'quota' systems. Under this kind of system, a country will require that at least a certain percentage of films put on distribution or programmes shown on television in its territory must have 'originated' in that country. Again, if the film qualifies under a co-production treaty to which that country is a party, it should qualify as part of the quota.

The EC operates a broadcasting quota under the 1989 Broadcasting Directive (often referred to as the 'Television Without Frontiers' Directive), which requires that 'a majority' (namely, more than 50%) of material broadcast in the EC must be 'European'. However, provided that the major co-producer is a European entity (and that means a Producer from any of the EC member states) a production made under a co-production treaty will qualify as 'European', therefore eligible to form part of the quota. Even if the European Producer is a minority participant, it is sometimes possible that the production will be regarded **in part** as European in content, and that part can go towards meeting the quota.

European broadcasters who have a quota to meet are therefore interested in spending money on new productions which qualify under co-production treaties, because this will enable them to acquire programming which meets the European content requirements, but without obliging them to pay for the total cost of production.

Disadvantages of existing co-production treaties in Europe

The operation of bilateral treaties (namely, where only two countries are party to it) has become increasingly less useful, particularly in the European production arena where productions frequently have to look to so many sources for funding that the involvement of any one co-producer may not be sufficient to qualify under any single co-production treaty. For example, if there are as many as three co-producers, bilateral treaties will no longer apply, as these envisage two co-producers only. Additionally, the requirements of the treaties as to the level of involvement of technical and artistic personnel of different countries often led to compromising the creative point of a production to a degree where it ceased to work (an example of this was television series or films which have been labelled as 'Euro-puddings').

To deal with this problem, in 1992 the Council of Europe agreed on the European Convention on Cinematographic Co-Productions.

The European Convention on Cinematographic Co-Productions

This Convention is (at the time of writing) the most recent development in the co-production area, having come into force on 1 March 1994. It only applies to films made with the intention of showing them in cinemas and which qualify as 'European works'. This is worked out on a 'points' system (points being allocated for the use of European artistic and technical personnel). The signatories to the Convention are Denmark, France, Germany, Italy, Luxembourg, Slovakia, Sweden, Switzerland, the UK, the Holy See and Latvia. It came into force by being **ratified** by five of the signatories (the act of ratification signifying their consent to be bound by the Co-Production Convention). These are Denmark, Sweden, Switzerland, the UK and Latvia.

The Convention applies:

- to co-productions where all the co-production partners (of whom there must be at least three) are parties to the Convention;
- to co-productions involving at least three co-producers from Convention countries ('Convention co-producers'), and one or more co-producers

from countries which are not party to the Convention. However, these non-Convention producers must not be making a contribution to more than 30% of the total cost of production.

What this means is that non-European financial involvement in European co-productions will not affect the production's ability to qualify as a European work.

The contribution made by any one producer must not be more than 70% or less than 10%. However, if there is a bilateral treaty between two of the countries from which the Convention co-producers originate, in this case the maximum is 80% and the minimum 20%.

The other effect of the Convention is that the member states have agreed that if a film qualifies under the Convention, it will be entitled to the national benefits, fund and subsidies of each of the Convention co-producers' countries.

For example, imagine a production made between co-producers from the UK, France, Denmark and Canada. The film has access to all the benefits it would have had under co-production treaties between:

- UK – France;
- UK – Denmark;
- France – Denmark.

This is notwithstanding the fact that their involvement might be less than the minimum participation required under each of those bilateral conventions.

In particular, those who are providing a minority **financial** contribution (between 10% and 25%) need not have made any **technical or artistic** contribution, so that even if the film is made mostly with UK finance, in the UK, with British actors and crew, it can still qualify for national benefits of French and Danish films. There also appears to be no requirement that the film is shot in any of the co-producers' languages (as would be the case with a bilateral co-production treaty).

To qualify under the Convention, the co-producers (and the film) must each be approved by the competent authority in their own country (in this country, the Department of National Heritage). Applications for approval should be made in advance (at least two months before shooting commences). One of the items (apart from script, budget and production schedule) which must accompany the application is the co-production agreement between the co-producers. This must provide for the distribution of receipts or territories between the co-producers.

The one drawback is that in the example of the Canadian co-production given on page 101 above, the Canadian co-producer would not be able to receive Canadian benefits, because these are only available under **bilateral** co-production treaties, and the film would not qualify under any co-production treaty with a non-Convention country by reason of the fact that there are more than two co-producers.

European funds/subsidies

The three most important sources of funding/subsidy for European productions are (at the time of writing):

- the Eurimages Fund;
- the European Co-Production Fund;
- the MEDIA Programme.

Eurimages

This is a Council of Europe initiative which the UK joined in April 1993. It is a fund, operating out of Strasburg, which provides financial support for feature-length picture films and creative documentaries produced by European co-producers from countries which are parties to Eurimages.

The countries which have subscribed to this initiative include the members of the EC/EU, the Scandinavian countries, Hungary, Poland, Switzerland and Turkey.

Eurimages provides interest-free loans for the production and distribution of co-productions involving three or more co-producers. The maximum amount of loan is presently around £500 000 per film and £110 000 per documentary. The involvement required of each co-producer (as long as the film qualifies as 'European') need only be largely financial, but as long as that co-producer is granted rights in the film and shares in the 'back end'. Each co-producer's contribution must not exceed 60% or be less than 10%.

Where the co-producers are from countries which are also members of the European Convention on Cinematographic Co-Production, they will also be able to claim purely national benefits as well as to apply for a loan from the Eurimages Fund.

European Co-Production Fund

This is actually a UK initiative (operated out of the same offices as British Screen Finance) which was set up in 1991 for a three year period and extended for a further three years. Its aim is to promote collaboration between Producers in the UK and other EC states by providing funds to enable them to invest in feature films and film development. This has extended to UK Producers who are co-producing films the same sort of benefits which (via British Screen) were originally only available to wholly UK productions.

The MEDIA programme

Finally, the European Commission offers a system of subsidies and grants to producers and productions under the MEDIA programme initiatives. This programme was set up for a five year period – 1991 to 1995 – with the self-professed aims of:

- creating a 'European audio-visual area' (promoting national industries at a European level and thus giving them the advantages of economies of scale provided by the European Single Market);
- 'setting up professional synergies' (cross-border networking between the professionals in the national film and television industries);
- mobilizing 'seed capital' (the investment offered by the programme is usually more of a start-up nature, enabling projects to be developed to a stage where other commercial investment is attracted);
- maintaining a balance between market forces (by giving priority to small and medium-sized enterprises, particularly to independent producers and to smaller countries or those with a less developed production industry);
- maintaining a balance between the media (cinema, television, video and the new technologies).

To meet these aims, there are some seventeen projects or initiatives which give financial or other help to Producers or aspiring Producers. Further details should be obtainable from the Department of National Heritage.

SPONSORSHIP

This is the raising of finance for a television production from a company which sells products or services, in return for that company being referred to in the production. It is **not** advertising as such, in the manner in which it is practised in relation to television programmes in this country, because the sponsorship itself should not involve any promotion of the product or service which the company provides to the public. Sponsorship in this form is something which only applies to television production. However, feature film producers can achieve a similar purpose by arranging for a commercial tie-up deal with a company. For instance, where a film shows characters drinking champagne, the producer may well be free to conclude a deal with a champagne producing company, that the champagne of that company will be shown to be used in the film in return for some kind of benefit to the production. The benefit may be anything ranging from free champagne to a relatively large sum of money. This is actually what is known as 'product placement', but it is a kind of deal which is not feasible where, as is so often the case in UK films, the film is being made with the participation of broadcasters, as broadcasters are not permitted to arrange or allow 'product placement' in productions made for them.

The BBC does not permit sponsorship in relation to its programmes, since it is prohibited from doing so under the terms of its licence from the government. It does, however, as viewers of sports programmes are aware, cover **events** which have been sponsored. The BBC itself cannot receive money from the sponsor of the event, and would almost certainly shy away from broadcasting any event if there were any suggestion that it had been created by a sponsor simply to attract broadcast coverage.

This does not mean that the BBC will not give an on-screen credit to the sponsor of the event in question. However, if the sponsor's name is included in the title of the event, the BBC will not necessarily use the sponsor's name in the title of the television or radio coverage of that event. This is something which usually only happens in relation to sporting events which have been sponsored. When filming a sponsored event for broadcast by the BBC, a number of guidelines must be followed, particularly in relation to events which have been sponsored by tobacco companies, in relation to whose products there are very strict advertising and publicity restrictions both in the UK and at the European level.

However, sponsorship has a more significant value to Producers (at least potentially) in relation to programmes broadcast on ITV and Channel 4. Sponsorship is permitted for these programmes, but must be carried out strictly in accordance with the standards drawn up from time to time by the ITC. The standards in force at the time of writing (the ITC Code of Programme Sponsorship) state that a programme is treated as being sponsored 'if any part of its cost of production or transmission is met by an organization or person other than a broadcaster or television producer, with a view to promoting its own or another's name, trade mark, image, activities, products, or other direct or indirect commercial interests'.

The principles applying to sponsorship are as follows.

- It is only allowed for whole programmes or programme strands (and not items of station presentation or continuity or viewers' competitions).
- Any programme can be sponsored except:
  - news programmes;
  - business and financial reports which contain interpretation or comment;
  - current affairs programmes;
  - programmes which, intentionally or inadvertently, have the effect of promoting the sponsor's service (for example, a programme about

sherry should not be sponsored by Harvey's Bristol Cream).

- The sponsor cannot have any influence on content or scheduling of the programme. This restriction in effect prevents the sponsorship of programmes which would normally be expected to provide criticism of or advice on the kind of products/services offered by the potential sponsor, such as a consumer affairs programme.
- The sponsor must be clearly identified at the beginning and end of the programme.
- No promotional reference to any advertiser or sponsor, or to any product or service is permitted **within** any programme.
- There can be no sponsorship by a person whose product or services would not be acceptable for **advertising** under the ITC Code of Advertising Standards and Practices. This includes any body which has objects 'wholly or mainly of a political nature', cigarette companies and makers of prescribed drugs. While sponsorship by religious bodies is permitted in theory it is subject to even greater controls under the ITC Code than sponsorship by commercial entities.
- Lastly, **product placement** is prohibited.

The ITC Code on Sponsorship contains strict provisions about when and in what form a sponsor can or cannot be mentioned (such as in trailers or front, end and 'bumper' credits).

There are also specific rules about programmes which feature viewers' competitions (for example, sponsors of such programmes cannot provide their own products or services as prizes). In addition, there are further restrictions on sponsorship by companies which provide betting and gaming services.

Coverage of events and locations which have been sponsored, or at which advertising and branding is present, may itself be sponsored (in effect 'double sponsorship'), but subject to restrictions as to showing any advertising or branding at the event. Additionally, television coverage must **not** be the principal purpose of the event. However, tobacco advertising requires more careful handling, as might be expected.

Lastly, in relation to character merchandising, it is **not** considered to be sponsorship if a programme maker licenses a product based on a character (or other material) appearing in a programme, as long as the programme was developed independently of the product, or the character(s) had a previous literary existence before any merchandising use. Additionally, the payments by the manufacturer of the product cannot be used to meet part or all of the cost of production or transmission of the programme. Normal character merchandising (Chapter 14, *Secondary exploitation*) is therefore not subject to restrictions under the Code. What **is** prohibited is the practice which has grown up in America, of toy manufacturers financing programmes featuring their products (such as *My Little Pony* cartoons).

Sponsorship in practice

Perhaps because of the restrictions placed on them by the ITC, broadcasters who commission a 'sponsorable' production from an independent producer are usually careful to reserve to themselves the right to seek sponsorship finance. The description 'sponsorable' refers not only to the acceptability of the programme under the ITC Code, but also to whether the programme will have an audience profile which is likely to appeal to the typical users of any particular potential sponsor's product or services.

The broadcasters' attitude in this respect is something which is difficult for an independent Producer to contradict. The Producer's bargaining position on any aspect of its relationship with a broadcaster is not usually that favourable. It is also an undeniable fact that broadcasters have to be extremely careful about the manner and context in which their programmes are sponsored. It is, after all, entirely up to the broadcaster as to whether the sponsorship is accepted and this enables the broadcaster to insist that it and it alone should contract with the sponsor and, often, keep the money paid by that sponsor in its entirety. If circumstances were different, and Producers were allowed freely to go and seek sponsorship, they could in theory take the credit for the sponsorship finance which they have introduced to a particular project, and this credit might be reflected in terms of enhanced benefits to the Producers in their deal with the broadcaster. One notable benefit would be the Producer being entitled to keep all or part of the rights in the programme.

<table>
<tr><td>

7

</td><td>

Production and financing agreements

</td></tr>
</table>

LEGAL ISSUES IN PRODUCTION

The next chapters will deal with the legal issues arising out of production. As it is the largest topic in the book, it seems sensible to split it into five chapters, which are:

- this chapter, *Production and financing agreements*;
- Chapter 8, *Hiring and firing*, the general principles of hiring and firing personnel who work on a production;
- Chapters 9 and 10, *Rights clearances* (including music);
- Chapter 11, other general topics, including completion guarantees and insurance, particularly Errors and Omissions insurance.

This arrangement is certainly not in order of importance, nor is it necessarily in the chronological order in which a Producer is likely to meet these issues. But it is logical to start with the central agreements under which the Producer is financed, as these agreements generally dictate the Producer's obligations and duties in relation to all production matters.

DIFFERENT TYPES OF PRODUCTION, FINANCE AND DISTRIBUTION AGREEMENTS

It is common to refer to the main agreements relating to the **production**, **financing** and **distribution** of a production as the PFD Agreements.

It may be that one agreement will govern all three aspects, but because there is usually a lot to provide for in one document, it is more commonly the practice that the production obligations and the financing of the production are dealt with in one agreement, with one or more separate agreements covering the aspects of distribution of the completed production. For that reason, while this chapter covers some aspects of distribution rights, Chapter 13 concentrates in more detail on the provisions of distribution agreements.

The production/financing agreement may differ according to the financing parties. Typically a UK feature film (which is still an all too rare creature) will have several Financiers, since no entity which finances British films has the money or the inclination to provide the total cost of production. The Financiers will often include British Screen Finance Limited and one or other of the television broadcasters (such as Channel Four or the BBC) together with a distributor or two who are interested in overseas rights. It is rare for Financiers to cash-flow the production (i.e. to provide the money to make the film up-front) for the reasons given in Chapter 6 (pages 91–2).

However, this then leaves the Producer with a problem of finding the money to make the film in the first place, even though the Producer can call for the Financiers to pay up once the film has been made.

Contrast that with the typical position, at least until 1993, where a production is being made for television and therefore commissioned and paid for 100% by a broadcaster. Historically, the broadcaster **has** cash-flowed the cost of production. That is now changing – the BBC has been known not to cash-flow feature films which it has commissioned, and the ITV Network Centre is commissioning independent Producers and Producer/broadcasters on the basis that the purchase price for the programme will be paid **on delivery** of it to the ITV Network.

The question of how the Producer pays for the film or programme to be made was considered in Chapter 6. First, it may help to analyse the different concerns of a person, either buying into a film or buying it outright, depending on whether that person is **cash-flowing** or paying on delivery.

CASH-FLOWING FINANCIER

If a Financier is parting with its money from the very start of production, the production agreement will go into much greater detail about the obligations of the Producer and give the Financier greater control and ability to interfere in the production process. Contrast this with a Financier, typically a distributor, who is paying on delivery – in that case, the Producer's obligations will be to deliver a film which meets a particular specification in terms of length, technical and pictorial quality, subject matter, principal cast, censorship rating etc. As long as that specification is met, the distributor is not particularly concerned about whether the Producer is producing efficiently or not – the distributor will only have to pay if it gets the completed film in the form agreed.

The cash-flowing Financier will typically require the production agreement to provide for more extensive protections. There follows a list of items which a cash-flowing Financier would want to see in a production/finance agreement between itself and the Producer. This does not mean that some of them would not be equally important for a Financier who is only paying on delivery.

Appendix E contains a summary of the contents of typical production and financing agreements. The column headed '100% Commission' sets out the normal requirements of a cash-flowing Financier. The position taken by other Financiers (who pay on delivery) is set out in the column headed 'Pre-Purchase'. It should be stressed that it is not an exhaustive review of the types of agreements referred to, but only a guide.

Production accounts/trust accounts

The cash-flowing Financier is naturally running a risk in giving the money to the Producer. If the Producer becomes insolvent during the course of production, the assets of the Producer are 'frozen' and only capable of being dealt with by the liquidator of the Producer. That is unless the assets are evidently the property of someone else. This is why it is prudent for the Financier to require the production funding to be placed in a separate bank account, and that it must not be mixed with the Producer's own money. In this way, the production funds will remain readily identifiable. It is also usual to state in the production agreement that the production account is a **trust account** and money standing to its credit is therefore the subject of a **trust** for the purpose of making the film. It is not practical here to explain in full detail how trust law works, except to say that it is a legal mechanism under which the benefit of property or assets, which are ostensibly held in the name of one person (the trustee), actually belongs to another (the beneficiary). This trust relationship automatically imposes specific legal restrictions on the way in which the property can be dealt with by the trustee. In addition, if the owner in name becomes insolvent, that property is **not** available to his creditors to repay them what they are owed by him, because it really belongs to the beneficiary. In the case of a trust account, the owner in name (i.e. the trustee) is the Producer; the beneficiary is the Financier. Thus, this device is intended to make it easier for the Financier to prove that money in the production account is not the Producer's, if a liquidator is appointed over the Producer's assets. Whether it works in practice or not is another question.

OVERCOST – WHEN THE BUDGETED COSTS ARE EXCEEDED

The cash-flowing Financier will also normally insist on **take-over rights** and other powers in case things start to go wrong with the production. The most obvious way in which things go wrong is that the film goes over budget. The Financier will therefore need a variety of contractual protections in this instance, one of which (and also the most drastic) is the right to take over the production, therefore setting aside the Producer.

The Financier takes the right to monitor and control the way that its money is being spent during the course of production. The Producer should have **some** flexibility in how money can be used. For instance, it should have the right to apply cost savings under one budget heading (for example if the fees to the actors turn out to be less than expected) to another budget area where there may be an overcost (such as extra fees to the lighting cameraman, if he or she is needed for a longer period than originally budgeted for). After all, the budget is only an **estimate** of what is needed to produce the film and the Producer is not expected to be accurate to the last decimal point. This is why it is common practice to have a contingency in the budget (normally around 10%). Some Financiers have been known not to allow for any contingency. This is unrealistic and unduly onerous on Producers who may well have budgeted relatively accurately, given the circumstances then existing, but cannot be expected to be able to foresee unexpected developments.

> For example, if the UK government suddenly declared war on another country, this may well have the effect of making certain things more expensive or scarce (since that is a usual effect of declaring war). It could also mean that certain people who would otherwise be available for work would not be because, for instance, they my have been called up to serve in the armed forces. All of these would have an effect on increasing the budget for a UK produced film, but at the time of drawing up the budget the declaration of war may have seemed totally unlikely.

Therefore, it is more normal for Financiers to agree to finance a contingency either for general use, or for use in case specific events have occurred. For example, on a production where there is a great deal of location shooting, there may be a specific contingency to cover extra costs where shooting has been delayed because of bad weather.

In a television production, the Financier will generally require the Producer to obtain permission before using the contingency. In feature film production, where there is a completion guarantee, the Financiers will usually leave approval of use of the contingency to the completion guarantor (Chapter 11).

A contingency gives the Producer some breathing space. However, if the cost reports being delivered to the Financier show an overcost which will or might result in the film ultimately going over budget as a whole, the financing contract will generally allow for a procedure similar to the following.

- The Producer must immediately draw up new budget arrangements to rearrange expenditure of the money so that an overall overcost can be avoided.
- If the Producer does not or cannot do this, or the Financier is dissatisfied

with what the Producer has been able to come up with, the Purchaser will have a number of options:

- to finance the overcost;
- to require the Producer to finance the overcost;
- to take over production, setting the Producer aside;
- to call in the completion guarantor (if there is a completion guarantee in force).

Whether or not the Financier can exercise any of these options depends on the provisions of the financing agreement.

Who finances the overcost?

This very often depends on who can be said to be at fault. The events which have led to the overcost may:

- be generally beyond the Producer's control (namely, caused by an **event of** *force majeure*, as lawyers like to describe these things) such as a natural disaster or war breaking out;
- be something which **theoretically** could have been avoided, but there is no implication that the Producer has deliberately brought them about, or that these were caused by the Producer's **negligence** (in that the Producer failed to exercise **reasonable** care and that failure led to the events happening);
- have been caused by the deliberate or negligent act of the Producer.

Depending on the attitude of the Financier, the Producer may:

- have been placed under a strict obligation to bring the film in on budget, so that the Producer will have to pay for the overcost, whether or not it can be said to have been caused by the Producer (this is sometimes referred to as a 'fixed price deal');
- be only liable for overcost if it was due to the Producer's **deliberate or negligent actions or failure** to take action.

However, any **fair** financing agreement should absolve the Producer from liability if the overcost arose due to an event of *force majeure* (Chapter 8, pages 131, contains further details on *force majeure*). In addition, even in circumstances where the Producer **is** liable, the Producer should insist on a statement in the contract that it will not be liable for overcost to the extent that the overcost has been caused or contributed to by the **Financier's actions or failure to act**.

For example, if the Financier has agreed to provide instalments of finance on particular dates, this will be because the Producer actually needs the money to meet expenses which it knows will be coming up for payment. If the Financier is late in paying, the Producer may have to take out a temporary loan to cover the costs arising in the meantime, rather than place itself in breach of its obligations to pay others. The cost of the loan may cause the budget to be exceeded, because of course it costs money to borrow money, and that cost would not have been allowed for in the original budget. In this instance, the Financier and **not** the Producer should be liable to pay for the extra cost.

Limits on the Producer's liability

If the Producer is liable to pay overcost, the obvious source of money to meet that liability will be the production fee, which is generally payable to the Producer out of the budget as recompense for its services in producing the film. Sometimes the Producer's liability to pay for overcost will actually be limited to the amount of the production fee itself. In other words, even if the overcost is a greater amount than the production fee, the Producer will not have to meet the extra amount. This is a restriction which the Producer might try to insist on if it has agreed to a fixed price deal, and certainly if the Financier has not allowed a contingency within the budget. Sometimes Financiers will agree to such a limitation on the Producer's liability, perhaps in recognition of the fact that many Producers may not have the financial wherewithal to pay more. However, a Producer should not necessarily expect this generosity, as where the overcost is large and is undoubtedly due to the Producer's default or negligence, the Financier may not want to restrict its ultimate power to recover the whole of the amount, if necessary, by litigation.

It follows from the various situations discussed that Financiers may in certain circumstances have to consider having to meet overcost which the Financier cannot recover from the Producer either immediately or at all. In these circumstances, decisions have to be made very quickly as the situation usually gets worse with every day's delay.

If the overcost is not too bad or if there is no completion guarantee, the Financier may simply agree to pay it. If it is a large amount and there is a completion guarantee in force, the Financier will probably call on the guarantee (Chapter 11).

TAKE-OVER AND ABANDONMENT RIGHTS

The right to **take over** production is an additional power which the Financier will often require, either in cases where there is overcost or otherwise where the Producer has committed a breach of the financing agreement. It must be stressed that, from the Producer's point of view, this power should be restricted to circumstances where the Producer has committed a **material** breach (namely, one which seriously affects the way in which the production was supposed to be produced). For instance, if the Financier could take over if the Producer had committed any kind of breach, this could lead to the Producer being ousted if it delivered a cost report one day late, or failed to submit one of the contracts with a minor member of the cast for the Financier's approval. These kinds of breaches would not normally be regarded as material.

The take-over provisions in the financing agreement will involve the Financier taking very much the same powers as the completion guarantor, in its agreement with the Producer as part of the completion guarantee arrangements (Chapter 11, page 191). It follows that where the Financier has the right to take over production, it will be taking over the **performance** and **benefit** of contracts which the Producer will have made (such as agreements for the actors and crew) for the purposes of production. These contracts must by their own terms allow them to be transferred (assigned) to the Financier. (The same applies in relation to the completion guarantor, if there is a completion guarantee in force.) As a matter of English law, if a contract says nothing about whether or not it can be transferred by one party to a third party, the position is that either party to the contract can transfer the **benefit** of the contract to a third party. However, it is not possible to transfer **obligations** under a contract to another person without the consent of the other party to the contract. This means that when a Producer has to transfer a contract (because the production has been taken over), the Producer will still remain **legally liable** to the other party to the contract for any failure in the obligations which the Producer originally assumed. However, the performance of those obligations will no longer be within the Producer's control!

For this reason the Producer, if wise, should seek an **indemnity** from the consequences of any action (or failure to act) on the part of the Financier in performing the Producer's part in the contracts which the Producer has taken over. Chapter 4, pages 41–3, deals with this.

> For example P, a Producer, has agreed to engage A, an actor, and (naturally) to pay A a fee. If F, the Financier, takes over production because the film is going seriously over budget, but fails to pay a part of A's fee, A will probably sue P. If P has an **indemnity** from F, P can claim on that indemnity and recover from F both the sums which P will have to pay to A, **and** the cost P has incurred in dealing with A's legal action, as long as the indemnity is properly worded.

RIGHTS/DISTRIBUTION RIGHTS

The average PFD agreement usually deals with the question of how the rights in the film will be owned, and who will exploit them. The Financier's motives for providing all or part of the finance may be simply by way of investment (looking to get repaid out of the proceeds of exploitation) or, more usually, in return for rights which the Financier can itself exercise. If the Financier is interested in rights, the Agreement will additionally contain provisions setting out how those rights are to be exploited, and how the resulting income is to be divided between the Financier and the Producer granting the rights. The position of a financing distributor, in terms of its obligations to the Producer, is not so different from that of an ordinary distributor, who is appointed by the rights owner of a film or programme (where the rights owner is not itself equipped to exploit the production).

However, the difference lies not in the **functions** which the distributor is agreeing to perform, but in the ultimate reward. An ordinary distributor may get only a commission for its services (i.e. an agreed percentage of gross revenue derived from exploiting the distribution rights), then have to pay over the balance of the income to the rights owner. A financing distributor, by virtue of paying up-front (what is known as 'a distribution advance') may also be entitled to a share of the net income, as well as being able to keep all gross income until the distributor's contribution to financing has been recouped from the proceeds which the distributor receives from exploiting its rights. This aspect is considered further in Chapter 6, pages 94–9.

The financing distributor may also require that the Producer **clears** certain exploitation rights in advance, by paying for them out of the budget. Chapter 5, *Development*, touched on 'use fees' payable to writers. Chapter 9 goes into much more detail as to how the right to use a contributor's services in a finished production (such as the writer's work, or the actors' performances) must be secured, and how that right is paid for.

The deal with the contributor may be on the lines that, if the production is more widely exploited, the contributor will be paid an extra fee (a 'use fee' or a 'residual'). The distributor will therefore require that a Producer must have clearly agreed with each contributor that he or she will grant all necessary permissions to use the contribution made, **and** what fees will be payable if the various possible uses occur. Paying a lump sum to cover all possible exploitation is referred to as a 'buy-out'. A distributor will require a Producer to agree 'buy-outs' with all contributors, wherever possible. However, it is not always possible, because union agreements do not always allow it.

The financing distributor may therefore require that certain minimum uses are paid for in advance out of the budget (for example, the right to show the production twice on UK television). Other uses must be **cleared**, even if not paid for, namely the contributor must give permission for the uses to take place, even if the use will attract another fee.

Where uses are **not** paid for in advance, the Producer should require the distributor to pay use fees as and when they become due.

BBC, ITV AND CHANNEL FOUR COMMISSIONS

Perhaps the most likely situation in which an independent Producer in this country will be concluding a PFD agreement is when commissioned by a broadcaster. Both the BBC and the ITV companies are under a legal obligation to commission at least 25% of their programmes (subject to certain exclusions such as news programmes) from independent Producers. The definition of independent Producer for these purposes is set out in Appendix F, but briefly, a Producer is only independent as long as a broadcaster does not have a substantial ownership interest in it.

In the case of all three main broadcasters (counting the fifteen separate regional ITV broadcasters as one network broadcaster), their main interest in commissioning a programme is to be able to broadcast it on UK television, either regionally or over the entire Network. However, it has been their practice, since all three broadcasters are equipped to exploit programmes in other ways (notably by overseas sales), to take **all** rights in the programmes which they commission, in return for providing 100% of the finance needed to meet the production costs. The question does not arise, in those circumstances, as to whether the price being paid by the broadcaster is the 'right' price for all rights in the production: since most independent Producers are not in a position to raise finance elsewhere or to provide it themselves, there are relatively few other market forces which could come into play to enable the Producer to try to keep back some of the rights. The Producer takes the terms offered by the broadcaster. If the Producer does not like them, the broadcaster can point to a range of other projects which it could commission instead, as there are some 1500 independent Producers in the UK. There are only three major network broadcasters in this country and each of these broadcasters has different criteria for selecting programmes (given that the BBC is a public service broadcaster, the ITV companies are purely commercial and Channel Four has a special statutory remit to cater to audiences not necessarily catered to by ITV). It is usually impossible for a Producer to use the threat of competition to improve its commercial position. The fact that the BBC likes a project does not mean that the ITV Network will automatically be interested in it as well, so there is often **no** real competition.

TERMS APPLICABLE WHEN COMMISSIONED BY ANY OF THE BROADCASTERS

The commissioning agreements, whether the commissioner is the BBC, an ITV company or Channel Four, will be pretty much the same as those described for PFD agreements when the Financier is cash-flowing the cost of production. As has been discussed, the Producer is usually required to part with all rights in the programme (and that will involve assigning the copyright in the programme to the broadcaster), as well as doing the work of producing it. In return, the Producer will receive from the budget:

- a production fee, expressed as a percentage of the budgeted cost of production – generally between 5% to 10% – the higher the budget, the lower the percentage which the broadcaster will agree to pay;
- a share of net profits realized from the exploitation of the programme (other than UK broadcast rights).

'Net profits' are discussed in more detail in Chapter 6, pages 98–9. They are found by deducting the cost incurred in carrying on the distribution function and some or all of the cost of production from gross exploitation income. How each broadcaster shares the net profits with the Producer is referred to in the section on each broadcaster below. However, in the current market a Producer cannot usually expect to receive more than 30% of the net profits generated from the exploitation of the production.

A comparative analysis of typical agreements (in summary form) under which broadcasters acquire rights in programmes is set out in Appendix E.

ITV COMMISSIONS – THE NETWORK CENTRE

It is actually easier to identify what ITV is prepared to pay in any particular case for basic UK broadcast rights because of the way in which the ITV companies have set up their arrangements to create a television network and to commission programmes for transmission over the entire Network.

The Network Centre

The ITV companies have obligations as regional broadcasters, and they produce and/or commission from independent Producers programmes specifically for regional transmission. However, for programmes which will be shown by **all** the ITV companies over the ITV Network, the ITV companies have set up a separate and independently run centre, the ITV Network Centre, which selects and buys programmes for transmission over the Network. The Network Centre is financed by the ITV companies, but they do not directly control how the money is spent. The Network Centre buys UK television rights in programmes for a certain number of transmissions over a certain period, and in return pays a licence fee to the rights owner of the programme. A large amount of programmes will be specially commissioned by the Network, because the Network's special requirements (both legal and commercial) would not always be met by buying ready-made products. For instance, this enables the Network to ensure that the programmes will comply with the Independent Television

Commission's standards (Chapter 12, pages 217–19, contains further discussion as to the broadcasters' concerns in relation to the nature and content of programmes).

Independent Producers – involvement of an ITV company for 'compliance' purposes

Technically it is open to any Producer (whether an ITV company which produces its own programmes or an independent Producer) to make a deal with the Network Centre to provide it with a programme or series. The original networking arrangements proposed by the ITV companies (after the ITV licences were awarded for the period beginning 1 January 1993) envisaged **only** the ITV companies having a direct arrangement with the Network Centre, either supplying their own programmes to the Centre or commissioning independent Producers. However, the Monopolies and Mergers Commission decided in 1993 that this was illegal, because it was anti-competitive to prevent independent Producers from having direct access to the Network Centre. So now, in theory, independent Producers can contract directly with the Network Centre. However, the nature of the arrangements put forward by the Network Centre is that the independent Producer must also attach one of the ITV companies to the project, to monitor production and ensure that the finished production will comply with the statutory obligations of ITV broadcasters. This is necessary because of the way in which the Broadcasting Act 1990 imposes obligations on the individual ITV companies to ensure that certain standards are met and that their programmes are produced bearing certain criteria in mind. If the programme supplied to the Network Centre does not comply with the requirements of the Broadcasting Act 1990, the Independent Television Commission ('ITC') will then have a particular ITV broadcaster to blame.

Financing the cost of production

Depending on the nature of the production, the licence fee payable by the Network Centre may be enough or nearly enough to cover the actual cost of production. Thus, in theory, the Producer has only to finance the shortfall and will then keep all other rights of exploitation in the finished production other than those which the Network Centre requires. However, the Network Centre (at the time of writing) will pay only the licence fee when the programme has been completed and delivered. So the Producer has, temporarily, to find that amount as well, if the cost of production is to be paid for. An ITV Producer/broadcaster will usually have sufficient funds available to cash-flow the cost of production or, if it has to borrow money, has sufficient assets to convince a bank that it is a good risk and is capable of meeting the financing cost (such as fees and interest charged by the bank). An independent Producer, not having the benefit of advertising income, usually does not have the necessary funds to hand and will then have to borrow. More often than not its only assets (against which to raise a loan) will be its rights in the project. In Chapter 6, pages 92–4, the process is described of Producers borrowing against future distribution income which a third party has agreed to pay in return for rights.

In theory, an independent Producer making a programme for the Network Centre could borrow from a film financing bank at least the amount of the licence fee. Unfortunately, this avenue is not at present open to independent Producers, because of the nature of the standard supply contract issued by the Network Centre. This contract is, according to the film financing banks, too uncertain to allow the bank to assume that the licence fee will actually be paid as long as the programme is delivered. This situation may well change, but in the meantime the only source of finance usually available to a Producer is that provided by an ITV company, which might well extract some or all of the remaining rights in the production, in return for cash-flowing the cost of production and making up the shortfall (if any) between that cost and the licence fee paid by the Network Centre. The ITV company will justify this on the basis that providing money is a cost (in terms of interest payable if the money is borrowed or interest lost if it is not) and the Financier who cash-flows is taking a risk, which is quite true (Chapter 6, pages 91–2). In addition, the ITV broadcaster might well be taking the position of a completion guarantor, in that if there is any overcost which the Producer cannot or is not obliged to meet, the ITV broadcaster will have to pay it, to ensure a finished programme can be delivered to the Network Centre.

Independent productions – financing by an ITV company

For all these reasons, the supply of the majority of ITV programmes (even those produced by independent Producers) is likely to be from the ITV company to the Network Centre. If the programme is being made by an independent Producer, the ITV company would then have a separate agreement with the Producer – what is, effectively, a PFD agreement. The terms offered may differ from one ITV broadcaster to another (even though there are guidelines which are intended to apply when an ITV company commissions an independent Producer). As for 'net profits', for the purpose of calculating what the Producer's share would be, the ITV broadcaster will, as well as deducting a commission for itself as a distributor and the costs incurred by it in acting as a distributor, deduct any shortfall between the licensee and the cost of production (with interest), in order to recoup its investment. The share of net profits payable to Producers ranges from 15% to 30%.

One particular point to note is that some ITV broadcasters are reluctant to allow the Producer to retain underlying format rights in projects originated by the Producer. In these cases the Producer must ensure that if the broadcaster does claim these rights (which would carry with them the right to make further films based on the format) the broadcaster can only make further programmes by commissioning the Producer.

THE BBC

One commissioning agreement

The BBC is both network scheduler and broadcaster in one, so the contractual position when an independent Producer is commissioned to supply programmes to be broadcast on BBC television is much simpler. There is only one contract, which again performs a function of a production and financing agreement. However, the distribution arrangements are usually touched upon in the main contract, at least to the extent of a provision which envisages such arrangements being settled and agreed separately and in more detail at a later stage.

Financing – BBC Enterprises

The situation is complicated only because the BBC has separated its functions as broadcaster from the commercial business of selling its programmes (and material associated with the programmes, such as books and merchandising articles). These commercial functions are performed by BBC Enterprises Limited, commonly referred to as 'Enterprises'. This is a limited company wholly owned and controlled by the BBC. However, the guidelines which the BBC have drawn up to cover programmes wholly financed by it and commissioned from independent Producers (referred to as 'The Working Practices') give the impression that Enterprises is an almost independent entity which goes its own way separately from the BBC. For instance, the Working Practices envisages that, in relation to each independent project, Enterprises is to be given the opportunity to invest, as opposed to the production being wholly financed by the BBC itself. From the Producer's view, there is no difference at the production stage if Enterprises invests, because the Producer deals only with the BBC and the finance is 'cash-flowed' by the BBC. Logically, there should be no difference at any stage, because the money being provided is the BBC's money, whether it is supplied by the BBC itself, or by Enterprises, which is wholly owned by the BBC. However, under the Working Practices, whether or not Enterprises makes an investment makes a difference to:

- the distribution of the programme;
- the way that net profits are calculated.

If the BBC alone pays the cost of production the cost is attributed to the exercise of the UK broadcast rights (plus simultaneous European cable rights, these being the right to show the programme, simultaneously with the BBC broadcast in the UK, by cable relay in certain European territories). This means that the production cost is written off, so that if any further income is realized from exploiting the programme (such as by home video sales or by sales to overseas broadcasters) this will be pure profit (after the distribution commissions and expenses on making these sales have been paid) as the cost of production will not need to be recouped from this income before profit is reached.

As to who exercises the distribution rights, the Working Practices envisage that the copyright in the programme will 'initially' belong to the BBC. The significance of using the word 'initially' does not mean that there is ever a possibility of the BBC relinquishing the copyright to the Producer. Since the BBC owns the copyright, the distribution rights are wholly within the BBC's gift. However, under the Working Practices, the BBC and the Producer are supposed to consult as to how best the programme can be exploited, and thus who should be appointed distributor, the choice being between Enterprises, the Producer itself (if it is capable of acting as a distributor) or a third party. The BBC not unnaturally has a preference for Enterprises, and in practice the Producer actually has to convince Enterprises (and not the BBC) that the Producer or someone else can do better, if Enterprises is **not** appointed distributor. The BBC's decision will be final, whatever the Producer's views on the matter.

It is probably fair to say that it is only if Enterprises is not particularly optimistic about the programme's distribution potential that the Producer will be appointed as distributor, as few Producers have the resources to match Enterprises as a distributor. If the Producer or a third party is appointed, this has to be under a separate distribution agreement (Chapter 13, *Distribution agreements*) between the BBC, as copyright owner, and the relevant distributor.

The same process applies in the case of who should own and exploit the 'secondary rights' (Chapter 14, *Secondary exploitation*).

If there is an Enterprises investment (an Enterprises investment being defined as Enterprises supplying 15% or more of the cost of production) Enterprises will have the **automatic** right to act as distributor. In addition, the amount of the Enterprises investment has to be recouped from programme sales before net profits is reached. The Producer will not see the 'agreement' between the BBC and Enterprises for the distribution of the programme, but the rates of commission which Enterprises will charge are set out in the Working Practices. Although it is fair to say that other qualities of a distributor may distinguish it from its competitors, the **main** way of comparing the performance of one distributor with that of another is by the commission rates which they charge.

Additionally, as with any other distributor, Enterprises will deduct from sales income the expenses incurred in carrying on its distribution function. The Working Practices state that expenses which are attributable to television sales can be deducted from income flowing from other forms of exploitation, such as the secondary rights. This is called 'cross-collateralization' (Chapter 13, pages 228–9, contains further comment on this expression).

The Working Practices additionally state that, where Enterprises is appointed to be distributor, it is the BBC's preference that the rights should pass to Enterprises by way of **assignment of copyright** and not by a licence (Chapter 13, pages 220–21, contains further discussion on the legal method of transferring the necessary rights to a distributor). If the Producer, on the other hand, were to be appointed distributor, the transfer of rights to it would certainly only be by way of licence from the BBC.

Whoever is appointed distributor, the share in net profits ultimately payable to the Producer is generally not more than 30%. This is a figure which is never really negotiable with the BBC, and of course the Producer has no bargaining power, since the BBC already owns the copyright in the programme. If the Producer has nothing further to offer, it will not normally be able to persuade the BBC to be more generous.

CHANNEL FOUR

This broadcaster deals with independent Producers in very much the same way as the BBC, largely because the Working Practices were extensively based on Channel Four's Terms of Trade. Until the last few years, Channel Four had had the most extensive dealings with independent Producers, being more or less a publisher-broadcaster since its inception in the early 1980s. 'Publisher-broadcaster' is a term used to describe broadcasters who are not also Producers, so who do not make their own programmes.

One difference between the BBC and Channel Four is that, although Channel Four has a distribution operation, it makes no artificial distinction between investment being made by its distribution arm. Channel Four is very direct and straightforward about rights and was certainly, at least until recently, more likely to be fair about relinquishing rights back to the Producer in the case of run-of-the-mill productions. Since the Broadcasting Act 1990, 'the Channel' as it is often called, has become more financially uncertain. It is funded mostly by the ITV companies, who used to sell Channel Four's advertising air time for it, but who will now be competing with Channel Four in advertising sales, as Channel Four will now be responsible for selling its own air time. In this uncertain climate, Channel Four is likely to be more rigorously commercial. As with the BBC, the net profit share which a Producer can expect is normally 30%.

Hiring and firing | 8

CONTRACTUAL ASPECTS

There are two aspects to deal with in contracts engaging personnel to render services on a production:

- the terms which apply to **how and when** they provide services and **the fee** payable for their services;
- the clearance of the **rights to exploit** the contributions of the person being hired in the finished production.

The second aspect is dealt with in more detail in Chapters 9 and 10 on rights clearances. However, the section which follows concentrates on the routine contents of contracts for services in the film and television industry.

As mentioned in Chapter 2, *The business*, personnel can be either **employed** (Schedule E for tax purposes) or **engaged** (Schedule D or freelance). The main points relevant to **employing** personnel are covered in Chapter 2, which deals with the considerations which employers of **any** type of personnel in any industry must bear in mind. However, there are separate and specific aspects of hiring personnel to work on film and television productions which will be covered below, and most of which apply whether the contributor is employed or engaged on a freelance basis. When a project proceeds to production, the majority of personnel will be engaged on a temporary basis for the life of the production period only.

The following issues must be kept in mind.

- The contract with the contributor has to comply with the basic require-ments necessary for a contract to be binding (Chapter 4, *The deal*).
- The tax position should be clear, especially if the contributor is engaged on a freelance basis. There may be other extra tax complications, depending on the normal place of residence of the contributor. The Value Added Tax position must also be kept in mind.
- If the contributor is a member of a talent union, the Producer may be bound to engage the contributor on the terms of the collective bargaining

agreement which his or her union has concluded with representatives of the main **users** of talent – the BBC, the ITV companies or PACT, the Producers' Alliance for Cinema and Television (Chapter 9, pages 150–4).

As long as these aspects are dealt with, the contract itself can be in almost any form the Producer wishes (unless an applicable union agreement requires the use of the union's pro-forma engagement agreement (Chapter 9, pages 152–4). It can be long and detailed or short and pithy. It can be in the guise of a formal contract or written as a letter from the Producer to the contributor (with the contributor signing and returning to the Producer a copy of the letter to show that he or she agrees to what it says). Evidently if it is short, that means that certain areas, which may have been covered in a longer agreement, have to be left out. The Producer has a range of choices:

- to deal only with those things that must inescapably be referred to (such as **what** the contributor will be doing, **how** he/she is supposed to do it, **when** he/she is required to do it and **how much and when** he/she will be paid);
- to deal with any eventuality which could potentially arise (such as what is to happen if the contributor gets involved in a scandal which might attract unfavourable publicity to the production).

UK Producers usually prefer the first approach because that might enable the whole contract to be on two sides of A4-sized paper (albeit relatively close printed). By contrast, the American preference is for the second approach. This may be due to the greater prevalence of lawyers in the American film and television industries!

It is suggested that the right approach depends on the **importance** of the contributors to the production and the amount of **money** involved. The more highly paid the contributor, the more important it is to have a 'heavy-duty' contract which protects both parties. Either way, it is worth commenting on the different topics that **could** arise in a contract for services and giving a flavour of what kind of detail should be included, depending on the circumstances.

THE NATURE OF THE SERVICES

The agreement should say what the contributor will be required to do (whether an actor, director, individual producer etc.). It might also provide for a certain standard to be met (for example, 'the Director will render to the best of his/her skill and ability all such services normally rendered by a first class director of films/television programmes').

It is also necessary to say **when** the contributor's services are required during the production period. The contributor may be needed for the whole production period (from start of pre-production to delivery to the distributor or broadcaster of the finished production) as in the case of the individual producer. Alternatively, some personnel such as actors will be needed only for part of that period. It is normal to define the relevant period and refer to it as 'the guaranteed period', to identify it as the time during which the contributor **guarantees** to be available to work on the production. The agreement will then state that his/her services are **exclusive** for that period, meaning that he or she cannot render services for anyone else. However, it is the nature of film and television production that some people may be needed at other times outside the originally agreed period. The most usual example is that of actors, who may be needed before they actually start work on shooting for costume fittings and rehearsal, or after shooting for 'post-synching' (namely, dubbing their voices on to the soundtrack where the sound quality of the original recording was not found to be good enough). The contract should therefore provide that the contributor will be available for a specified number of days outside the 'guaranteed period'. This extra availability can either be on what is called a **first call** or **second call** basis.

Being on **first call** means that the contributor has to drop everything and work when required. Being on **second call** means that existing professional commitments can be finished before the contributor has to answer the Producer's call. Since first call status effectively stops the contributor from taking other work, it naturally costs more to keep people on first call than on second call.

PAYMENT AND TAX ISSUES

The contract naturally has to be clear about how much the contributor will be paid and when. It is normal to pay an agreed fee in instalments evenly spaced throughout the guaranteed period. As with any other commercial deal, it is not good practice to part with the whole of the agreed fee until all of the work has been done.

Depending on the nature of the services, the contributor may also ask for expenses (travel and accommodation) to be reimbursed or paid for from the production. The Producer should only agree to pay either expenses which it has approved in advance of them being incurred **and/or** expenses which are evidenced by proper receipts and bills. If the contributor has an agent, the agent will want to receive the fees on the contributor's behalf (so that the agent's commission can be deducted by the agent before paying it over to the contributor). The Producer must obtain **written** authority **from the contributor** (ideally in the contract itself) to make payment to the agent. The obligation in the contract is to pay the **contributor**. If the Producer pays someone else, that liability will not have been met, and the Producer would face the risk of having to pay all over again. However, if the Producer has written authority from the person otherwise entitled to payment, that will be sufficient.

The question of whether, in addition to the fee for the work done, further sums may be payable at some later date if the contributor is to share in the proceeds of exploitation, is covered in Chapter 9, *Rights clearances I*, pages 150–54.

There are two other tax issues to consider which relate to the question of whether income tax has to be deducted before the fee is paid.

- As a general point, if the contributor is self-employed and the producer pays without deducting tax and national insurance contributions, there must be some protection in the contract in case the Inland Revenue takes the view that that person is **actually** employed.
- If the contributor is a foreign entertainer (someone who is not resident in the UK and is a performer of any type, not just an actor or sportsman) the Inland Revenue has regulations which require basic rate tax to be deducted from payments to entertainers/sportsmen before those payments are made.

EMPLOYED OR SELF-EMPLOYED?

On the question of PAYE, the Inland Revenue has issued guidelines about where PAYE must be deducted, notwithstanding that certain personnel themselves may regard themselves as self-employed. Most actors will be treated as self-employed by the Inland Revenue. However, for technical personnel, the Inland Revenue has a comprehensive list of grades where PAYE need **not** be deducted. Where personnel fall **outside** those grades, it is unsafe not to deduct tax from them. If in any doubt, a Producer should contact the Inland Revenue. This is vital to get right because if a deduction is not made, the Inland Revenue will almost certainly require payment from the Producer of the amount which it believes should have been deducted. The Inland Revenue is legally entitled to do this and it is much easier than trying to collect it from the individual recipient.

FOREIGN ENTERTAINERS

Where payments are to be made to foreign entertainers, the Producer should liaise well in advance with the Foreign Entertainers Unit ('FEU') of the Inland Revenue.

The main point of this kind of deduction is to prevent foreign entertainers from avoiding paying tax altogether. It was often the case that, for example, US actors or other performers who were rendering services here would not declare the income which they had been paid here when filling out their tax return to the American IRS. However, it is not the intention of the regulations that entertainers should pay two lots of tax on the same income – thus if tax **is** deducted under the regulations, the foreign entertainer/ sportsman is given a credit for the tax paid against his/her domestic tax bill, which can then be set against that bill when the time comes to pay it. Normally, therefore, the only disadvantage from an entertainer's point of view (although quite a major disadvantage if the fee is large) is one of cash flow, in that he/she does not get the gross amount until a tax bill becomes payable at home. However, there is an added disadvantage if the tax rate payable by the entertainer in his/her home territory is **less** than UK basic rate tax. In that case, the extra tax paid here is not actually reclaimable. The FEU provides on request a Payer's Guide to payments to foreign entertainers, which is 21 pages in length and which explains the requirements in full.

PROTECTION AGAINST INLAND REVENUE FINDINGS THAT TAX SHOULD HAVE BEEN DEDUCTED BEFORE PAYMENT

Whenever engaging self-employed people, including foreign entertainers, it is prudent for a Producer to include provisions in the agreement of engagement which:

- allow the Producer to make deductions from the fees or other sums payable, if required by law or a governmental authority;
- enable the Producer to reclaim amounts which should have been deducted if the Inland Revenue claims these amounts from the Producer. This ability to seek repayment from the contributor should be reinforced by authority being given to the Producer, in the contract, to retain money which might otherwise become payable to the contributor in the future (such as use fees or net profit shares) until the Producer has been reimbursed for the sum paid to the Inland Revenue.

CREDITS/PUBLICITY

If the contributor is of sufficient status, he or she may also be entitled to expect a credit on screen on all copies made of the production. The producer should restrict any obligation to accord a credit to copies made 'by or under the control of' the Producer. For instance, a Producer should not be responsible for what does or does not appear on 'pirated' copies made without the Producer's consent. Additionally, the key contributors to a production may ask for a credit in major paid advertising (namely, substantial advertising on publicity which has been specially paid for). As it is the distributor (or broadcaster) who usually arranges for advertising, the Producer should remember that distributors commonly refuse to undertake to provide for credits in certain kinds of advertising. Thus, the Producer must ensure that the credit obligation of the Producer in the contract with the contributor is excluded in similar circumstances. The standard exclusions are listed in Chapter 13, on pages 231–2. However, to save space in the contract, it is sometimes just as good to say simply that the obligation will be subject to the 'exclusions customarily applied by distributors in the film and/or television industries'.

The Producer should normally exclude **any** liability for 'casual or inadvertent' failure to provide a credit (so that the Producer will not be in breach of the agreement unless the failure was deliberate). It is also common for Producers to try stating that they will not be liable for the failure of distributors or other end users of the production to accord the agreed credit, so long as the Producer has told the distributor/end user what credit the distributor is entitled to receive. Additionally, Producers often try to restrict their liability, even for deliberate breaches of the credit obligation, to using reasonable endeavours to correct the failure in future (Chapter 4, pages 43–4, contains further comment on 'reasonable endeavours'). The contributor, if wise, should anyway insist on the Producer being under a duty to try to **correct** credit failures (whether deliberate or made by error) but the Producer should be careful to make sure that this only applies **prospectively**, and that the obligation is to use only 'reasonable endeavours' to correct. Equally it should be made clear that the use of the words 'reasonable endeavours' will not imply that the Producer has any obligation to spend substantial sums of money or to commence legal action (for example against a distributor who has failed to accord a credit).

WARRANTIES

'Warranties' is the term used to describe statements made as to fact by a person who is a party to a contract, which are highly relevant (or in legal terms 'material') to whether or not the other party would actually want to conclude the contract. For instance, in agreements where rights are granted by one party to the other, it is naturally essential to the other that the rights actually belong to the first party and that he or she has the power to grant them.

There is, therefore, usually a warranty (or even several) to this effect.

OTHER OBLIGATIONS

The level of detail needed in the contract about the obligations of the contributor (leaving aside the main services to be provided) depends on the status of the contributor and the amount of money involved. Here are a few examples:

- keeping the Producer informed of the contributor's whereabouts and telephone number;
- using best efforts to keep in good health, so as not to jeopardize the Producer's ability to get insurance on the contributor's life and health and, if required, submitting to medical examinations for insurance purposes;
- not carrying on any hazardous pursuits which might invalidate insurance policies or not be covered by insurance;
- obtaining or assisting the Producer in obtaining all necessary work permits or membership of unions which are necessary to allow the contributor to render services as required;
- not to do anything which might or will adversely affect the reputation of the production and/or the Producer.

SUSPENSION/TERMINATION

When the engagement is either important or lengthy, the Producer will want to be able to suspend it, or even terminate it in certain circumstances.

Provisions relating to being able to suspend services usually appear only in contracts which involve very large sums of money and/or a very long period over which services are to be rendered. Events which might lead the Producer to wish to suspend are:

- if the contributor for some reason fails to perform as required, either deliberately or because of his/her incapacity;
- if **an event of** *force majeure* occurs which prevents, interrupts or delays production.

An event of *force majeure* is something which is genuinely beyond a particular party's (in this case the Producer's) control. Examples are:

- fire, casualty, accident, riot or war, act of God or the Queen's enemies, strike, lock-out, labour conditions, judicial order or enactment (i.e. a change in the law), incapacity or death of any leading artist, the individual producer, the director or a senior technician on the production.

Suspension can have one or more effects, depending on the contract.

- While it lasts, the Producer may not have to pay instalments of the fee which would otherwise be due (although the contributor should insist on continuing to be paid expenses).
- The period of engagement may actually be extended by the period during which the suspension lasts.
- However, the contributor would usually be required to carry on

performing those of his or her duties under the contract which are not actually affected by suspension and not to agree to work for anyone else unless the Producer consents.

Agents who represent actors or other major personnel often try to limit the Producer's powers to suspend or the effects of suspension in the following ways.

- The Producer can only suspend the actor/other contributor if the key crew and principal cast are also suspended.
- The actor/other contributor should have the first option to resume the services for which they were originally engaged if suspension led to termination of their engagement, but production is actually resumed in the future.
- The actor/other contributor should be able to take on other work during the period of suspension.

While suspension provisions may not often be necessary, termination provisions are very useful in all contracts, except those which deal with very short periods of engagement. Events which could give rise to termination are:

- if the contributor fails to perform or is unable to do so for more than a specified period;
- if a *force majeure* event occurs which affects the production for longer than a certain specific period;
- if the contributor's conduct affects his or her reputation adversely or prejudices the production or its successful exploitation;
- if insurance on the contributor's life and health, where required, is not obtained or not obtainable;
- if work permits or other necessary consents are not obtained or obtainable.

The contract should state clearly which procedure needs to be followed when the contract is to be terminated. For instance, it is sound practice to agree that an agreement can be terminated only by notice **in writing** to the other party, and the termination will take place either immediately or after a certain period following the date of the notice of termination.

If the agreement has been terminated by reason of the failure or breach of one party, it is common for the contract to state that termination will **not take effect** until the party in breach has been given a specific time (for example fourteen days) to put matters right, assuming this can be done. This period is often referred to as a **cure period**. If the breach has not been cured within the period, the contract will then terminate.

As to what the effects of termination should be, the usual practice is to state the following specifically in a contract.

- Both of the parties' obligations to each other will come to an end (especially those which involve further payment), **except** obligations which specifically say that they are still to survive termination of the contract. (An example of this might be a statement that warranties given by one party or another are to continue in effect, even if the agreement is terminated.)
- Each party will remain entitled to require performance by the other of obligations which were due to be performed **before** the date of termination (for example, to pay a fee for services which have already been rendered).
- Termination will not affect any grant of rights or consents given to the agreement. So, for example, an assignment of copyright from the contributor to the Producer will not be reversed simply because the contract has been terminated.

This last effect is the most important from the Producer's point of view.

RIGHTS OF THE CONTRIBUTOR IF THERE IS A BREACH BY THE PRODUCER

It is of course quite possible, although it has not been dealt with specifically above, that the contributor may want the right to terminate the agreement if the **Producer** fails to perform. However, it is usually in the contributor's interest to keep the contract going (so as to avoid arguments that, by terminating, he or she has forfeited the right to be paid the agreed fee). In that case, the only protection which the contributor will usually require is the right to 'down tools' and stop work without being found to be in breach of the agreement, if and as long as the contributor is not actually being paid what the Producer owes.

On the other hand, from the Producer's viewpoint, it is particularly important to ensure that the legal options open to the contributor are limited, if the Producer does breach the agreement after the production has been made. Examples of such breaches are where there has been a failure to accord credits as agreed or where the contributor fails to receive an agreed net profit share which has become due. It would therefore be wise of the Producer to include the following wording (or something similar) in the engagement agreement.

> If the Producer is in breach of any of its obligations under this Agreement or under statute law or common law enforced in any part of the world, the rights and remedies of the Contributor will be limited to the Contributor's rights (if any) to recover damages in a legal action and in no event will the Contributor be entitled by reason of any such breach to injunct or restrain the distribution, exhibition, broadcasting, advertis-

ing or exploitation of any film/programme produced by the Producer.

Unless restricted in this way, the contributor may take out an injunction to prevent further breaches – if the injunction effectively stops the production from being shown, this would be disastrous for the Producer (Chapter 15, *Legal proceedings*).

SERVICE COMPANIES – INDUCEMENT LETTERS

To enable more efficient regulation of their tax affairs, self-employed personnel frequently set up 'service companies'. The contributor with a service company has usually agreed with the company that it will be entitled to his or her exclusive services. Therefore, a Producer wishing to use the services of the contributor has to contract for them with the service company.

The form of the contract will be very much the same as if the Producer were contracting directly with the contributor. However, because the contract is not with the contributor, the Producer will not be able to sue the contributor if the contributor does not perform as required. Contract law dictates that the Producer's claim is against the company. (Chapter 4, page 43.) Unfortunately, most service companies are mere 'shells' without any independent business or assets, and a claim against such a company is worthless. This will be particularly so if the contributor severs all connections with the company by winding it up.

Therefore, when contracting with a service company, the Producer should require the contributor to sign an 'inducement letter'. This is a direct contract between the contributor and Producer under which, as an inducement to the Producer to sign the contract with the service company, the contributor agrees certain things. These will include:

- to perform what is required of the contributor under the main agreement;
- that if he/she does not perform, the Producer can sue the contributor directly;
- that if the service company ceases to exist, the contributor will be substituted as a party to the agreement with the Producer;
- an assignment of copyright/consent to exploitation of the contributor's services (and a waiver of moral rights where necessary).

An example of a typical inducement letter is set out in Appendix G.

9

Rights clearances I

LEGAL PRINCIPLES

Whenever the contributions of individuals are made to a film or television production, the Producer must 'clear' the rights to the products of those individual's services. That means that terms must be agreed between the Producer and the contributor which will allow the work of the contributor to be exploited, as part of the film or programme, by all the means and in all the media which are likely to be relevant. The same process must take place if the Producer uses pre-existing copyright material – permission must be obtained to use that material.

'Clearing' as opposed to paying for rights

There is a distinction between, on the one hand, 'clearing' the rights, and on the other hand, paying for them. When a production is made, the Producer may well know at that stage that certain types of exploitation are certainly going to happen (for instance, UK network television transmission if the production has been commissioned by the BBC). However, other types of exploitation (for instance, sales to overseas distributors or broadcasters, or release on home video) may not be **guaranteed** to happen, although naturally all concerned would like to see the production exploited as widely as possible. So it is the practice of Producers to **clear** the right in individual contributions to the production. Clearing rights in material is getting consent in principle to exhibit or broadcast those contributions (as incorporated in the finished production) by those means and in those media which are not currently planned, but in which it is hoped that sales will be made. When a sale **is** made, a further fee (the amount of which will have been agreed at the time the rights were cleared) will become payable. Examples, in the case of a production commissioned by the BBC, will be sales to an overseas broadcaster or by distribution on video. On this basis, the Producer (or whoever may have taken over the Producer's responsibility to pay money to the contributor) will only pay if and when the particular right is exercised. This practice will be explained further when considering the operation of the various industry collective bargaining agreements. These have been concluded to save Producers having to negotiate individually with each contributor (and those agreements also guarantee certain minimum pay and other terms for the contributors). However, first it may assist to see rights clearances in context by considering the legal rights which individual contributors have in what they provide to the production and thus, why their consent is necessary to enable full exploitation after production.

RIGHTS OF CONTRIBUTORS

These can be summarized as follows.

Copyright

This will apply to the work of writers (literary works of copyright), designers (artistic works of copyright) and composers/lyricists (musical works of copyright).

It will also be necessary to clear copyright when a Producer wishes to use pre-existing artistic works (paintings, sculptures) which have been created by an artist whose work is still in copyright. Remember that a building can also be an artistic work of copyright, and so can works of craftsmanship. The use of photographs will also involve clearance of copyright.

Lastly, rights of copyright in films and sound recordings means that use of extracts from pre-existing film/sound recordings in any film and television production will also require the consent of the copyright owner.

Moral rights

Since 1989 in this country, the question of moral rights will arise whenever use of a copyright literary, dramatic, musical or artistic work takes place. Moral rights are also an issue in relation to the work of the director of a copyright film.

Rights in performances

The copyright law of the UK protects the rights of live performers by requiring the consent of the performer to the making of a film or sound recording of any performance given by him or her. The right to consent (or withhold consent) is also extended to any person who has an **exclusive recording contract** with a performer, in respect of that performer's live appearances. That person will usually be a record company.

Recording a performance without consent of the necessary people, or exhibiting and exploiting a recording made without consent will entitle those people to sue the infringer.

Rental and lending rights

As part of the European Community's moves towards improving and harmonizing the laws of individual EC member states on copyright and in relation to other so-called 'intellectual property', the EC has adopted a Directive on rental and lending rights of certain persons. (A 'Directive', once adopted, requires each member state to change its law (so far as may be necessary) by a certain outside date, to reflect the terms of the Directive.) The Directive on rental and lending rights requires that certain individuals must be given the legal right to consent to or prohibit the originals or copies of the products of their artistic or performing abilities being rented or lent out. This right is given to the authors of copyright works (for these purposes literary, artistic, dramatic and musical works **and** films, but not sound recordings); to the Producers of and performers on phonograms (i.e. sound recordings); to the performers in films; and to the film Producer in relation to the first recording of a film.

'Rental' means making available for use for a limited period of time and for direct or indirect economic or commercial advantage (such as through a video shop). 'Lending' means making available for use, for a limited period of time and not for direct or indirect economic or commercial advantage, when it is made through establishments which are open to the public (such as a public library).

Some people take the view that 'rental' will not only include the normal commercial hire of films (on video or disc) or records, but will also encompass 'pay-per-view' television (where viewers pay a fee for each specific film/programme which they have chosen to see) and other kinds of exploitation of films and records along these lines. While the right to consent or object to rental or lending can be **waived** by the original right holder, or even transferred to another person, the author or performer who has transferred or assigned his rental right in relation to a sound recording or a film always has a right to 'equitable remuneration' for the rental. This right cannot be waived. What 'equitable remuneration' means is as vague as the rest of the Directive. What it will entail for the UK film and television industry will not be made clear until the British government passes laws to bring the Directive into force in this country, and maybe not even then. However, this book will try to give some guidance below (pages 149–50) on how to deal with the Directive when it comes to clearing rights.

Other property rights

Where locations outside a studio are used for filming, the Producer will need consents from the owner of the property to be present there. Otherwise, any activities on the owner's property will be 'trespass'. In addition, there may be other consents to obtain, such as from the police or local authorities.

HOW TO CLEAR THE VARIOUS RIGHTS

This section contains guidelines on how the rights referred to above can be cleared. In certain cases, where arrangements with contributors are made under collective bargaining agreements, the accepted form of agreement for use under that collective bargaining agreement should accomplish the transfers and consents which are about to be described. Otherwise, in concluding contracts with contributors, Producers should always ensure that they consider the issues set out below.

Clearing copyright

Assignments

When specifically commissioning a copyright work for a film or programme (usually a script), a Producer's most complete form of clearance will be to take a transfer of the copyright (referred to as 'an assignment'). Taking an assignment of copyright will give the Producer the right to use the work in the proposed production and, in addition, the right to control all further exploitation of the finished film or programme. However, the exploitation right will of course be restricted by the terms on which the copyright was assigned or the effects of law which the Producer cannot avoid (such as, for example, the moral rights of the original author or his rights under the Directive on rental and lending rights).

Consider the following example:

A writer ('W') assigns the copyright in her script to P, the Producer. However, W does not waive her moral rights. P also agrees to pay W 2% of the net profits made from exploiting the film which has been made from the script, and W has been very tough and insisted that if her share is not paid at any time, P will become obliged to reassign the copyright in her script to her. Lastly, assume that UK law has already been altered to bring the Rental Rights Directive into force. This all means that P **must** pay W her share of profits, or will forfeit the right to exploit the film; P must also respect her moral rights (pages 144–5 below). And P may also have difficulty if there is any possibility that W may decide that 2% of net profits is not 'equitable remuneration' for her rental right. That is, if the wording in the assignment was wide enough to make sure that the lending and rental rights were actually transferred to P!

As to the length of time for which copyright is to be assigned, this will more often than not be for the full period of copyright (although it is possible to agree that the copyright has to be reassigned after a shorter period of time or, as in the example above, after a particular event, such as non-payment, has occurred. Remember, however, that if the assignment is to be for the entire period of copyright protection, it should acknowledge the fact that copyright may be extended or even revived after the work has fallen into the public domain (as seems likely under the Directive harmonizing the term of copyright protection (Chapter 3, page 22)).

It is also very important to get the wording of the assignment right, to leave absolutely no doubt that it was an **assignment** (rather than, say, a licence) which was intended.

The following wording is recommended:

[The Author] assigns to [the Assignee] the entire copyright and all other rights of whatever nature in and to [the Work] including all vested, future and contingent rights to which [the Author] is now or may in the future be entitled to under the laws in force in any part of the World TO HOLD the same unto [the Assignee] absolutely for the full period of copyright protection in [the Work] throughout the World including all reversions, renewals and extensions and after that so far as is permissible in perpetuity.

This wording will cover **all** rights (not just copyright) and not just those rights which presently exist, but other rights which might be conferred on authors in the future. A particular example of this is the rental right.

Producers may find that writers and other creative individuals, even if they are prepared to assign their copyright, sometimes object to giving away potential future rights before they know what they are! However, from the Producer's point of view, to do otherwise runs the risk that the future exploitation of the entire production (which is, after all, usually the fruit of a number of creative talents) may be halted by a new right given to one individual contributor, who refuses to give consent on reasonable terms to that right being exercised. Sensible compromises for this kind of dilemma are usually possible if both parties keep an open mind.

Licences

It is becoming more and more frequent that Producers may not get outright assignments of copyright works which they have commissioned for the production. An assignment will also generally be out of the question where pre-existing material (such as film clips, photographs or underlying material) is concerned. This is not a problem as long as the Producer gets consent to carry out all those acts which are restricted by the copyright in the work which the Producer wishes to use (Chapter 3, pages 24–5) which are necessarily involved in the making and exploiting of the film. These will be:

- the right to copy the work (for example filming or photographing a work, or incorporating music or a sound recording on to a soundtrack);
- the right to make further copies, by making copies of the finished film or programme;
- the right to present or show the work in public (when exhibiting the film or programme itself);
- the right to broadcast the work (or include it in a cable programme);
- the right to adapt the work (as many pre-existing works might need adapting, editing or altering in order to make them fit within the film or programme).

There is nothing wrong with a licence, and it can be as effective as an assignment of copyright from the Producer's point of view, as long as the Producer remembers that since the licence is only a form of **permission**, it can be **withdrawn or terminated** by the person granting it. It is, however, possible to agree with the person granting the licence that he or she should **not** be able to terminate it, and it is recommended that Producers do this. To show why this is important, the following is an example of how the Producer could face disaster:

If in our example above, W had only granted a licence, she could (in the absence of further agreement to the contrary) terminate the licence if P broke the terms of their agreement in some way, such as by not paying W what is due to her. If the licence is terminated, P's rights to do any of the acts, in relation to the script written by W, will cease as well. As the script is indivisible from the film (as it usually is!), this means that the film can no longer be exploited, unless another agreement with W is reached.

This risk can be avoided, if W and P agreed that the licence would be **irrevocable**, and that if P did breach any of the terms of the licence, W would restrict herself to suing for damages, and in particular would not be able to resort to any other action, such as termination or (just as bad from the Producer's and distributor's point of view) an injunction preventing further exploitation of the film.

It should be added that an assignment can have the potential drawbacks of a licence, if the person in whose favour the assignment was made agrees that he/she has to **re-assign** the rights if there is a breach of the terms of the assignment.

Formal requirements to create assignments/licences of copyright

As a matter of law, **assignments** of copyright must be in writing and signed by the person assigning his or her copyright. Otherwise, they will not be effective (except, perhaps, as an **agreement to assign** copyright).

Licences need not be in writing to be effective, except if they are **exclusive** licences when, again as a matter of law, they must be in writing and signed by the person granting the licence. An **exclusive** copyright licence granted to someone will give him or her the right to do whatever he or she is licensed to do, to the exclusion of anyone else, **including** the copyright owner.

However, even if the law does not require that agreements relating to rights clearances must be in writing, they **should** be, for the same reason that any agreement ought to be – otherwise, there may be no firm evidence of what has been agreed. More practically, a distributor or broadcaster will require, under its contract with the Producer, that there be written documents dealing with rights, which the distributor/broadcaster can use as reference in its exploitation plans, and from which it can be seen at a glance what does or does not need to be paid in the future, when certain forms of exploitation take place.

When copyright clearances may not be required

Fair dealing exceptions

UK Copyright Law allows certain exceptions (where it is in the public interest) to the normal rule that copying or exhibiting a work of copyright requires a copyright owner's permission. The main exceptions are known as the 'fair dealing' exceptions because they each allow the use of works of copyright or parts or extracts from them when it is for:

- criticism or review;
- reporting on current events.

In either case, the use must be 'fair'; if it is for criticism or review, an acknowledgement must also be given to the work and its author. If the use is in reporting current events **and** in a film, broadcast or cable programme, no such acknowledgement is actually required by law.

The 'current events' exception does **not** apply to photographs, so specific consent from the owner of the copyright in a photograph will be necessary for its use in news and current affairs programmes.

The use must be 'fair': this means that it must not be used to an extent where it actually competes with any use made by the copyright owner, or (possibly) where the use will actually damage the copyright owner.

> For example, if an arts programme is reviewing or discussing a film, the showing of a brief clip would usually be acceptable, without having to seek the permission of the copyright owner. However, if there is more than one clip from the film shown in the programme, and each is of a considerable length (and perhaps even the ending is shown), the copyright owner of the film could legitimately claim that consent should have been required for this use. (In practice, at least where new films are concerned, it is the usual practice to get specific consent from the copyright owner or distributor, because they will generally be the only source of the footage required.)

An interesting use of the 'fair dealing' exception for news and current events was made by BSB (as BSkyB then was) which used, in BSB's sports news coverage, excerpts of BBC broadcasts (broadcasts being protected by copyright in the same way as other works of copyright) of football matches. These extracts were brief, but featured some or all of the goals. On screen, BSB acknowledged the source of the pictures. The BBC objected to this use but, in court, the use was found to be covered by the 'fair dealing' exception. Key factors influencing the court's decision were the fact that BSB had tried to agree terms with the BBC for the use of the footage before actually using it and the BBC had refused; and that BSB had drawn-up (and scrupulously observed) strict and detailed guidelines to ensure that use was kept to a fair minimum and that (even though not strictly necessary) the BBC's ownership was acknowledged.

Another more recent example where the 'fair dealing' exception was used was the case involving the Channel Four programme *Without Walls*, which was discussing the self-imposed censorship by Stanley Kubrick of *A Clockwork Orange*. Kubrick had withdrawn the film from distribution in the UK after it had caused public outcry, following allegations that it inspired violence. In discussing this, the programme (some 25 minutes in length) showed extensive clips from the film, totalling more than half the actual length of the programme itself. The distributor successfully obtained an injunction preventing the broadcast of the programme on the basis that, since they had a contractual obligation to Stanley Kubrick for the film not to be shown, they would suffer substantial damage as a result of clips being shown. However, on appeal, the injunction was lifted and the court found this to be fair dealing.

Public display of artistic works

The Copyright, Designs and Patents Act 1988 permits the inclusion in films and television programmes of buildings, sculptures, models for buildings, works of artistic craftsmanship, in each case permanently situated in a public place or in premises open to the public. The Act does not say in absolutely clear terms what is meant by a 'public place' or 'premises open to the public'. For instance, are the grounds of a hotel 'premises open to the public'? Naturally, members of the public do go into the hotel grounds, otherwise the hotel would not have any guests. On the other hand, the hotel usually reserves the right to exclude any person it wishes from its premises. This might make it necessary to get permission to film, say, a work of sculpture in the hotel grounds.

Incidental inclusion

If a work of copyright (of any kind) is **incidentally** included in a film, broadcast, sound recording or artistic work, no permission is required of the copyright owner. However, the meaning of 'incidental' is not expanded on. The view is generally taken that it applies only to the inclusion of works over which the maker of the film or sound recording had no control (i.e. **accidental**).

For example:

A television news crew films an interview with a politician who is opening a new shopping mall. In the background, 'muzak' is playing.

In an episode of a soap opera, two of the characters are playing a scene in the kitchen, where the radio is playing a 'Top Ten' hit.

In the first example, the use is incidental; in the second example, it is generally thought to be not incidental, because the Producer had the choice of whether the radio should be switched on or off when the cameras were rolling.

Other examples might not be so obvious: what if the television news crew interviewed a captain of industry in his office, sitting at his desk, with a David Hockney picture shown prominently behind the interviewee's head? Obviously, the interviewee could have been shot from another angle, avoiding the picture. In those circumstances, it might then be unwise to try to rely on the 'incidental inclusion' exception.

The only possible argument against this point of view is as follows: the exception applies when another work is 'incidentally' included in an **artistic work**. However, the only kind of artistic work in which one could argue that inclusion of another work might be truly 'incidental' (in the sense that the photographer had no choice whether to include it) is a photograph.

However, the Act does not refer to photographs only, but to 'artistic works', which is a very wide category indeed. Furthermore, even a photographer always has a choice about the direction in which he or she points the camera, so one could argue that the inclusion of any other work could never be 'incidental'. Thus, to give the exception some meaning in relation to artistic works, one would have to argue that 'incidental' does not mean 'accidental' but simply that the artistic work which has been included is not the main subject and purpose of the work in which it has been included.

However, since it is really better not to have to go to court to try to prove the real limits of this exception, it is probably wise to assume that the only time when the exception can be safely relied on is for outside broadcast units of sports or other public events.

Moral rights (or 'droit morale') which cannot be transferred to any other person (except the creator's heir or heirs)

The two most important moral rights are:

- the right of paternity (i.e. to claim authorship of the work);
- the right of integrity (i.e. to object to derogatory treatment in relation to the work).

These rights are given to:

- the **author** of **copyright** literary, dramatic, musical or artistic works;
- the **director** of a **copyright** film.

When the work falls out of copyright, the author/director's moral rights will also come to an end.

As these rights were introduced in the UK with effect from 1 August 1989, they should not apply in relation to works created before that date.

Additional rights to be borne in mind are the right to:

- prevent false attribution of the authorship of a copyright work to oneself (for instance, this would give David Hockney the right to take action if someone tried to pass off one of their paintings as a Hockney);
- the right of a person who has commissioned the taking of a photograph for **private and domestic purposes** to prevent it from being issued to the public or shown in public. In this case, even where the photographer has retained copyright in the photograph, the person who commissioned it can stop the photograph being exploited.

Moral rights are considered in more detail below.

The right of paternity

The right to be identified as author of a work is only enforceable (according to the Copyright, Designs and Patents Act 1988) after it has been inserted **in writing** by the author/director. This can be done in a contract with a Producer. Some lawyers believe that it should be asserted in a very formal way, e.g.:

> [The author] hereby asserts his/her right to be identified as the author of [the work] in accordance with Sections 77 to 78 of the Copyright, Designs and Patents Act 1988.

This author does not think that that degree of formality is strictly necessary, but agrees that it is better to be safe than sorry, as can be seen on page iv of this book!

The right of integrity

The right to object to derogatory treatment is of greatest concern to Producers in the film and television industry because it is very wide indeed.

- 'Treatment' means **any** change to, or deletion from, or adaptation of, a work other than a translation of a literary or dramatic work, or an arrangement of a musical work which involves more than a change of key or register.
- Treatment is 'derogatory' if it amounts to 'distortion or mutilation' of a work or is 'otherwise prejudicial to the honour or reputation' of the author/director.

These expressions are very vague in meaning and there have been very few cases in court in the UK to shed any light on them, or to give an idea of what penalties would be handed out to anyone who infringes moral rights. Alterations to any film or television production made after 1 August 1989 may theoretically be objected to by:

- the director;
- the writer(s);
- the composer;
- the choreographer;
- the set designer;
- the production designer.

That is, unless they waive their rights.

Waiving moral rights

Moral rights can be waived under English law (unlike, for instance, French law). The Copyright, Designs and Patents Act 1988 enables authors to give general or specific waivers, to give them conditionally or unconditionally, irrevocably or revocably. As the Act is ambiguously worded on this point, it is not clear whether a moral rights waiver **has** to be in writing, but as with any other form of legal right, it is unwise to rely on the owner not exercising it, without written evidence that he or she has actually agreed not to do so. Any waiver should therefore be **in writing** and signed **by the right owner**. As with assignments of copyright, the waiver can be included in a document which deals with other arrangements (most usually in the contract which deals with the creation and exploitation of a work, such as a writer's agreement).

However, and not surprisingly, it is common for writers (and increasingly directors) to object to waiving their moral rights, when the law have given those rights to them. On the other hand, Producers are reluctant to run the risk that one contributor to a film or programme can object to any editing or alteration (as it is of course the right of integrity which causes most concern) which distributors or other end users think is necessary for the effective exploitation of the finished production.

Here are two examples of problems which commonly arise in negotiation and how they can be dealt with in practice (if the financiers, broadcasters or distributors are happy).

P, a film Producer, presents W, a writer, with a contract to sign which requires her to waive her moral rights in the script she is writing for P. The contract states that she will receive a credit if the film is made based on her script, both on screen, and in major paid advertising of the film wherever the director's name is mentioned (this being a fairly good deal on credits, especially if the director is well known).

W's agent objects on W's behalf to waiving her moral right to object to derogatory treatment, and also asks for a statement in the contract that W actually asserts her moral right to be identified as author of the work.

P knows he may have to change the script in the course of shooting, and also that certain parts of it may get cut out when the film is edited. He has agreed to give W what he believes to be a generous credit and that is as far as he wants to go in identifying W as writer of the script. On the other hand, he does not wish to antagonize W – her work is very good, and she has been prepared to accept reasonable fees for what she has done.

P suggests:

- on the paternity point, that the assertion of her right to be identified is accepted but W must agree that this right is fully satisfied by the agreement to give credit as stated in the contract;

- as far as integrity is concerned, that W must waive this right in P's favour but that he will only be permitted to make minor on-the-floor changes without consulting with W, so that on any more substantial changes, W will (subject of course to her availability) be consulted and her views will be duly considered. However, P will have the final say.

W's agent **should** find this acceptable.

D, the writer/director of a feature film, who regards himself as an 'auteur', has brought his latest project to P for production. P arranges all the finance and sees to the commercial side of getting the film made. However, D refuses to waive his moral rights of integrity as director. P, on the other hand, has to be able to allow for the editing requirements of distributors, broadcasters and other end users. D **might** accept as a compromise that his consent is not required for:

- editing to comply with legal or censorship requirements of any territory where the film is being shown;
- editing to enable the interposing of commercial breaks;
- editing to meet slot length requirements of a broadcaster, or to meet broadcasting standards applicable to a broadcaster or to insert public service announcements;
- subtitling and/or dubbing as may be reasonably required in non-English speaking territories.

Otherwise, P will consult with D before any other kinds of changes are made. It is then a matter of bargaining power whether P or D (the consultation having taken place) has the final decision about whether the change can be made, assuming that D does not like it.

If it is agreed that a waiver should be given, the following wording is suggested.

The [author/director] hereby irrevocably waives the benefit of any provisions of law known as moral rights to which he/she is or may become entitled under the law in force in any part of the world [subject only to the obligation of [the Producer] to accord credit to the [author/director] in accordance with the terms of this Agreement].

The last part of the wording set out above reflects the commercial reality. If the waiver forms part of an agreement which also commits the Producer to giving the creator of the work a credit as such, on screen or elsewhere, then any waiver of this right should really be made subject to that commitment. If the author actually insists on asserting his or her moral rights (rather than waiving them subject to the credit requirements), the Producer can salvage the situation by the means suggested in the example given on page 146. Either way, the Producer's obligations **must** be made subject to the standard credit restrictions imposed by broadcasters or distributors (i.e. those circumstances in which the author, and practically any other contributor of the film, will not be entitled to receive a credit come what may (Chapter 13, pages 231–2)).

As a final comment, sometimes writers or directors, as a last resort, will require the right to remove their name from the credits if they do not approve the changes made to their work in the process of making or editing the production. However, this should not be easily conceded by the Producer because it will be very expensive to re-edit the credits, unless done at a very early stage.

Clearing rights in performances

Since it requires the consent of the performer (or a person who has an exclusive recording contract with that performer) to record his or her performance, the obvious way to clear this sort of right is to get the performer's consent!

It should preferably be in writing, and if the performer has an exclusive recording contract with someone else, consent of both performer and the other party to that recording contract should be obtained as a matter of caution. 'Performers' quite naturally include any person one would normally regard as such – actors, singers, dancers, trapeze artists, circus artists, mimes and the like; but it could also include sportsmen and women who give a type of performance (such as ice skaters or gymnasts). 'Performances' mean live performances which are dramatic (including dance and mime) or musical; readings or recitations of a literary work; or a performance of a variety act.

The normal and wisest practice is to get consent from anyone whose voice, or voice and appearance is being recorded. This will include interviewees on news and current affairs shows, and contestants. In fact, lawyers tend to include the relevant consent wording in contracts with contributors who are not even due to appear on screen. This is particularly sensible because even if the rights given under the Copyright, Designs and Patents Act 1988 are not relevant, the Act provides that the copyright in any recorded speech will belong to the speaker (regardless of who made the recording). Equally, there is the question of rental and lending rights which the contributor may have.

To clear these rights, the following wording is suggested:

[*] hereby irrevocably gives all consents which are or may in the future become necessary under any law in force in any part of the world to enable:

(a) the fullest possible exploitation of the [film/programme] (incorporating [*]'s contribution by all means and in all media (whether now known or to be invented in the future) throughout the world; and

(b) the promotion and publicizing by all such means and in all such media of the [film/programme] and its exploitation.

* Insert as applicable, writer, director, Producer or other contributor.

A specimen consent/clearance form is set out in Appendix H. It should, of course, be added that not every person will give consent if asked and not every person **can** be asked. For instance, a documentary reporter making a programme about the allegedly shady activities of a businessman will certainly be unlikely to persuade him to sign a consent form as well as giving an interview. It is always a question of assessing the risks, and making an appropriate decision as to whether to dispense with the formality of getting consent (Chapter 12, pages 205–208, considers the other legal danger areas which might require some form of agreements with individuals, such as defamation or infringement of rights of privacy/publicity).

Rental and lending rights

It is difficult to comment, in advance of legislation which is yet to be passed by the UK government, on how to be sure to clear these rights. However, the consent wording suggested just above (since it is so general) should have the effect of giving consent to rental and lending. What one cannot do is require the contributor to forego his or her right to 'equitable remuneration'. Almost certainly, a Producer will have agreed to pay the contributor something for the services or rights which have been contributed and the contributor by signing the contract will have agreed (either happily or reluctantly) to accept it as full payment. Some people have taken to including the following wording in contracts with contributors:

> For the avoidance of doubt, the assignment or grant of rights made or intended to be made in this Agreement includes without limitation those rights known or to be known as the lending right and the rental right in and to [the Work]/[the products of the [assignor/author/performer]'s services] and the [assignor/author/performer] acknowledges and agrees that the remuneration payable under this Agreement is an equitable pre-payment of any sums which may subsequently become due to the [assignor/author/performer] in respect of exploitation of the lending and rental or other rights.

While there is no harm in using this wording, the point has to be made that since no one has any way of knowing what will or will not be regarded as 'equitable', this may not prevent the contributor coming back at a later date and, like Oliver Twist, asking for more.

Having summarized the purely legal background, the following sections of this chapter will take each major type of contributor/contribution in turn and examine:

- the mechanisms which have been created in film and television industries to assist in clearing rights (such as union agreements);
- certain particular commercial peculiarities to be remembered.

UNION AGREEMENTS

Contributors to film and television productions are quite frequently represented by trades unions, who have each separately agreed with production organizations (the BBC and ITV companies) and with the representative body of independent Producers, PACT (the Producers' Alliance for Cinema and Television) collective bargaining agreements – namely, standard terms on which the members of that union may be engaged to work on productions. The major unions (from the point of view of rights clearances) are:

- British Actors' Equity Association ('Equity') representing actors and other performers (excluding musicians);
- the Writers' Guild of Great Britain ('WGGB') representing script-writers;
- the Musicians Union ('MU') representing musicians.

(BECTU is the union which represents technical personnel but, apart from directors, the question of rights clearances does not generally arise in agreements with BECTU members.)

It has been illegal during the last few years for unions to operate a 'closed shop' (so it is of course possible for Producers to engage, for example, actors who are not members of Equity). However, if the Producer works for the BBC or an ITV company, or is a member of PACT, **and** engages an Equity member, the Producer is bound to observe the terms of the agreement between the broadcaster/PACT and Equity. In addition certain unions (notably Equity) have, at least until recently, imposed in their collective bargaining agreements fairly onerous consultation procedures which have to be gone through if a Producer wishes to engage a non-Equity Member (the point being to discourage the use of non-union labour unless strictly necessary). There is doubt as to whether the imposition of such procedure is strictly within the letter of employment legislation which abolished the 'closed shop'.

In any event, it is still rare in practice for Producers in film and television production to use non-union talent, and even then the union agreement usually forms the basis of the terms on which the artist or other contributor is engaged. That way, the Producer has a ready-made framework for the deal with the contributor and (should it turn out to be necessary) can establish that the deal was fair (at least, as far as the relevant union is concerned, were the contributor to be a member of the union).

This book does not set out to describe in detail the contents of each separate union agreement. For each union, there are usually three agreements which differ from each other in quite significant respects (namely, one each with the BBC and the ITV companies, and the third with PACT). The agreements are also subject to periodic re-negotiation, so the only reference work which a Producer should use to find out the contents of the union agreements should be the agreements themselves.

However, they all operate along similar lines since they are each out to achieve similar purposes (although perhaps by slightly different routes). These purposes are:

- to lay down minimum financial remuneration for the contributor's work;
- to stipulate basic and guaranteed working conditions (for example, restrictions on nightworking or nudity for actors);
- to establish the right for the Producer to exploit the contribution made by the contributor **but** to ensure that the contributor can share in the financial rewards of exploitation.

It is this last function which is relevant from the point of view of clearing rights.

Typically, a union agreement states that the contributor should receive no less than a certain amount of money for a particular amount of work ('the minimum guaranteed fee'). Then if the production is exploited, the contributor may be entitled to receive further payments ('use fees' or 'residuals') in respect of each type of exploitation (for example, a sale of the television programme in which the contribution is used by network television in the US, or release of the programme on video).

These use fees are calculated in one of two ways, depending on the union agreement. Sometimes, the agreement may require that the contributor be paid a **specified percentage of the fee which he or she was originally paid** for work done, if a particular form of exploitation occurs.

For example, A, an actor, is paid £10 000 to appear in a television programme. Assume that the Equity/PACT Agreement (relating to television productions) states that certain uses are deemed to have been purchased by payment of the basic artist's earnings (such as one UK terrestrial network television transmission), but that if the programme is released on home video, A will be due another 7.5% of his original earnings (£750). Again, assume that the programme is shown a second time on UK television, another 35% of the original earnings will be due (£3500). If the programme is sold to US television, the residuals will really start mounting up as, for instance, a sale to US network television will attract a much larger percentage of the original fee.

The disadvantage of this system becomes apparent if, for instance, the production features a lot of actors and the money received from a particular form of exploitation is actually less than the residuals which would be payable to the actors if the exploitation takes place.

For this reason, some union agreements operate on a royalty basis, namely that the contributor receives a **percentage of the money realized from the additional form of exploitation**.

Under agreements which do not use a royalty basis for calculating residuals, it is wise (and common practice) for Producers to pre-purchase as many uses as possible within the fee which the Producer has available to pay a contributor from the production budget.

For example, if P has £10 000 available in the budget to pay A, an actor, but wants to be sure that the fee pays for **two** UK network transmissions, **plus** world video, **plus** sales to syndicated television and PBS in the US, the agreement with A should state that these uses are deemed to have been paid for and included in the £10 000 fee. This will work as long as the £10 000 fee is enough to cover the guaranteed minimum fee which A should have received for his work, plus all the relevant percentages of that fee which would have been payable for those uses (assuming that these are 35% for a second UK showing, 7.5% for video, 15% for syndication and 10% for PBS). Assume for the purposes of the example that A had done two weeks' work, and that the minimum guaranteed fee for that amount of work is £1120 (at a rate of £560 per week). If that **minimum** fee is treated as the basic artist's earnings, it is obvious that a total fee of £10 000 will be more than enough to cover both the basic fee and the percentages of that fee needed to purchase the extra uses which the Producer requires. In fact, however, A's agent is adamant that the £10 000 fee will only cover the specific uses which P has asked for. Any other use **must** be separately paid for. Thus, a complication could arise when P makes another kind of sale (such as US network television) and has to work out what A's basic fee **should have been**, so that say another 75% of that figure can be paid to A. However, for an intelligent production assistant with a calculator, this should not be difficult to work out. Briefly, it involves adding together the percentages of the different use fees plus 100%, dividing the total fee by the total of the percentages and then multiplying by 100 the figure thus found. In our example, this works out as follows:

	%
Artist's earnings	100
Second UK transmission	35
Video	7.5
US syndication	15
PBS	10

167.5% Total percentage

$$\frac{\text{Total fee}}{\text{Total percentage}} \qquad \frac{10\ 000}{167.5} \qquad = \qquad £59.70$$

£59.70 × 100 = £5970 = notional basic artist's earnings

Fee sale to US Network TV
£5970 × 75% = £4477.50

The operation of these agreements can be even more complicated by the fact that they usually have different use fee/residual scales depending on the type of production for which the contributor was engaged. For example, the PACT/Equity Agreement has different use fees depending on whether the production was originally made for theatrical release or for television. At the time of writing, the WGGB/PACT Agreement has different fee scales for each of the different types of production such as:

● higher budget feature films;
● lower budget feature films;
● single television films;
● television series and serials with format provided by the Producer to the writer.

(This is dealt with further in Chapter 5, page 80.)
    One last point to note is that the union agreement itself may state that it is only to apply for a limited period in relation to the products of the contributors' services. For example, the PACT/Equity TV Agreement current at the time of writing is limited to seven years after which, if the production is still being exploited, the Producer must pay the actor fees in accordance with the PACT/Equity Agreement then in force.
    The way in which union agreements are used in practice is that the Producer engages the contributor by a fairly short letter or agreement of engagement, which states that the terms of the union agreement will apply to the contributor's engagement, (This is what is known as 'incorporating by reference' the provisions of another, lengthier, agreement.) Doing this quite obviously makes life a lot easier than having to negotiate a full-scale agreement from scratch, but two things **must** be borne in mind.

● It is essential for both sides to the letter of engagement to know exactly what is in the agreement they are agreeing to incorporate.

- If any of the terms of the other agreement should **not** apply, then this must be specifically stated in the letter of engagement. (For example, if the PACT/Equity Agreement states that rehearsal days should be paid for at one half of the minimum guaranteed daily salary, and the actor has negotiated that he be paid the full daily salary, this needs to be stated in the letter/agreement of engagement.)

Some unions have drawn up a 'pro forma' contract of engagement for use under the union agreements (as is the case with Equity and WGGB under their agreements with PACT). This saves the Producer from having to draft an agreement, and enables the parties to fill in the 'variables' on the standard contract form (such as names, addresses, fees, etc.). These 'pro forma' contracts do provide for space to include any 'special stipulations' (namely, amendments to the standard terms of the union agreement or extra provisions on matters not dealt with by the union agreement).

Where, as is sometimes the case, the union agreement does not provide for a specific type of exploitation, this must be specifically agreed on between the Producer and the contributor, and the terms on which the contribution can be exploited must be specified as part of the 'special stipulations'. However, more often than not, this will not happen at the time of negotiation of the original contract because the type of exploitation is something which is yet to be invented. Again, this shows why it is convenient from the Producer's point of view to persuade the contributor to agree that the fee paid will cover new forms of exploitation yet to be invented (if, of course, the terms of the union agreement do not prevent this).

COLLECTING SOCIETIES

There are other representative organizations or bodies which can simplify the process of rights clearances in relation to pre-existing copyright works (such as music, recordings or artistic works). These bodies do not usually **own** the rights they are administering, with the exception of the PRS (Chapter 10, pages 164–6). They simply act on behalf of rights owners, by negotiating and granting licences to end users and collecting and dividing the resulting income to the rights owners.

The majority of collecting societies represent the owners of music rights and so are dealt with in more detail in the section below on music (Chapter 10, pages 164–8). However, others exist and are also mentioned in the remaining sections of this chapter, where relevant.

(Appendix A contains the current addresses and telephone numbers where each of these bodies can be contacted.)

Having looked at the general principles, the following sections look at specific issues in clearing rights in new contributions or pre-existing material used in film and television productions, these being:

- performers   ⎫   covered in
- writers   ⎪   the remainder
- directors   ⎬   of this
- locations   ⎭   Chapter
- music and recordings ⎫   covered
- film and television clips ⎬ in
- artistic works   ⎭   Chapter 10

PERFORMERS

'Performers', for these purposes, are actors, dancers, singers or musicians. This is because they will be giving 'performances' under the Copyright, Designs and Patents Act 1988 (pages 136 and 148–9). Under that Act, specific written consent must be obtained to record and exploit any such performance. Additionally, if either actors or musicians **improvise**, there is a possibility that their contribution (or part of it) is protected by copyright, so a Producer should also obtain an assignment of copyright from a performer.

It is standard practice, even where a person appearing in a film or programme is not a 'performer' in the legal sense, to ask that individual to sign a written consent form. A typical example of a consent form is shown in Appendix H.

Actors

Equity, the actors' union, has agreed collective bargaining arrangements with the BBC, ITV and with PACT. Broadly, if an actor is engaged under any of these, his or her consent will be given for future uses (even those which are currently unknown), but on the basis that the broadcaster/ Producer will have to agree a fee for any such use once it has been invented. Equity members have authorized Equity to negotiate such fees on their behalf. However, Equity takes the view that it is not so authorized in respect of pre-1988 ITV programmes. In those cases, any new use must be cleared with each actor, and therefore it remains open for an individual actor to block a new use. Since 1989, the ITV companies and Equity have agreed that residuals for overseas sales of ITV programmes should be paid on a royalty basis.

At the time of writing, there is some dispute as to the basis of paying residuals for secondary television use in the UK (such as sales to Sky TV or UK Gold). When UK Gold was set up, Equity would not (when negotiating terms on which old programmes featuring its members could be shown) accept a royalty (but insisted on a residual), as they took the view that the price negotiated for the sale of programme material to UK Gold was not necessarily a properly commercially negotiated price, given that the person selling the programmes to UK Gold also owned most of the shares in it.

As discussed above, the PACT/Equity Agreements (which consist of three elements, one relating to television productions, another relating to feature film productions, and the third containing terms common to both types of production) calculates residuals/use fees on a percentage of the actor's fee, although a royalty can be paid for certain uses.

There is an additional union, the Film Artistes' Association ('FAA') which represents 'crowd' actors, stand-ins or doubles. Under the PACT Agreement with the FAA, artists are not entitled to residuals or repeat fees. Although the PACT/Equity Agreement also covers identifiable or speaking walk-on actors (as opposed to the normal extra), this is obviously more expensive to use than the FAA/PACT Agreement, since it does require repeat fees to be paid for additional UK television transmission.

Musicians

The Musicians Union Agreements with the industry and users of the services of musicians do not require much comment. They enable musicians to be engaged for recording sessions of a maximum length, in return for a session fee (plus transport costs for instruments where these are to be provided by the musician). The cost of the session often depends on the nature of the music to be recorded (such as signature tunes or incidental music), the hours at which the musicians are required to turn up and whether the music is to be used in one production or in a number of episodes of a series or serial. The payment of the session fee allows certain basic uses of the musicians' work, but further work attracts additional payments. Usually, however, the Producer has the opportunity to choose (at the time of the session or for a limited period after) to pay a higher fee which will pre-purchase more extensive rights (this is referred to in MU parlance as a 'combined use fee').

The MU Agreements with end users provide for musicians to be engaged using payment vouchers, which record what the musicians have been paid, and which set out the consents required under the Copyright, Designs and Patents Act 1988.

WRITERS

Most scriptwriters are WGGB members and it is common practice to engage a writer on standard WGGB terms, unless he or she is a major screenwriter and can require special treatment (and as a result can negotiate his or her own terms).

In either case, the Producer will normally take an assignment of the copyright in the script which has been commissioned (as under the WGGB/PACT Agreement for instance). As explained above (pages 140–41) an exclusive licence can be perfectly acceptable, as long as the Producer gets all the necessary rights to exploit the script in the finished production.

The WGGB/PACT Agreement sets out a scale of fees for each of four different types of production (Chapter 5, *Development*, page 81 contains more detail).

For each different type of production, there is a schedule of:

- fees for the writing of each stage of the script, e.g. treatment, first draft, second draft;
- fees for all the different types of exploitation (UK network transmission, cable and satellite, video, etc.).

There can be an area of dispute over secondary rights of exploitation (such as 'book of the film' rights, or publication of the screenplay, or merchandising). These forms of exploitation are not covered by the WGGB/PACT Agreement, nor does it deal with the financial terms which should operate where the writer has created the original format for a television series.

DIRECTORS

Directors, along with other 'behind-the-camera' personnel, do have unions, and those unions do have agreements with broadcasters and Producers, but this book will not consider those agreements, not only because their contents are usually fairly straightforward, but also because these personnel do not generally have rights which require to be cleared, or if they do, clearing those rights is not particularly complicated. To the extent that most behind-the-camera personnel have any legal interest in the products of their services, it is usually in the nature of copyright, such as designers (whether productions, set or costume designers) or choreographers. The way in which copyright is cleared has been covered above (pages 138–44). Moral rights should be dealt with at the same time as taking copyright, usually by asking the contributor to waive his or her moral rights. Again, if the transfer of rights in the contributor's contract is sufficiently widely expressed, it should also cover any lending or rental rights to which the contributor could possibly make a claim.

The one area of real controversy (and where there is the greatest possibility of change) is in relation to film and television directors. Up until fairly recently in this country, where directors were engaged under union agreements, it was under the agreement with the relevant technical staff union (formerly the ACTT or BETA, two unions which merged in the past few years to form BECTU, the Broadcasting Entertainment Cinema and Theatre Union). These agreements, certainly as far as the independent production sector was concerned, did not provide for use fees, but allowed technical personnel (including directors) to be engaged on a 'buy-out' basis. So, however successful the production in terms of distribution throughout the world, the director would not normally share in the proceeds of that success. A few years back, certain directors joined together to form their own union, the Directors Guild of Great Britain, which has put forward its own standard terms of engagement. These provide for more extensive rights to be given to directors as part of their minimum contractual entitlement (such as residual payments and a limited moral rights waiver). However, these terms have not been generally accepted by the production entities who use directors' services, and certainly not by PACT.

What could make a difference, however, is the effect of EC laws being made to harmonize the copyright laws of the member states of the EC. On the continent, it has been accepted that the author of a copyright work can only be a 'natural person', and never a non-human entity such as a company. In the UK we have accepted, ever since copyright law recognized film and sound recordings as works of copyright, that they can be 'created' by a company. The definition of the 'author' of films or sound recordings is 'the person by whom the arrangements necessary for the making of' the work 'are undertaken'. Under English law, the expression 'person' can mean an individual **or** a company. In almost all cases, films and television programmes made in the UK are therefore treated as having been made by companies, since the individuals involved in making programmes have invariably found that it is more convenient and sensible to do business through a company.

This issue of the nature of the author of a film is a direct conflict between our law and continental practice, and this conflict has been fought out in the context of the EC Harmonizing Directives. It will be remembered that under the Directive on rental and lending right, the 'author' of a film, **as well as** the Producer of it, has the right to authorize or prohibit rental or lending of the original or copies of the film. This makes the assumption that the Producer is **not** the author (as the Producer certainly would be under UK copyright law). As to who **is** the author, the Directive states that 'the principal director' shall be considered as the author or one of the authors of a film although EC member states, in making laws to implement the Directive, may provide for others (such as the writer(s)) to be considered among a film's authors.

The same provision is included in the Directive harmonizing the term of protection of copyright (which, it will be recalled, provides for copyright to last for 70 years after the death of the author of a work). However, to avoid confusion (by reason of some but not all member states designating other persons, as well as the director, as author) the period of protection for films is to expire 70 years after the death of the last to die of certain individuals (whether or not they are co-authors), these being:

- the principal director;
- the author of the screenplay;
- the author of the dialogue;
- the composer of specifically commissioned music.

Directors not unnaturally see this development as giving them the bargaining power they previously lacked to bring about an entitlement to share in the proceeds of exploitation of a film or television programme. As holder of a rental and lending right, they will be entitled to 'equitable remuneration' from the exploitation of that right, from a date no later than 1 July 1997. As to whether the right will be backdated to apply to films/programmes created before the Directive comes into force, the Directive leaves that very much up to the member states to decide.

At present therefore directors, at least in the future, will have the right to insist on sharing in the proceeds of exploitation of a film or television programme when it is hired out in video form or when it is exploited in any other way which can be called 'rental' or 'lending'. What remuneration would be 'equitable' remains to be seen, but it naturally provides an incentive for Producers to negotiate a collective agreement with a representative body of directors, because it should not then be open to individual directors, having authorized that body to negotiate on their behalf, to question the basis on which remuneration is agreed to be paid.

LOCATION AGREEMENTS

This section covers the rights and protections needed to use private or public property for the purposes of filming on the property.

When filming in any place, there are two aspects to be considered. First, the material in that place (such as works of art) which itself may require clearance to show it in a film or programme (Chapter 10, pages 185–6). Secondly, and this is the aspect concentrated on below, there are the legal areas which have to be covered in hiring a location.

Public places

When filming in the street, if the equipment and people necessary for filming are large in number or otherwise very space-consuming, the production will need to get a permit from the authority/authorities responsible for the area in which filming takes place. This will often be the local authority, as well as the police (whose co-operation will generally be necessary if there is likely to be any effect on traffic movement). However, filming in London may need the authority of several bodies, including the local council, governmental bodies, the police, as well as the owners of private property **outside** which filming is to occur. The British Film Commission is intended to assist in these situations by identifying what consents will be necessary and smoothing the way towards getting them.

Private property

Anyone who is present on private property without the permission of the owner is a trespasser. Trespassing is not a criminal offence, which explains why the expression 'trespassers will be prosecuted' is not a threat capable of performance, unless the trespasser also does something criminal while trespassing. However, a trespasser can be sued in a civil action. So it is necessary to get a licence from the owner to be present on his or her land or in his or her house. (A 'licence' is simply the legal terminology for the permission to do something which one would otherwise not be legally entitled to do.)

A location agreement is simply a specialized form of licence. It should cover aspects such as:

- exactly what the production company will be doing on the premises;
- how long they will be doing it;
- where access and exits will be needed;
- whether or not any part of the property is 'off limits' to the production;
- whether or not any temporary alterations to the premises will be needed (such as building a mock extension, or a summer house in the grounds) and what happens to those alterations afterwards. Usually the Producer has to pay for the property to be reinstated to its normal state;
- the rights which the Producer will have in the finished production to feature both the premises and **everything in the premises** including:

  - all rights of exploitation and publicity;
  - the right to portray the premises as something else (whether a fictional place or otherwise). For example, the entrance to 'Caius College' in *Chariots of Fire* was in reality another Cambridge college, because Caius did not grant permission for filming outside of its premises;

- the fee payable for use of premises and exactly what it covers. It is prudent for the Producer to make it clear that it is a 'buy-out', so that nothing further will be payable if and when the production is exploited;
- a waiver of any rights of privacy or publicity by the owner. (It may seem obvious that, by letting a film crew on to one's premises, one is not

concerned about these matters, but in America for instance such an inference cannot be taken for granted.);

- warranties that the owner **alone** is entitled to give all necessary consents and permissions. The main immediate practical point of this is to 'flush out' the truth if anybody else has an interest in the property and their consent is required;
- credits for the use of the premises. (If it is **not** intended that the owner of the premises should be mentioned in the credits, it is prudent to say so in the location agreement.);
- the options of the owner, if there is any breach by the Producer of the location agreement, should be restricted to a legal action for damages, and not an injunction (Chapter 8, pages 133–4 and Chapter 15, pages 247–51);
- the question of insurance against any loss or damage to or caused on the property and who takes responsibility for that insurance. The owner of the premises has certain legal duties to try to ensure the safety of persons whom he/she allows on to the property. Those liabilities cannot, as a matter of law, be side-stepped or excluded in a contract, if the owner's failure results in a personal injury to or death of anyone. However, the owner can reasonably expect the Producer to take proper care, and that all members of cast and crew should also do so (the Producer being responsible for their behaviour). The owner should also require that the Producer has proper and adequate insurance to cover all loss and damage which the Producer/cast/crew might cause (whether to persons or property).

10

Rights clearances II

MUSIC

As a practical matter, the question of the music to be used in a production generally crops up towards the end of production period. Producers also have a tendency to defer dealing with it because of a lack of confidence about the legal issues involved. The subject does sometimes seem dauntingly complex because to use a particular piece of music may involve having to deal with several different persons or organizations who have an interest in it.

These complexities arise because, in relation to any piece of music appearing on a film or television programme soundtrack, there are generally two copyrights involved, for which the rights often have to be cleared.

> For example, a Producer, P, wishes to use in a feature film a segment of the song *Night and Day*, written by Cole Porter. The song is still in copyright, so the right to use it for the film must be cleared with the copyright owner. P. has paid for a new version of it to be recorded. There will be copyright in the sound recording made, but P will own the copyright, because P is the person who has 'undertaken the arrangements for' the making of the recording (this being the definition of the 'author' of, and therefore first owner of the copyright in, sound recordings under the Copyright, Designs and Patents Act 1988). However, change the example and assume that P wishes to use the Ella Fitzgerald recording of *Night and Day*: *that* recording is still in copyright and permission will be needed from the copyright owner of the recording to use it, as well as permission from the heir(s) of Cole Porter who owns the rights in the song *Night and Day*.

What rights need to be cleared?

From a legal point of view, **music** falls into two categories – specially commissioned or pre-existing. Whatever the type of music, the rights to be cleared will be the right to:

- **copy** the music (namely, to **record** and synchronize the recording with the visual images of the production) – this is referred to as the **synchronization right**;
- **perform** the music publicly/broadcast it/include it in a cable programme (the **performing right**).

If a Producer is using a pre-existing **recording** which is still in copyright (as in the example above, the Ella Fitzgerald recording of *Night and Day*), the following rights also need to be cleared, namely the rights:

- to **dub** the sound recording (i.e. to copy it on to the soundtrack);
- to **perform** the sound recording publicly/broadcast it/include it in a cable programme (the **performing right**).

The copyright owner

Music

The owner of all or any of the rights in a particular music may be:

- the original composer (in the case of a song, this expression also covers the lyric writer);
- a music publishing company (such as BMG or PolyGram Music Publishing) to which composers often assign or exclusively license the copyright in their work so that the work can be properly commercially exploited. To assist it in this exploitation, a music publisher will usually control all rights **except** the performing right (below);
- the Performing Right Society Limited ('PRS') which controls and administers the **performing right** in all music written by its members; or
- the Mechanical Copyright Protection Society ('MCPS') which licenses the recording of music (namely the exercise of the **synchronization right**) and collects and distributes the income from such licensing for MCPS members who have authorized it to represent them for these purposes.

Sound recordings

Again, the owners of the rights in a sound recording may be:

- a record company (such as PolyGram or EMI);
- the British Phonographic Industry ('BPI') which is sometimes authorized by its record company members to license the **dubbing** of records; or
- Phonographic Performance Limited ('PPL') which is authorized on behalf of record companies to license the **performing right** in records.

Just occasionally (but very rarely) the copyright in a sound recording may be controlled by performing artist(s) or by a company which is controlled by the artist(s). However, it is normally safe to assume that if the rights are controlled by a record company, there will be no need for further consents from the performers on the recording, as these should have been obtained by the record company to cover all possible uses of the recording (including using it for film and television).

There is also a possibility that a payment may have to be made to the Musicians Union ('the MU'), in respect of the **performance** of the musicians and others appearing on the recording (Chapter 9, page 156 and page 168 of this chapter).

Collecting societies

Music

Performing Right Society Limited ('PRS')
The PRS is a body which has a membership of composers and publishers of musical works of copyright. It licenses its rights and collects royalties on behalf of its members, operating on a worldwide basis by affiliation to foreign collecting societies which, in their own territories, administer the same rights as the PRS. It can therefore collect income paid for the use of its members' music in those foreign territories, as well as collecting income for use of music in the UK which is written by foreign composers.

The PRS controls the **performing right** – this is the short name for the rights:

- to perform the music in public;
- to broadcast the work;
- to include the work in a cable programme.

The PRS operates by taking an **assignment** of the performing right from its members. In effect, when a composer joins the PRS, he or she agrees to assign the performing right in all of his or her musical works (past, present and future) to the PRS. The only other right which the PRS sometimes controls is the **synchronization right** in music written by its members specially for films.

From a Producer's point of view, since the person who needs a licence of the performing right is the person **exercising** that right as and when it is being exercised (in the case of feature films, the cinemas where they will be shown and in the case of television programmes, the broadcaster) the Producer does not normally need to clear rights in advance with the PRS because it is common practice for the 'end user' to have a direct arrangement with the PRS. For instance, broadcasters generally have a so-called 'blanket licence' with the PRS. This licenses the broadcaster in advance so that the broadcaster can play the music of PRS members without seeking specific permission every time, but on the basis that it makes a periodic 'return' to the PRS of all the music actually played during the relevant period, so that the licence fee for that period can be calculated. The broadcaster then pays the PRS what is due. This is one of the reasons why the Producer of a programme commissioned by a broadcaster is generally required under the production agreement to complete a **music cue sheet**, in respect of all music used in the production. This sheet will usually set out information in respect of every piece of music used, such as:

- the title of the piece;
- the name of the composer/arranger;
- the music publisher who owns the music;
- the performer(s);
- if a pre-existing recording is used, details of the recording;
- how the music has been used (i.e. whether it is background or featured, as defined below);
- the exact timing of the music used (to the second).

This information can then be used by the broadcaster in its return to the PRS for the period when the programme is shown.

It is worth noting here that a new arrangement of a particular piece of music (which involves more than a change of key or register) will itself attract separate copyright. On that basis, two separate permissions may have to be obtained.

> For example P, the Producer in the previous example, wishes to use the recording by Ella Fitzgerald of Cole Porter's song *Night and Day*. The permission of Cole Porter's heir(s) must be obtained in relation to the music itself. Additionally, though, assume that the recording features a special arrangement of the song by Nelson Riddle. Technically speaking, therefore, the rights in the re-arrangement will belong to whoever owns the copyright in Nelson Riddle's output, and the permission of that person must also be obtained.

The PRS normally charges the same rate however the music is used in the production, but certain overseas collecting societies (who will collect from foreign broadcasters who transmit a programme which includes the relevant pieces of music) charge a different rate according to the **classification** of the music used as either 'background' or 'featured'. These definitions are as follows.

- **Background** music, also known as incidental music, is music which is heard by the viewers, but is not performed by anyone shown on the screen, nor is it audible to any of the performers/characters appearing in the production.

- **Featured** music is music performed by artists in the programme or apparently audible to characters in the production (for example, where a radio is playing while actors are playing a scene).

(The PRS's address and telephone number are shown in Appendix A.)

Mechanical Copyright Protection Society ('MCPS')
As mentioned above, MCPS controls synchronization rights to music owned by its members on behalf of those members who have authorized it to do so. Some of its members (usually music publishers) will wish to control these rights themselves, and therefore do not ask the MCPS to act for them.

As a body, its function is to represent composers and music publishers but, unlike the PRS, it does not necessarily represent all composers and music publishers. However, like the PRS, it has reciprocal arrangements with foreign collecting societies and can collect fees for overseas use, as well as collecting licence fees here for use in the UK of music which originated abroad.

The MCPS also has blanket arrangements with certain broadcasters, whereby the broadcasters are entitled to record MCPS members' works in programmes on payment of an annual royalty fee.

Independent Producers who are commissioned by a broadcaster can sometimes take advantage of the broadcaster's blanket licence (so that music recording rights need not be paid for out of the budget, but will be covered by the annual licence fee which the broadcaster has to pay to the MCPS in any event). However, this should always be checked with the broadcaster and the MCPS. Whether or not the Producer can avail itself of the blanket licence is generally dependent on the broadcaster owning (and retaining) 100% of the copyright in the programme itself. So if a Producer retains all or part of the copyright in the programme, the Producer will have to clear the music and pay for it out of the production budget.

MCPS may not always be authorized to represent the composer/ publisher in the case of particular pieces of music which a producer may wish to use. However, the organization can be very useful in finding out who **does** own music (the PRS is also useful in this respect) and will be helpful in establishing contact with the rights owner. (In the case of **recordings** it is usually fairly easy to identify the rights owner, as the information is shown on the record label or packaging. If for some reason this information is not readily available, the BPI and PPL should be able to trace the copyright owner.)

If a Producer has quite a lot of different pieces to clear for one production, it is preferable to try to deal with MCPS for a synchronization licence for all of them – one-stop shopping is always easier. MCPS is usually authorized by publishers to deal with television uses; but other uses (such as for theatrical feature films) may have to be negotiated directly with the publisher.

However, even where it is possible to deal with MCPS, this will not usually mean that the Producer ends up paying the same standard rate for all music used in one production. The licence fee payable is always a matter of negotiation, and will be fixed taking into account:

- the amount of music used (generally measured in units of 30 seconds, so that using 40 seconds would involve paying for two units);
- the licence period – a Producer will want either full period of copyright or perpetuity (which comes to the same thing in practice, but is shorter to say) whereas the publisher may not be prepared to grant so long a period (as mentioned below);
- the territory (which could be the whole world or just specific countries;
- the media licensed (for example all kinds of television only, all theatrical, all non-theatrical rights).

If the licence period offered by MCPS/the music publisher is less than the full period of copyright, the Producer may well not want to use the music concerned. This is because the production itself will not be usable after the licence period has ended, unless the music is removed from the soundtrack. In some cases, this may not be a problem, if the production itself has a limited shelf life (such as a quiz or game show) but it will not be practical for feature films or expensive productions which it is hoped will continue to be sold in the future.

Separate permission has to be obtained to exploit music on videos and the fee for this use is assessed on a different basis. There is a standard rate for use of music on videos manufactured in the UK which MCPS recommends to music publishers and which they usually accept. This is a royalty based on the published dealer price of each video sold, pro-rated according to the proportion which the length and music used bears to the total duration of the material incorporated on the video. This applies to UK manufactured videos, but it is also possible to get worldwide video clearance.

Sound recordings

Phonographic Performance Limited ('PPL')

This body is equivalent to the PRS and licenses the 'performing right' in sound recordings owned by its members (usually record companies). The members, as with the PRS, have assigned the performing right to PPL, which then concludes licences with end users (the main end users being the broadcasters).

British Phonographic Industry ('BPI')

The BPI is more of an industry body, representing the commercial interests of record companies, than a collecting society, but sometimes has the authority to grant dubbing licences on behalf of its record company members.

The main example of this is blanket dubbing arrangements with BBC, ITV and Channel Four. Producers should check details of what territories and media these agreements cover with the commissioning broadcaster, as well as whether the independent Producer can take advantage of these arrangements.

The Musicians Union ('MU')

Existing recordings usually embody the performances of musicians and/or singers or other performing artists. Performers have rights (see Chapter 9, pages 136–7 and 148). It is very unlikely that when the musicians were engaged to make the recording, they did not give permission for the recording (incorporating their performance) to be exploited by all means. However, the MU do require that when a Producer uses existing recordings, it should make a payment to the MU to clear the rights of the original performers on the recording. Rather than argue with the MU as to its entitlement to require such a payment, PACT have arrangements with the MU as to the amounts of those payments, and it is most important **before the recording is used** to check what should be payable with either the MU or PACT.

CASE STUDY

To show how rights in music are dealt with in practice, it may be helpful to go through the process by looking at a particular case:

P, the Producer of the film discussed in Chapter 6, pages 94–100, *Freud's Little Secret*, has decided to use:

- specially commissioned music, to be composed by C, who is a former rock star and has retired from touring and making records to concentrate on writing music for films;
- existing music, including *Beim Schlafengehen* from Richard Strauss's *Vier Letzte Lieder*, *Dazed and Confused* by Led Zeppelin, *Reach Out, I'll Be There* by the Four Tops.

Remember that the project is a feature film, but that it will be shown on Channel Four.

Arrangements with C/C's music publisher/C's record company

Music

Synchronization licence
Even if C were not already rich and famous, it will be unlikely, even though the music C is composing will be a fresh copyright, that P could get an **assignment** of the copyright, as most composers will already have a pre-existing agreement with a music publisher, under which all the composer's output, past, present and future, will be exploited by the publisher.

C is no exception and in fact, because he is so eminent in the rock music world, he has set up his own music publishing company, SoSoSongs Limited. P therefore has to obtain from SoSoSongs (which owns all rights in C's music) a **synchronization licence** (referred to as a 'sync licence' for short), to enable the music to be recorded on to the soundtrack. This is an agreement quite separate from the arrangements to be made with C for his services in writing the music.

Composer's agreement
Separately from the synchronization licence, C has agreed that he will be providing such services as:

- writing the music and some accompanying lyrics;
- recording it, performing on the tracks themselves and engaging the other musicians required to perform it;
- producing and mixing the sound recording.

A soundtrack album is also planned, and therefore the arrangements with C also allow for C's services in re-recording or re-mixing for the album version as necessary.

Record rights
It is very common these days, in British films and television programmes at least, for composers to provide a complete package (namely the composer not only **composes** the music, but also **records** the actual version which will be incorporated in the soundtrack). If this is the case, the film Producer should be able to get an assignment of the copyright in the **recording** because, unless the composer is also a recording artist, his or her **recorded** output is not generally already spoken for (unlike his or her musical compositions which will already be contracted to a music

publisher). Therefore, C is free to assign the copyright in the **recording** and P is entitled to require it to be assigned, because P is paying the cost of making it.

However, in this example, C is a recording artist and it is safe for P to assume that C may be under a contractual restriction not to make any recordings (as a performing artist) for anyone but his record company or allow anyone to exploit such recordings without the separate permission **from the record company** with whom C has a recording contract. If P is wise, he should get this consent before the recording is made and **in writing**.

The deal with SoSoSongs must allow for the music to be recorded, dubbed on to the soundtrack and for the film to be exploited by all means and in all media in which P needs to exploit the film. The best deal is an all-media worldwide buy-out. In the circumstances, P is likely to get that sort of deal, because SoSoSongs is C's company, and he is in a position to ensure that it grants these rights. However, in other circumstances if the Producer is particularly short of money or the music publisher is being particularly tough, the deal might be to split the rights up into different media, which will be paid for at separately negotiated prices, and perhaps at different times. If this kind of piecemeal deal is envisaged, the split of media is usually:

- theatric: theatres, cinemas and other places to which the public are admitted in return for a fee for viewing the film;
- non-theatric: films shown in circumstances where exhibition of films is not the primary purpose and where no specific admission fee is charged (for example schools, colleges, military bases, oil rigs and aeroplanes);
- video for home use: sale of video recordings in any form for playback at home for private purposes and where the only money paid is for purchase or rental of the video;
- standard television: non-pay terrestrial television;
- non-standard television: cable and satellite television, including pay-TV and subscription television;
- other uses: these days, sync licences should also cover multi-media uses.

When use in a particular medium is not paid for up-front, the Producer **should** negotiate an agreed fee for that use, which will become payable when that type of use is made. The alternative to this (as in the case of uses which may not have even been devised) is to agree to negotiate a fee when the issue arises. However, that leaves the Producer in the unsatisfactory position of not being able to use a production in that way if the contributor does not agree a commercially viable fee at the time. Where the production has been commissioned for broadcast, it will also usually mean that the Producer is in breach of its agreement with the broadcaster, who will require a warranty that all material will be cleared so that it can be exploited, subject only to payment of an ascertainable fee.

An all-media worldwide buy-out is usually granted for specially commissioned music. In actual fact, where the music has been specially commissioned, it is common practice for a sync licence to be issued by the music publisher at little or no charge (often for a £1 nominal fee). This is because it is highly advantageous for the publisher for the music to be used in a film or television production, because it means that the music will be widely publicly performed and broadcast and this will result in an automatic source of income, in the form of performing right royalties, every time the production is exhibited in cinemas or shown on television, payable to the PRS by cinema exhibitors or broadcasters (page 164 above).

The following wording is typical wording for the grant of synchronization rights:

> . . . to record and reproduce and authorize the recording and reproduction of [the Music] either as embodied on the recording to be made under this agreement (or any part or parts of that recording) or otherwise in any manner, medium or form throughout the world whether now existing or to be invented in the future in synchronization with the visual images of [the Film] and the soundtrack of [the Film] and trailers thereof and advertisements therefor either alone or together with any other musical, literary, artistic or dramatic works in connection with [the Film] or which are in [the Film] – **this wording covers synchronizing the music on to the soundtrack**.

> . . . to exploit [the Music] or any part or parts thereof (subject to the rights (if any) of the PRS) by means of the performance in public of [the Film] or any part or parts thereof or by means of trailers or advertisements for [the Film] by all means or methods now known or to be invented in the future – **this wording covers the performing right**.

> . . . to reproduce [the Music] (either by way of copies of recordings embodying [the Music] or otherwise) or any part or parts of [the Music] in synchronization with the visual images of [the Film] and the soundtrack of [the Film] and with trailers and advertisements for the Film in all languages and in any gauge, medium, form or format and to exhibit, distribute, broadcast, sell, rent, turn to account or otherwise exploit [the Film] without further payment (save for payments (if any) to the PRS) whether by way of mechanical fees, royalties or otherwise in all media and by all means and methods whether now known or to be invented in the future including without limitation by means of

theatrical and non-theatrical exhibition, radio and all television broadcasting (including pay cable and satellite television and whether 'free' or 'pay' and whether 'standard' or 'non-standard' television) and by means of videograms including cassettes, discs and tapes and by all other audio-visual devices and by any means whatsoever – **this wording enables unlimited copies of the music (as included in the production) to be made**.

However, this agreement must also, since P is contemplating a soundtrack album, deal with the **mechanical reproduction right** in the music (namely, the right to record it and make copies of it in the form of sound carrying devices such as records, CDs and tapes, for distribution and sale to the public). P must take this right in order to be able to exploit it, by licensing it to a record company, R Co.

While there will be a flat fee to the music publisher for the use of music in the film, the right to issue it in the form of records will, however, usually be in return for a **royalty**, based on the selling price of each record sold. As with performing rights, the royalty payable in respect of the mechanical reproduction rights will be paid by the person who exercises it, namely the record company which manufactures and sells copies of the recording, in this case R Co.

MCPS and BPI (representing publishers and record companies respectively) have agreed a standard mechanical reproduction rate payable by record companies to music publishers on the published dealer price of records sold. In the present example, R Co will pay SoSoSongs at this rate. However, because C's music will not be the only music used on the soundtrack album, the royalty payable to C's music publishing company will be **pro-rated**. This means that the royalty payable by R Co at MCPS/BPI rates on each record sold will be divided by a fraction found by comparing the extent of C's music on the album in relation to the other music. In this example, assume that the royalty will be divided by a fraction of seven-tenths, because there are ten tracks on the album altogether and seven of these are C's music. (Another way of doing it would be by comparing the actual duration in playing time of C's music with all other music on the album, but it is usually easier to work it out by the number of tracks).

As this is a feature film project, there is an additional complication. As one might expect, SoSoSongs cannot grant performing rights, which are owned by the PRS (although SoSoSongs will be a beneficiary of the income collected by the PRS, as will C). However, if the film is likely to be exploited in the US, the PRS will be involved in granting synchronization rights. This is because of certain vagaries in US law, by virtue of which the US equivalents of the PRS (ASCAP or BMI) are not entitled to collect public performance fees from cinemas which exhibit films.

The PRS circumvents this loss of potential income by taking from its composer members the film synchronization rights in **specially commissioned music**. In the present case, the PRS will grant this right to P, under its standard form US theatrical performance licence, which will require P to inform the PRS when the film is first shown theatrically in the US, and then to pay the agreed fee, the amount of which will depend on the amount of music used in the film.

Agreement with C

P's agreement with C will cover the creation of the music and of the recording. The fee agreed to be paid for C's work is a lump sum fee (if it had been an agreement for music for a TV programme, the fee might well have been calculated per minute of music actually composed or used in the programme). It also includes all recording costs, as C is making all arrangements for the recording of the music, including contracting the session musicians. This raises a number of points.

- The copyright in the recording might be said to belong in the first instance to C, as the person undertaking the arrangements for the making of the recording. However, P should be able to require an assignment of the copyright in the recording from C, as P has paid for the recording to be made. C should agree to this, if the assignment is made subject to P paying C a share of the income which P might make from exploiting that particular recording.
- As C has agreed an all-inclusive fee (to cover the recording costs) P needs to be sure that the fee paid to C **will** actually cover all the costs of recording the music. It is sensible to take an indemnity (Chapter 4, page 41) from C against any additional costs which P might be asked to pay by a third party (such as session musicians claiming an additional use fee, on the basis that C did not pay the musician for all uses worldwide) in spite of P's arrangements with C.
- P will also, if wise, take the right to deduct from any fee or income payable to C (for example, record royalties) any money which might become payable by C under the indemnity.

On this subject, as P is arranging for a soundtrack album, C will naturally require a royalty for the use of the recording on the soundtrack album. This royalty is not for the use of the **music**, for which C's music publishing company will be paid (page 172 above), but rather in recompense for C's services as a **recording artist** on the recorded version which will appear on the album. The royalty is usually based on 90% or 100% of the published dealer price (namely, the wholesale price) of records sold, and the amount of the royalty, in this instance, has been agreed with C to be 13%. This is a reasonably high royalty, because C is well known and because he has done extra work by producing the original recording. In general, the royalty payable to composers ranges from 2% to 10%, depending on the extent of services which he or she has actually rendered in bringing the recording into being (such as performing, conducting or producing). The royalty payable to someone who merely produces a record is 2–3%. (Remember, this royalty is purely for the services C has performed on the recording. As composer of the music, he is compensated for the use of the **music** by his share of the income payable to SoSoSongs, his music publisher.)

Again, C's royalty will be pro-rated, because his recordings are not the only ones to appear on the album.

Additional points to bear in mind are as follows.

- If there have been additional recording costs to get the music, as originally recorded for the film, into a form where it is suitable for release on the album, C may agree with P that these costs should be deducted from C's royalty before it is paid to him.
- P might also require that part of the fee paid to C for his original services, which represents a fee for working on the recording, should be treated as an advance against C's royalties; so again, it would be deducted and recouped by P from C's royalty. For example, if £10 000 of C's fee were to be treated as payment for recording services, the first £10 000 of C's share of royalties would be paid to P to recoup this fee.

The royalty payable to C will be coming out of the royalty which P will negotiate with R Co, the record company which is distributing the soundtrack album, and which is paid to P in return for a licence from P to manufacture and sell copies of the recording which P has brought into being for the film.

Thus, in agreeing to pay a royalty to any person such as C, who has participated in making the recording, P must ensure that it is not paying out any more than it is due to receive from R Co, and that the royalty will be calculated in the same way.

For example, R Co agrees to pay a royalty calculated on 90% of the retail price of each record sold, but after a 25% reduction for packaging costs. The top rate of royalty agreed to be paid by R Co to P is 18% but this is only payable on sales of the album in the US. For other less lucrative territories, the rate is scaled down. In its deal with C, P should state that the agreed rate payable to C of 13% represents a specific proportion of P's royalty and will be calculated on the same basis (and subject to the like reductions and deductions as P's royalty from R Co). Thus the 13% will only apply to sales in the US. The royalty for other territories will be proportionately less, depending on the decrease in the rate payable to P; C's royalty will be calculated in exactly the same way as P's.

Since R Co is selling the album and receiving the resulting income, C is fairly likely to ask P to require R Co to pay C his share of the royalty direct. This is common practice in the record industry, as royalty participants wish to protect themselves from the potential insolvency of 'middle men', such as P, who might go into liquidation, leaving C with an unsecured right to income which P is due to receive (Chapter 4, page 38 and Chapter 6, page 99 contain further explanation of why this is undesirable). Record companies are generally happy to account direct, as long as they have firm instructions in writing from the person whom they are primarily due to pay (Chapter 8, page 127 explains why such instructions are important) as it requires very little extra work on the part of the record company.

One last complication arises by virtue of the fact that C is a recording artist. C, as a performer on the recording, must of course give his consent to the recording of his performance and the exploitation of copies of that recording (Chapter 9, pages 136 and 148). However, if his record company has an **exclusive** recording contract with him, that company's consent must also be obtained, because C is not able, without the record company's consent, to make recordings for anyone else. If P has been sensible enough to remember this in advance, his deal with C should have provided that:

- C would take steps to ensure that this consent is given;
- any fee/royalty demands by its record company in return for its consent would be payable out of C's fees and royalties.

If P did not remember to do this before the recording was made (and therefore a substantial part of the music budget has been spent), there is a grave and very real risk of being held to ransom by C's record company, without any come-back against C, as there would be nothing to stop the record company from claiming a separate payment, and no reason why P should expect C to have to foot the bill.

Lastly, as C will certainly be a member of the PRS, the agreement with him should contain a warranty that he will arrange for the grant to P of a PRS theatrical performance licence in relation to the US exhibition of the film. The PRS will then contact P with a copy of their standard licence and will notify the fee (which becomes payable when the film opens in the US) when they know details of how much of C's music appears in the final film.

One last thing should be mentioned. If C had been a very new or relatively unknown composer, the publishing rights to his music might just have been still available, since getting a deal with a music publisher sometimes depends on the composer being able to prove that he or she has some background of composing money-making music. If the publishing rights are available, it would be theoretically possible for P to take an assignment of the copyright in the **music** which C had composed (excluding any rights already belonging to the PRS). However, in this situation, C will be bound by the rules of the PRS, one of which requires that if P wishes to register with the PRS as publishers of the music (which P must do, to be able to collect its share of PRS's income), P should agree to exploit the music on C's behalf (as any normal music publishing company would agree to do). This is intended to inhibit Producers from taking assignments of the publishing rights in music simply in order to be able to collect the PRS income (and therefore not having any interest in taking other steps to see that the music is exploited in other ways). As this burden is imposed on P, it is not necessarily better for P to take an assignment of copyright rather than leaving the copyright with C and merely taking a synchronization licence; taking the copyright would mean that P will have to sign an administration deal with the real music publisher who will do the work of exploiting (or trying to exploit) the music in return for a commission (generally between 10–15% of the income). If C does assign the copyright to P there needs to be a rather more complicated agreement between the two parties than a synchronization licence. The agreement will have to deal with all the possible means of exploitation of the music which P will agree to try to bring about as publisher (such as the mechanical reproduction right, namely making records; sheet music sales; further synchronization licences to other productions) and state how the income generated from these sources will be shared between P and C. P's share (the so-called 'publisher's share') will never be more than 50%. This is because again the rules of the PRS prohibit composers, when assigning their rights in their music, from assigning more than 50% of the income which arises from exploitation of the performing right. This is designed to protect composers from giving everything away in return for a tiny fee. The maximum percentage split is, however, reflected in relation to income from other types of exploitation under a music publishing agreement (except sheet music sales, for which the composer usually gets a royalty) so that composers stand to receive between 50–90% of the music publishing income, depending on their eminence and bargaining power.

In the present example, assuming that C's publishing rights had been available, it would certainly have been worthwhile for P to take the copyright, because of the soundtrack album deal – P would then receive the mechanical royalty (at the rate agreed between MCPS and the BPI) for each record sold. However, it has to be said that if C were such an untried composer as not to have a publishing deal before being commissioned by P, it is unlikely that any record company would be interested in issuing the music on a soundtrack album.

The agreement with C should also contain some further warranties:

- that C is free to enter into the agreement and to perform the services required of him;
- that the music is original and not copied from other works;
- that copyright subsists in it;
- that no rights have been granted in it to any other person (apart from the PRS and C's music publisher).

Existing music/recordings

Remember that P is also planning to use a piece by Richard Strauss, some Led Zeppelin music, and a Four Tops track.

P needs to obtain a synchronization licence from the publisher of each of these pieces of music **and** from the copyright owner of the recorded version which he wishes to use.

Music

Usually, when using compositions by a classical composer, such as Richard Strauss, the work may well be out of copyright, because the composer has been dead for the requisite number of years. If so, this will remove the need for a music synchronization licence (but **not** for a licence in respect of the recording, unless the Producer makes a new recording, as the recording is quite likely to still be in copyright). However, in the present example, Richard Strauss died in 1949, so his **music** is still in copyright. The identity of the publisher (if not actually shown on the label of any recording of the music) can be found out from MCPS. As mentioned above, MCPS may also be authorized to act on behalf of the publisher to negotiate and agree a licence.

Dazed and Confused (composed by Jimmy Page) is published by Warner Chappell Music. *Reach Out, I'll Be There* (composed by Holland, Dozier, Holland) is published by Jobete Music. Again, MCPS will either put P in touch with these publishers or act on their behalf, if so authorized.

The music publishers may refuse permission for the music to be used. However, if they agree that it can be used, they may well have their own standard form of 'sync licence' which they like to use. Alternatively they might expect P to proffer a draft for their review. They will certainly have their own standard rates per minute or 30 seconds of music used, and this amount will vary from publisher to publisher. Again, the amount may be too much for the budget, in which case P will have to choose some other music. This underlines the need to make decisions about music as early as possible and the importance of **never** synchronizing it on to the soundtrack until permission to use it has been given – to do otherwise again exposes a producer to demands for extortionate fees by shrewd music publishers and record companies.

Recordings

The same process has to be gone through with the record companies for a dubbing licence in respect of the recording of each of these pieces of pre-existing music. However, if using classical music, a Producer does have the advantage of being able to shop around, as there is usually more than one available recording of well-known classical pieces, and one record company may charge less than another.

  As for the public performance right, P should not need to have dealings with the PRS (for the music) or PPL (for the recording) at this stage. Their rights arise when the music is publicly performed, so it is generally the end user – such as cinemas and broadcasters – who needs a public performing licence.

Fees payable

The fee which P pays to the music publisher for the music, or to the record company for the recording, will depend on the territory, media, amount of music used and the licence period. P will probably want an all media worldwide licence in perpetuity – this is very expensive and again, therefore, he may have to decide to use other music (however enamoured the director may be of a particular piece) depending on the budget.

US-composed music – the *Rear Window* case

One last thing to bear in mind which might be relevant when using old (pre-1978) recordings of US-composed music is the decision in an American court case, known as the *Rear Window* case. Before 1978, US copyright law gave a divided period of copyright protection to authors/composers of copyright works – a first period of 28 years and then a renewal period of 28 years (now extended to 47). However, the second period only comes into force if the author/composer (or his heirs if he was dead) **renewed** the copyright in the last year of the first period of protection. The point of this was to protect the author/composer's heirs; because only the author/composer or his heirs were entitled to the second term of copyright, it could only be renewed by those persons.

This stopped the author/composer from assigning all his rights for a pittance so that no benefit would ensue to his heirs after his death. It **was** possible for an author/composer to agree with someone to whom he was assigning his rights that he would assign the copyright renewal term to that person, once it had been renewed. He could not, however, validly assign it in advance (i.e. so that it would automatically belong to the assignee when renewed). If he **had** agreed to assign the renewal term, and was alive at the time of renewal, the author/composer would be under a binding obligation to renew copyright and assign it for the remainder of the term. However, if he were dead, the *Rear Window* case made it clear that his heirs would **not** be contractually bound by what he had agreed to do, and would therefore not be obliged to assign the renewal term. This is what happened in the *Rear Window* case. In this case, the author of the short story on which the Hitchcock-directed film was based had granted the necessary rights to the makers of the film to allow them to make it (Chapter 5, pages 66–9 describes the rights required). The film makers then produced the film (technically referred to by US lawyers as a 'derivative work' and what we would call an adaptation). The author, who had agreed to assign the necessary rights for the renewal term, died before the time for renewal was due. His heirs renewed the copyright, but were not obliged to grant the rights to the owners of the film (as the court decided when the film makers took action to try to get the rights for the second period of protection). Thus the film, as a derivative work, could no longer be exploited in the US until the story from which it was derived fell into the public domain – the film maker's rights lasted only during the first term of copyright.

This leaves Producers with a potential problem with **any** 'derivative work' created before US law was changed in 1978 to provide one term of copyright protection. Sound recordings are another form of derivative work (usually), in that to make them requires a licence to the music featured on the sound recording. Thus, Producers should steer clear of using recordings of US-composed music which was created before 1978 and which was still in its first term of copyright protection when the recording of it was made.

FILM AND TELEVISION CLIPS

Another form of pre-existing material which Producers commonly use in their productions are film clips or archive material. It is common practice for Producers to employ a specialized film researcher when the production makes extensive use of clips. Film researchers should be able not only to identify and find the source of clips which a Producer requires to use, but they should also be able to manage the process of seeking and getting an appropriate **licence** to use the clips.

As with music, the cost of clips greatly depends on the source. If the availability of rights in the clip is limited, or use of the clip in the production would be too expensive for the budget, this could be disastrous for the Producer if this is discovered too late in the process when the clip has already been incorporated into the production. It is therefore infinitely preferable to do some research into what the implications of using a particular clip (in terms of cost and otherwise) will be before the budget is fixed, or before the Producer becomes wedded to the idea of using that particular material.

Again, film clip licences are granted according to media, territory or licence period required. What is required will be dictated either by the Producer's contractual obligations or by the likely potential exposure of the finished production. For example, if a Producer is commissioned by the BBC to produce an historical documentary, the Producer may only have to pay for the use of clips for two transmissions on standard television (i.e. BBC Network Television) and Simultaneous European Cable Relay rights (the right to show the programme by cable relay in certain European territories, but only at the same time as the programme is being transmitted on BBC television). However, the production agreement with the BBC will also require all other relevant rights to be **cleared**. This means that in relation to any use which the BBC believes it may wish to make in the future a fee must be negotiated, but it will only become payable when the particular use actually takes place. For example, the fee to permit use on pay television will only become payable when the programme is sold to a pay-TV broadcaster.

However, it is unlikely that the BBC would ever want **theatrical** use to be cleared (page 170 contains definitions), because most BBC productions are not being made with theatrical distribution in mind. However, if the production and financing agreement with the BBC does state that this use needs to be cleared, a Producer must either clear it or negotiate with the BBC for the requirement to be dropped.

The process of using and clearing clips

The first step is to find physical material embodying the clip which the Producer wishes to use. It is essential to remember that the owner of a **physical copy** of the material in question may not actually be the copyright owner of the **film embodied on the material**. This is especially so with older films, where there may be several different copies in existence held by different archives. Thus, even if a fee is agreed with the owner of the copy for providing it, this fee will not necessarily clear the right in the **underlying copyright** in the film.

Finding the copyright owner can be a tricky business because the ownership of productions may change hands up to five or six times. This is where film researchers can be useful.

The fee charged by either the supplier of the physical material or the copyright owner will depend on the length of the clip used (either per minute or by the actual length, in feet, of footage).

The cost of using material from feature films can be very high indeed (thousands of pounds per minute). Some film companies habitually never give permission for the use of the films which they own.

Even when the rights owner has been found and a price has been negotiated, there may be further consents needed. For example, the use of certain Marx Brothers' films requires the consent of the heirs of the particular brother(s) featured in the clip. Certain film directors also have a power of veto over use of clips from their films. This particular consideration applies to all clips featuring performers (musicians and actors) but it is even more essential to remember that if the clip featured **music**, rights to use the music will also have to be separately cleared (i.e. the **synchronization right in the music** itself and, if the music was not especially recorded for the original production from which the clip is taken, **the dubbing right** in respect of **the pre-existing recording** which was used). These separate permissions would not, of course, be necessary if the Producer of the original material, from which the clip is taken, contracted with the performers of the music on terms which allowed its use by all means and in all media. However, with old clips, that is very difficult to establish and rights owners are not often prepared to take any risks – they therefore often refuse to give any assurances (or warranties) about the rights which they may have in third party contributions featured in the clip, but instead place the responsibility for clearance squarely on the Producer seeking to use it.

In the case of **television** clips, finding a copy of the material is generally easy, because the original broadcaster keeps archives. However, broadcasters do wipe old tapes sometimes and a researcher may have to root out old copies elsewhere. For instance, old 1960s comedy programmes are sometimes only available because one of the principals involved has kept a copy for his own personal use. On the question of getting the consent of **performers** in television programmes, the first step in tracing the performers is usually to contact the appropriate union. In relation to actors, sometimes Equity (the actors' union) will have the power to negotiate a fee on their behalf, but sometimes there may be no choice but to deal directly with the actor. Actors are sometimes not keen to see their old performances revived and used in another context, and this explains why they occasionally refuse permission.

The rights owner of the copyright in television clips will often be the original broadcaster, but sometimes the rights will belong to a production company or to a foreign broadcaster. Additionally, there may also be a question of moral rights arising if the Producer is intending to edit the clip or show it in a particular context.

As mentioned previously (Chapter 9, page 141) there may actually be no need to obtain a licence from the copyright owner to use an extract if that use can be brought within one of the **fair dealing** exceptions to copyright protection. However, even when an exception is technically available, it is advisable to ask for permission first and try to negotiate a reasonable fee. The Producer should only resort to taking advantage of the exception if the rights owner refuses permission or (which comes to the same thing) asks an exorbitantly high fee. That way, the Producer may avoid having to go to court to **prove** that the case was within one of the exceptions (as Channel Four did in the *Clockwork Orange* case – Chapter 9, page 142).

Television commercials

The rights owner in commercials can usually be traced through the advertising agency responsible. Use of commercials may well involve having to get separate consents from all performers in the commercial (actors, voice-overs and musicians) because their original consent will almost certainly not have covered the use of extracts of the commercial in another context.

Music videos

Clearance to use a music video will usually have to be obtained from a record company, as it is generally the case that record companies arrange and pay for (and therefore own the copyright in) promotional videos featuring their contracted artists. However, occasionally the featured artist(s) may have produced and paid for the video, and in those circumstances may own the copyright.

The collecting society Video Performance Limited ('VPL') was set up in 1984 by the major record companies, and administers **the public performance and broadcast rights** in music videos. Thus, when using a music video in a television programme, a Producer may be able to take advantage of the arrangements between the broadcaster of the programme and VPL (if any).

Documentation

The agreement setting out the licence to use a clip may be in one document only (below is an example) drawn up either by the Producer or by the rights owner, or contained in an exchange of letters. If the rights owner insists on using its own standard form licence, the Producer must be careful to see that the licence includes all necessary details and does not contain any unwelcome surprises. The rights owner will probably be particularly concerned about the **context** in which the clip is going to be used, and will be keen to commit the Producer to a particular type of use. For example if the Producer, when originally seeking permission, stated that the clip was to form part of a 'tribute' programme to one of the performers shown in the clip, the rights owner will want this to be specified in the licence. Then it will be a breach of the terms of the licence if the clip is used in a programme criticizing that or any other performer or the production company originally responsible for the clip. The owner will also often want to be credited, and may also demand a free video cassette of the finished production in which the clip appears. As a minimum, the licence **must** deal with the:

- fee;
- rights granted (i.e. medium/number of transmissions);
- territory for which the rights are granted;
- time period during which the rights can be exercised (for example five years or for the full period of copyright);
- length of clip allowed;
- fees payable for further uses.

This last will be very important, for example, to a broadcaster who agrees to finance from the original budget only two UK terrestrial network television transmissions, but is keen to ensure that the production can be sold overseas or to a satellite/cable broadcaster. It considerably smooths the path to further exploitation not to have to go back and re-negotiate an additional fee for every film clip which might be featured in the film to be sold – it is much simpler if the broadcaster can go ahead with the sale on payment of an already ascertained fee.

Ideally, it is better for the Producer if the licence agreement for clip use contains some sort of assurances that the rights owner actually does own the rights and is entitled to grant them. Sometimes this is achievable, but all too often (especially with US film distributors) the opposite happens and the rights owner's licence will specifically state that the owner give no warranties as to ownership, and will have no responsibility if the Producer is faced with any legal action or other claim arising out of use of the clip. In these circumstances, the Producer has to balance the desire to use the material against the risks involved. When commissioned by a broadcaster, the Producer will be obliged (under the terms of the commissioning agreement) to refer a decision on this aspect to the broadcaster.

A sample licence agreement:

To: [Production Company]

Dear Sirs

1 In consideration of the sum of £   (receipt of which we acknowledge) [being £   per minute] for [   ] clip(s) ('the Material') as more specifically described in Part I of the Schedule, [belonging to us] [controlled by us], we hereby grant to you the right to use and adapt and to incorporate the Material in your proposed [series of] [television] film(s) entitled ['   '] ('the Film') and to exploit the Material as part of the Film by means of [e.g. two network television broadcasts thereof throughout the United Kingdom and simultaneous European cable broadcast].

2 It is agreed that the further rights of exploitation of the Material as part of the Film specified in Part II of the Schedule will be exercisable by you upon payment to us of the relevant fee in respect of such exploitation specified in Part II of the Schedule.

3 We further warrant and represent to you that we [own the copyright] [are the exclusive licensees of the distribution rights] in the Material throughout the [United Kingdom] and the various territories specified in Part II of the Schedule and are entitled to make the grant contained in this letter and we agree to indemnify you against all claims actions demands costs or other liabilities howsoever arising in any way from a breach of this warranty.

4 This Licence will be governed and construed in accordance with English law, and the parties hereby submit to the non-exclusive jurisdiction of the English Courts.

Schedule

Part I

Details of clip(s)

Time of Production **Subject Matter**	**Length of Clip**

Part II

Territory **Fee**	**Medium**

Signed . . . .

For and on behalf of

[OWNER/LICENSOR OF CLIPS]

Dated . . . .

AGREED AND ACCEPTED

Signed . . . .

For and on behalf of

[Producer]

Dated . . . .

PHOTOGRAPHS AND OTHER ARTISTIC WORKS

Photographs are included in the definition of 'artistic work' in the Copyright, Designs and Patents Act 1988. The full definition of what constitutes an 'artistic work' is:

- a graphic work, sculpture or collage, irrespective of artistic quality;
- a work of architecture being a building or a model for a building;
- a work of artistic craftsmanship.

'Graphic work' includes:

- any painting, drawing, diagram, map, chart or plans;
- any engraving, etching, lithograph, wood cut or similar works.

'Sculpture' includes a cast or model made for the purposes of sculpture.

If the artistic work is protected by copyright, then permission to feature it in a film or television production will be needed, unless the use is one which exempts the user from having to obtain permission. The exceptions of **fair dealing** and **incidental inclusion** have already been covered (Chapter 9, page 141). However, it should be noted that the exception for fair dealing for the purpose of reporting current events does **not** apply to **photographs**. There is an additional exception, which removes the need for permission to include a building or a sculpture or work of artistic craftsmanship in a film or a broadcast, as long as the work is **permanently** situated in a public place or in premises open to the public.

As to whether a work is in copyright, with most artistic works, the period of protection is the life of the creator plus 50 years (to be increased to life plus 70 years – Chapter 3, page 22). The same applies to photographs created after 1 August 1989 (when the Copyright, Designs and Patents Act 1988 came into force). However, photographs taken before that date have protection for only 50 years from the date of first publication of them, or 50 years from 1 August 1989 if the photographs were unpublished on 1 August 1989.

Obtaining clearance

As with film clips (perhaps even more prevalently) the owner of the physical copy of a photograph is rarely the copyright owner, so two permissions will then be needed. Finding the copyright owner can be difficult – if he or she cannot be found then use of the work will be risky. Owners of the copyright in works of fine art can usually be traced through the Design and Artistic Copyright Society Limited ('DACS'). This is a collecting society representing many painters, sculptors and photographers, both British and foreign. As with other collecting societies, if DACS does not actually represent the copyright owner for the purposes of agreeing a licence and negotiating a fee, it will usually assist in tracing and putting the Producer in touch with the owner. Again, as with clips, there should be a document recording the terms on which permission is given – the fee will depend on the rights required and the amount of time during which the work is shown on screen.

Completion guarantees and production insurances | **11**

INTRODUCTION

In earlier chapters, the subject of completion guarantees and the insurances which a Producer will need to put in place have regularly cropped up. This chapter explains in more detail what is required but, in relation to insurance, concentrating particularly on Errors and Omissions insurance.

COMPLETION GUARANTEES

A completion guarantee is a 'performance bond' (which is a particular type of contract of insurance) which Financiers of films and television programmes sometimes require to protect the investment they have made. Completion guarantors are specialist companies which offer a form of insurance coverage against certain kinds of events which could prevent a production being completed. Although giving a completion guarantee can be very remunerative, it is also very risky which explains why there are not many completion guarantee companies in existence.

Evidently contributors to the financing of a production would lose their investment, without a hope of return, if the film/programme were not completed for some reason. There are quite a lot of reasons why a film/programme might not be finished, although running out of money is usually head of the list.

It is therefore wise practice to take out a completion guarantee (or, to use the North American name, a completion bond) which will either:

- guarantee that the film is completed and delivered on time; or
- guarantee to repay the Financier its investment if the film cannot be completed.

In feature film production, guarantees are required almost without exception – Financiers are usually unwilling (if not incapable) to provide a blank cheque to a production. They therefore want to be sure that if and when the sum of money which they have agreed to supply runs out, the excess amount will be available to finish the job. In television, even where an independent Producer is commissioned by a broadcaster on the basis that the broadcaster pays 100% of the production cost, completion guarantees are still comparatively rare. The broadcaster has more commonly acted as its own guarantor, but usually reserving the right to recover budget excess (or overcost) from the Producer, either in all circumstances or if the overcost is due to the Producer's wilful default or negligence. (Chapter 7, pages 112–15, contains more detail.)

Guarantees can be expensive, like most forms of insurance – the fee charged by completion guarantors for providing a guarantee is about 5% to 6% of the production budget of the film although, as guarantors commonly give refunds (referred to as the 'guarantee fee rebate') if the guarantee is not called upon, the final fee can be as little as 1.5%. (In fact, it has been the practice for Financiers to save money, by paying only half the fee in advance, and then only paying the second half if the guarantee is called upon.)

Guarantors take the right (which should also be a specific obligation to the Financier to whom the guarantee is given) to monitor a film from the very first day of production. This means that a completion guarantee company has to have extensive knowledge of production practice and techniques to do its job properly. Monitoring production gives the guarantor the opportunity to nip any trouble in the bud, either by stepping in and taking over production, or by exercising some lesser form of control. The guarantor's objective, as with all insurers, will be to minimize the extent of its financial liability.

Documentation

The documents forming part of a guarantee 'package' are usually:

- the guarantee itself – between the guarantor and the Financier(s);
- the Producer's agreement – between the guarantor and the Producer.

This latter agreement will give the guarantor the right (and authority) to monitor the production and, if necessary, to assume control of it, and will usually entail the production company providing other documents to safeguard the guarantor's position.

The guarantee

The Financier will often be a bank or some other entity which is cash-flowing finance in return for a promise that the Producer will pay over the amounts which distributors are agreeing to pay to the Producer for rights in the film, if and when the film is delivered to those distributors.

This way of lending production finance, known as 'discounting distributor advances', is considered in more detail in Chapter 6, pages 92–4.

The Financier's risk is that the distributor may be able to refuse to pay the advance, because the film is not delivered to it, or the film does not meet the contractual specifications set out in the distribution agreement (for example, if the distribution contracts stipulated that the stars of the film would be Meryl Streep and Robert De Niro, and the Producer makes a film with two different actors; or if the film materials delivered to the distributor for making prints and for publicity purposes are not of the required technical standard).

From the Financier's point of view, it is essential that the guarantor agrees to guarantee the delivery of substantially what the distributor is agreeing to pay for.

Since a guarantee is not only a vital service, but is also expensive, it is highly advisable and commercially justifiable to seek legal advice on its contents. For that reason, this section will give only a brief review of some of the major points to note.

'Conditions precedent'

The guarantor's **financial** liability under the guarantee will normally not come into play until a number of specific pre-conditions (or 'conditions precedent' in legal terms) have been satisfied. These are as follows.

- **An amount equal to the 'strike price' must have been paid into the production bank account**: the strike price is the total of the contributions to the financing of production which the guarantor is agreeing to protect.

  The Financier will want the strike price to be the same amount as the sum which that Financier is providing, but where there is more than one Financier, the guarantor will not want to accept financial liability until the **entire budget** has been funded.

  This is a matter of negotiation – the Financier's view will depend on the financial stability of the other persons who are agreeing to contribute to production funding.

  However, the Financier will expect the guarantor to monitor the production from the outset, to ensure that it is being kept on schedule, even if the guarantor's financial obligations have still not come into effect.

- **The budget must be funded on an 'as needed' basis**: it would evidently throw out the calculations of the film's financing requirement if finance was not provided when it was required. For instance, if the Producer does not receive instalments of the finance when it is needed, the Producer may have to incur extra costs (such as interest and paying lending fees to other sources of finance) in borrowing the cash to make up the shortfall. This will add to the final cost of production. The guarantor will not want to be obliged to pay that extra cost.

- **The guarantee fee must have been paid**: since usually only half of the fee is paid in advance, the guarantor will want to be sure that the second half is paid, before the guarantor starts spending its own money. Again, it is only the guarantor's **financial** obligations which do not come into effect until the fee has been paid in full. The Financier will still expect the guarantor to monitor the progress of production.

Recovery of guarantor's expenditure

If the guarantor pays out its own money to complete production, it will want to be one of the persons who are entitled to recoup their contribution to the production cost from the first proceeds of exploitation of the film. The guarantor should not expect to get its money back before the primary Financiers of the film. The usual recoupment order for the sharing out of exploitation income is:

- payment of distributor's commission and expenses;
- recoupment by the primary Financiers of their contributions towards the cost of production of the film (plus interest and other financing charges) if their contributions were made by way of equity investment;
- repayment to the completion guarantor of money advanced by it, plus interest;
- payment of deferments (Chapter 6, pages 95 and 98).

The guarantor will only agree to deliver the **essential** items required to exploit the film – therefore, a lot of items which a distributor will normally expect will tend to be excluded from the guarantee (as in *Exclusions* below). In this case, the Financier may well have to advance more money than was originally agreed to pay for these non-essential delivery items (to make sure that the distributor will accept delivery and pay the distribution advance). Alternatively, the Financier may have spent extra in an attempt to avoid calling on the guarantee (which may at the time have seemed commercially sensible if the extra money required appeared to be less than the amount of the second half of the completion guarantee fee). So the recoupment order agreed with the guarantor should permit the Financier to recover those extra costs, and not just the amount it was originally **committed** to advance.

Exclusions

Guarantees are usually drafted so that guarantors will not have certain responsibilities. The normal matters which are excluded from a guarantor's obligations are:

- **defects** (either in the ownership or in some other respect which might lead to legal claim) **in the underlying rights, copyright or screenplay of the film**. This is why Errors and Omissions insurance is vital (pages 196–200 below). However, the exclusion should not apply to copyright material which a guarantor itself has made or commissioned for the film and for which it should naturally take full responsibility;
- for **extra costs** which may have to be **incurred if a film as delivered** to a distributor **does not qualify for a certificate** from the British Board of Film Classification, or a rating from the Motion Picture Association of America. However, the guarantor should agree to ensure that the film will qualify for a rating no more restrictive than '18' or 'R' in the US, as long as the script is suitable;
- the **artistic quality of the film** (as opposed to the **technical** quality for which the guarantor **will** be responsible);
- for the **cost of cutting, re-editing, re-recording, dubbing**, making foreign language versions of the film, 'cover shots' for television versions, or making other changes to meet the *ad hoc* requirements of the distributor (so the Financier should ensure that the cost of all these, if they are items which the distributor can contractually insist on, are covered in the production budget);
- **additional delivery items** (in other words, delivery items which the distributors have asked for which exceed the basic essential items which are needed to enable the film to be distributed);
- **if any event of *force majeure* occurs**. However, this should **not** completely absolve the guarantor – the Financier should insist that the guarantor can only exclude the guarantor's responsibility for late delivery of the film to the extent of **postponing** the agreed delivery date for a specific period. That period will be one which is equal to the duration of the event of *force majeure*, plus a reasonable time to enable the guarantor to resume production. The guarantor should then agree, come what may, to complete delivery or to abandon production and repay the Financier by an outside date (usually 60 days from the delivery date which would have applied if the event of *force majeure* had not arisen).

Abandonment

The guarantor will have the right to decide to abandon the production and to pay off the Financier, rather than completing the film, if the guarantor takes the view that the production is not capable of salvage. In this case, in view of the fact that the Financier would have been entitled to interest (from the proceeds of exploitation) and may have also incurred extra costs, the guarantor's repayment obligation should cover the principal amount of the Financier's investment **and** interest and any additional funds which the Financier provided towards the cost of production.

Guarantor's insurance

The guarantor will usually insure each film with an insurance company or with Lloyd's to make sure that the guarantor can meet the cost of production if the guarantee is called on. This is a form of reinsurance. As the guarantor's insurer will be the one who ultimately has to pay out (if the guarantee is called on) the Financier should, if possible, ask for a direct contractual right to require payment from the insurer. This is normally achieved by the insurer writing to the Financier what is known as a 'cut-through' letter, agreeing to pay the Financier directly if the guarantor fails to pay for the overcost, or fails to pay up if the film is abandoned. This is essential protection if there is any possibility that the guarantor is or may become insolvent (which has been known to happen).

Release

The guarantor may ask, once a film has been successfully completed and delivered, for a document releasing it from its obligations. The Financier will want to make the release only partial, to this extent:

- that it does not apply to the guarantor's obligations if there is a legal problem with copyright material commissioned or made by the guarantor;
- that it will not apply if, at the time that the Financier releases the guarantor from its obligations, there were facts, then unknown to the Financier, as a result of knowing which the Financier would not have given the release.

The Producer's agreement

The guarantor agrees separately with the Producer to give the guarantor appropriate rights of control, so that it can perform what it is guaranteeing (to the Financier) to do. The guarantor is also looking for assurances from the Producer that the costs allowed for and the arrangements already made for production should, barring accidents or unforeseen circumstances, result in the film being made on budget, on time and as exactly as everybody wants it to be.

Most essentially, the guarantor will require the Producer to give it the right to step in and take over production, if the guarantee is or may be called on. The guarantor will therefore take the right to assume control of the production bank account, and of the film materials shot and soundtrack recorded so far.

Producer's obligations to the guarantor in the Producer's agreement

The Producer will be asked to agree in favour of the guarantor to perform very much the same functions as it agrees to do for the Financier under the production and financing agreements (Chapter 6) namely:

- to produce and deliver the film on time, as required by the production and financing agreements **and** as required by any agreement relating to a pre-sale of the distribution rights;
- to keep to budget, script and production schedule;
- to get the guarantor's approval on contracts engaging artists and production personnel;
- to deliver frequent financial reports to the guarantor during the course of production, and to give access to the production records and accounts so that the guarantor can inspect them;
- to give the guarantor's representative free access to the studio and any locations where the film is being shot, and during the cutting and editing process;
- lastly, to report to the guarantor, as soon as possible, any circumstances which significantly affect the Producer's own financial situation.

It is not only control which the guarantor is interested in, but also in being able to take action against the Producer if it is the Producer's default which has led to the guarantee being called on. In many cases, this right of action may not be much help to the guarantor in recovering the amount it has had to pay out to complete the film, but it is supposed to concentrate the Producer's mind!

However, a Producer might well find a very conscientious guarantor something of a nuisance during a production which is going fairly smoothly, and should therefore try to temper the strictness of the guarantor's controls or approvals. For example, the Producer should:

- reserve the ability to make minor changes to the script and production schedule without having to get approval;
- ask the guarantor to pre-approve the Producer's standard contract form used in taking on production personnel, so that each individual contract with each person does not have to be approved in advance of its being signed (but only the variables, such as the fee payable);
- require the guarantor to exercise its rights reasonably and not in such a way as might hinder production;
- require the guarantor to consult before giving any instructions to the

Producer, and to allow the Producer at least 24 hours to comply with any such instructions.

Personnel

The guarantor will take the right to suspend, dismiss and replace any artists or production personnel. In this respect, both Producer **and** Financier will want to be consulted before the guarantor takes any step of this nature. A Producer would also want to ensure that, in exercising its rights, the guarantor will not be entitled to do anything which would put the Producer in breach of any contract of engagement, or in breach of a distribution agreement (for example by firing one of the principal actors, when it is a requirement of the distributor that that actor appears in the finished film).

Take-over

It is rare for a guarantor to take over production, as problems can usually be dealt with less drastically. But if the guarantor does take over, it will require the Producer to give it control over all personnel and equipment, and the benefit of all other contracts which a Producer has entered into in connection with the film. It is therefore important for the Producer to have ensured in its contracts with production personnel that they agree to perform their obligations for the benefit of the guarantor, should take-over occur.

The guarantor will also contract directly with the film processing laboratory or post-production house to ensure that it can take control over all material already shot. As for the production bank account, the Producer's mandate to the bank when opening the account should have included a direction to the bank to comply with the completion guarantor's instructions (so that the guarantor can take over the bank account) and the completion guarantor will also take a 'power of attorney' from the Producer, so that he can take action and do everything necessary to complete production, in the name of and on behalf of the Producer.

From the Producer's viewpoint, the guarantor's rights should be restricted to the following extent.

- It should not be entitled to borrow money on behalf of the Producer.
- If the Producer manages to raise sufficient finance to put right the situation which causes the guarantor to step in in the first place, the Producer should be allowed to resume control over production of the film. (Naturally, this assumes that the other existing Financiers are happy with the terms on which the Producer has raised the new money.)

Charge or other security

Since the guarantor will want the ability to enforce its right to be repaid its financial outlay (as described above), the guarantor will take a charge over the film and related assets of the Producer (Chapter 6, pages 99–100).

This charge will take second place in order of priority to any charge given to the Financier(s), since the Financier(s) rank higher in the list of persons to be repaid their investment into the film. What this means, in practice, is that the guarantor either cannot enforce its charge without the consent of the Financier(s) or, if it does, has to repay the Financier from any money which the guarantor gets, before it can start repaying itself.

PRODUCTION INSURANCES

The sorts of production insurances that will be taken out for both film and television productions are:

- pre-production and cast insurance;
- negative and videotape, faulty stock, camera, editing and processing insurance;
- supplementary perils including props, set and wardrobe; all risks camera, sound and miscellaneous equipment; third party property damage; extra expense and production office contents and money insurance;
- employers and public liability insurance;
- contingent personal accident insurance;
- Errors and Omissions insurance.

In certain cases (particularly for films) essential element insurance (otherwise known as abandonment insurance) may also be required. This covers situations where the Financier/distributor makes it a condition of the financing arrangement that particular persons such as a specific actor or director must be involved in the film. If, during production, the actor or director falls under a bus, the insurance will cover the abandonment costs.

In certain circumstances, political risk insurance may also be required. This covers situations where filming may be interrupted through acts of political or civil disturbance.

Further detail on the cover provided by most of the insurances mentioned above can be obtained from film and television insurance brokers. No further comment is made here, because the application for most of these insurances does not cover many legal issues. However, one general point applies to all kinds of insurance, and in particular applying for them. As a matter of law, a person seeking insurance is under a duty (which continues after insurance is given) to **disclose** all facts or information known to him which are relevant to the insurance in question. A failure to disclose this information can result in the insurer disclaiming liability.

An example would be if a Producer applied for medical insurance on the life and health of a particular actor whom the Producer knew to have a debilitating disease, without disclosing this knowledge to the insurer. There is a temptation not to disclose facts such as these, because the insurer will generally exclude liability for loss suffered as a result of the fact disclosed. As a result, the Producer would not be able to claim for loss suffered on days when the actor was not available. However, if the fact of the illness was not disclosed, the Producer runs the risk that the insurer will declare the entire policy on the actor to be invalid. Then, even if the Producer suffers loss through the actor suffering an entirely unrelated mishap (such as being run over by a bus), this may not be covered by the insurance.

It is, however, worth commenting in detail on Errors and Omissions insurance, as this closely concerns the question of whether the Producer has complied with those laws which commonly affect film and television productions. (The laws in question, and the procedure to see that they are complied with, are covered in more detail in Chapter 12.)

ERRORS AND OMISSIONS INSURANCE

Errors and Omissions (or 'E&O') insurance is the name usually given to a kind of insurance also sometimes known as copyright and libel insurance, or Producer's liability insurance.

Not many insurance companies offer this type of coverage, so those that do provide it do not differ much in the extent of cover and the price they require for it. The procedures which a Producer has to go through to get it are also much the same from one insurer to another.

Risks covered against

A typical E&O insurance policy will cover against claims made by third parties during production or exploitation of the film or television programme, and arising out of:

- copyright and trade mark infringements;
- libel or slander;
- infringement of an individual's right of privacy or publicity;
- plagiarism or unfair competition or breach of confidence or of an implied contract, resulting from unauthorized use of ideas, scripts, titles, formats, performances or other material.

Rights of privacy and publicity are not particularly relevant here (as yet), but are naturally danger areas if the production is to be shown in the USA.

The policy will not generally cover a Producer for a claim made as a result of breach of contract (for example, a breach of the contract under which underlying rights are required). Other exclusions will be claims by employees, or claims relating to physical injury (which should be covered under other production insurances).

Period of cover

The policy will usually last for three years (renewable on payment of an additional premium) and should be in place and taking effect from the very first day of production. Claims can just as easily be made at that stage; and as soon as production starts the level of expenditure on production, and thus the potential loss for Producers, Financiers and distributors, increases with every day that passes. An example of a typical claim at this stage is a claim by a writer or another Producer (who has read about the film or programme in one of the trade magazines) that the production is based on a treatment or script which that person submitted to someone on the production team, and which was turned down. Such a claim will usually be either that the writer/Producer's copyright has been infringed, or (if what was submitted does not really merit copyright protection) for breach of confidence. (Chapter 3, pages 27–31).

Persons insured

The insurance should be taken out for the benefit not only of the Producer, but also of the Financiers and all other persons who either have a financial interest in the film or are exploiting it (thereby adding themselves to the list of people who may be sued if the film is alleged to infringe somebody's rights). This obviously includes the distributors of the film.

Premium payable and amount insured

With most insurance policies, the premium differs according to the degree of risk which the insurer thinks is likely to arise. However, E&O premiums are usually much the same amount from one film to another. If the insurer thinks there is a higher risk, it usually increases the amount of the 'deductible'. This is a kind of compulsory 'excess' amount of a claim which the insured parties will have to pay before the insurer's liability comes into play. A deductible can be as high as US$500 000 or more.

The standard amount of cover is usually around $1 million for each claim and $3 million in the aggregate (namely, for all claims the maximum amount payable in total will be $3 million). The amounts are usually expressed in US currency because companies which offer E&O insurance cover are invariably American.

How to obtain E&O insurance

This type of cover is generally obtained through insurance brokers who deal in production insurances, rather than Producers dealing directly with the insurance underwriters. (This is the case with all production insurances.)

The Producer is required to fill out a form giving full details of the production, so that the underwriter can satisfy itself that all necessary clearances have been obtained (Chapters 9, 10 and 12) and then will have a fair idea of the risk areas (if any). The questions clearly entail giving a description of the production and the media in which it is planned to exploit it.

It will be a matter of particular interest to the underwriter if real living people appear or are portrayed as themselves in the work, and whether or not those people have consented to appearing, or as the case may be, being portrayed. If no consent has been given, the underwriter will have to be convinced that no consent was necessary.

To take an example, a Producer ('P') makes a mini-series about the life of Margaret Thatcher. If she has not been consulted about it, nor has she consented to it being made, there is a risk that P may face claims as follows:

- for libel if (as is entirely possible) Mrs Thatcher is depicted unfavourably;
- for breach of the rights of privacy or publicity if the mini-series is shown in territories where such rights exist.

If it seems likely that any such claim if made would be successful, the underwriter ('U') will completely exclude such claims from the insurance policy cover. However, P may be able to convince U on legal grounds that there is little to fear either:

- on the libel front, because either Mrs Thatcher is shown as an angel of goodness and light or because everything unfavourable can be established as fact and has already been published elsewhere (although this may not convince U that there is no risk);
- from a right of privacy/publicity claim because the mini-series does not depict anything which is not publicly known or that, as a public figure, Mrs Thatcher has lost her right to object. (These and other defences are sometimes available under the laws of countries where such a claim is likely to be made.)

If U accepts these arguments, it will give cover, but will probably increase the amount of the deductible in respect of any claim for libel or breach of publicity/privacy by Mrs Thatcher.

While P may be able to show that it has a complete defence, this may not deter Mrs Thatcher from starting legal proceedings; and litigation is expensive for the person being sued from the very moment it starts, and even if that person is eventually shown to be in the right, he may not recover all of his costs. By imposing a deductible, U automatically reduces its liability for legal costs if a claim is made.

Another potential risk area is where real life events have been fictionalized. A person who featured in the original events may not actually be identified as him or herself in the drama, but that person may still have a libel claim if he or she can show that people did actually identify the character appearing in the drama with him or her. There can also be a problem where some real person's name has been used in a fictional production, if that person can show that his or her acquaintances thought that the character was meant to be a portrayal of him or her. (Chapter 12, pages 207–208).

The underwriter will therefore wish to see that the Producer has gone through standard clearance procedures to avoid this kind of risk.

The underwriter will normally expect as a matter of course that title and copyright searches (and, if necessary, legal reports on those searches) have been obtained (Chapter 5, pages 60–61 and Chapter 12). Sometimes, though, the underwriter will dispense with this if the Producer shows that one or other search/report is actually unnecessary.

Producer's lawyers

If the Producer is using an external lawyer to do some of the production legal work, the underwriter will ask that the Producer's lawyer sign the application form to acknowledge that:

- he/she has read and understood the insurer's standard clearance procedures and advised the Producer on them;
- all necessary rights and releases have been obtained; and
- the finished production has been viewed for any likely problems.

However, the lawyer will **not** usually sign the form, simply because not all of these things will be or have been in the lawyer's control. Only a lawyer who is actually in-house at the Producer could claim to have been involved in all matters covered by E&O insurance. Instead, the external lawyer will write a letter to the insurance broker confirming that he or she has seen the clearance procedures, advised the Producer of them and will take appropriate steps to try to comply with the clearance procedures, **to**

the extent asked by the Producer to do so.

In sending this letter, the lawyer will also expand on any answers in the application form which need further explanation (such as why a title report has not been obtained), and will disclose any material information which may affect the insurance and which has not already been disclosed (page 195 above). If a lawyer is not involved, it is still a good practice, when sending in the insurance application form to the broker, to expand on answers given in a covering letter, to the extent that any further detail is relevant.

Once the application has been accepted (and they can be processed very quickly if necessary), cover will be issued immediately.

It is worth stressing again that this is not an insurance which can be left till the last minute, but should be in place from the **first** day of production.

Script and content clearance

DANGER AREAS

Both for the purposes of obtaining Errors and Omissions insurances (Chapter 11, *Completion guarantees and production insurances*) and for general peace of mind, one of the most important legal aspects of production is the vetting of the script and the finished but unedited production to ensure that it contains nothing unlawful. The purpose of this process is to avoid any legal claim against the Producer or any other person exhibiting the production (such as distributors or broadcasters). Additionally, broadcasters have statutory duties with regard to the contents of their programmes, and Producers commissioned by broadcasters to make programmes have to bear those duties in mind – not least, because the production and finance agreement between the Producer and the broadcaster will require the Producer to warrant that those statutory duties will be observed.

The areas to be considered when vetting a script or a production are:

- copyright (and to a certain extent, trade marks);
- defamation;
- other legal danger areas such as obscenity/indecency and the Official Secrets Act;
- contempt of court;
- the broadcasters' statutory duties as regards programme contents.

Each of these areas is considered in turn.

Copyright

What copyright is, and when licences need to be obtained has already been covered in this book (Chapter 3, pages 22–5 and Chapter 9, pages 138–44). However, the danger area to bear in mind is the **incidental** appearance, in a script or a production, of material which is in copyright, and which has been overlooked in identifying the material in which rights have to be cleared.

> For example, a script features a scene where a little boy is the centre of attention at a children's party. His father enters the room, wheeling an elaborate cake on a trolley. The script calls for the children to gasp in admiration at the cake. However, when the scene is actually being shot, the director and the actor playing the father agree that notwithstanding that it is not in the script, he should loudly and tunelessly whistle *Happy Birthday to You* when wheeling in the cake. This tune is (perhaps as a surprise to many) still in copyright and therefore it must be cleared, otherwise it will have to be edited off the soundtrack.

Incorporating material in a film or television programme before it has been cleared, or even without realizing at the time that it needed to be cleared, can be a very expensive business. If permission cannot be obtained after the event to use it, the production has to be re-edited. Even if that is possible, without extensive re-shooting, it is still going to cost money. If it does require re-shooting, it will be very expensive indeed. Where the owner of the material is prepared to grant permission, but for an exorbitant fee, the Producer may have to weigh the cost of paying the fee against the cost of extensive re-shooting – either way, it will probably result in the production being over budget. It is therefore essential to consider whether **anything** which appears in shot or on the soundtrack is protected by copyright.

Trade marks and passing-off

'Trade marks' is a term used to describe marks, logos, names or brands under which businesses operate, and which distinguish one business from another.

It can consist of words or pictures or a combination of the two.

> For example, a purchaser of a packet of Kellogg's cornflakes will note the name *Kellogg's* at the top of the packet in a red stylized script. The name *Kellogg's* is a trade mark in itself, as it operates to distinguish these products from other breakfast cereals, but the stylized logo type in which the name is shown will also separately qualify as a trade mark. For that reason, using a different name but in the same style and manner may well amount to trade mark infringement.

(Further detail on trade marks is contained in Chapter 14, *Secondary exploitation*.)

The problems for Producers in relation to trade marks (either names or logos) mainly arise when referring to fictitious companies in drama or comedy. If the trade mark/logo of the fictitious company is sufficiently close to the trade mark of a real company, this could amount to trade mark infringement. Additionally, if the fictitious company is shown in an unfavourable light in the production, the real company could also possibly also claim to be identified with the fictional company and take action for defamation (described below), even if the similarity was entirely inadvert.

'Passing-off' is the name of a legal action available to those who are entitled to claim ownership of unregistered trade marks. Protection is given by the law to persons who have established a particular **reputation** with the public under or in connection with a certain name. 'Reputation' in this sense means that the user of the name has established an association in the minds of the public between the name and any product or service in respect of which the name is used. If someone else uses that name, to the actual or potential confusion of the public, the person who established a reputation in using it may be able to sue for 'passing-off'. (More detail on this is contained in Chapter 14, pages 239.)

In this context, it is worth going into more detail about the extent to which the title of a film or television production can be protected. To the extent it can, the Producer will wish to ensure that the title of its production is not too similar to any films or programmes which already exist.

If the title is registered as a trade mark, the owner of the registration may be able to stop it being used as a film title.

Equally, the use of the title may bring a claim for passing-off. However, the **reputation** of the original user of the title should, if the action is to be successful, have been established in a similar field of activity or in relation to a similar type of product – ideally film or television productions or, at the least, a book on which members of the public might think the new film has been based. Otherwise, a court might be reluctant to find that the use of the title would lead the public to confuse the film or programme with some activity or product of the person claiming that passing-off has occurred.

Under English law, a title will not generally qualify for copyright protection as it is considered that the creation of a title does not involve sufficient skill and labour (one of the requirements of eligibility for copyright protection – Chapter 3, page 23).

Furthermore in the United Kingdom and in Europe, as there is no system of copyright registration even if a title were capable of protection, no central system to register ownership of that title exists.

This means of course that if a use of a title cannot be protected, its use by more than one company cannot be prevented either. Although it is relatively unusual for two films to be released with exactly the same name it does happen from time to time. If English production companies are involved there is little to prevent this situation occurring, if neither title is a 'trade mark', either registered or unregistered. However, the position is slightly different in the United States.

In the United States, there is a central copyright registry at which it is possible to register all forms of copyright work (as that phrase is understood in American legislation). However, as with English law, a title alone is not sufficient to merit copyright protection. On the other hand, it would appear that there **is** some sort of passing-off-right in relation to titles of films which have been released. Any Producer seeking to use as the title of a film to be released in the US, something which has already appeared as a title of another film, should seek US legal advice.

In addition, the Motion Picture Association of America ('the MPAA') provides a Title Registration Service for feature films, use of which is compulsory for all its members, and voluntary for any other Producer or similar entity. The Title Registration provides protection for feature film titles for varying periods of time.

It would appear that the Sam Goldwyn Company has been able to obtain **permanent** protection for the title *Wuthering Heights* (although the MPAA do not seem to be exactly sure how this was achieved). Under the current rules, it is possible to obtain permanent protection for a title. However, another company may only be prevented from using the registered title if the original registrant can show that it will commence a 'remake' within two years of the date of registration or it will re-release the film within one year of the date of filing for registration.

It is also important to bear in mind that the registration of a title is only binding on subscribers to the service and only applies to feature films to be released in the United States. A subscriber company which may have already registered a particular title would probably not have any course of action against a company which is not a subscriber to the service. Of course, if no title has already been registered, a production company may wish to consider becoming a voluntary member to the service for the purposes of registering a title. However, the fees for doing so are quite high – the annual subscription charge is at least $300, a service fee of at least $200 is payable for the first title registered and further fees are payable if an arbitration hearing is required to decide on who should have prior right to use a particular title.

It is also advisable to obtain a title availability search in the United States Copyright Registry, which will detail other **copyright** works which have the same or similar titles. This may indicate if there are likely to be any potential problems with a title in the United States at least. The Companies which carry out the search charge a fee of several hundred US dollars and the search usually takes about a week (expedited searches have a higher charge).

Defamation

Libel and slander

Defamation is the general term which covers both slander and libel. **Libel** is the term used to describe defamation of a more permanent nature (which is written down or recorded). **Slander** describes spoken defamation (or more rarely, defamation to be implied from gestures or actions). It is usually fairly easy to identify the difference between libel and slander. (Lawyers specializing in this area have what they regard as highly amusing arguments about whether teaching a parrot to use insulting epithets to other people would be libel or slander.)

Who can be sued?

A defamatory statement about a person entitles that person to take civil legal action for injunction and damages against any person making the statement (Chapter 15, *Legal proceedings*).

In the case of libel, that does not just expose to claims the person who originally made a statement, such as a journalist in a newspaper or current affairs programme, but **everyone** who is legally responsible for the making of the statement. In the case of a newspaper statement, that will mean the editor and proprietor can also be sued; in the case of a television programme, the 'victim' of the statement can sue the production company **and** the broadcaster.

What is 'defamatory'?

To be defamatory, a statement must damage the reputation of the person about whom it is made in the eyes of 'right thinking people'. This latter phrase is one which originates from one of the many legal cases where the definition of the expression 'defamatory' was laid down for the future reference of lawyers (which is probably why it sounds a little archaic).

In a claim for defamation, the victim has to prove that the statement was made to a third party and that it has the appropriate 'lowering' effect on his or her reputation.

It is a **defence** to a defamation claim that the statement is true. The fact that the statement is true, however, does not prevent the object of that statement from suing in the first place. Defending defamation proceedings is extremely expensive, however justified the original statement was (as the editor of *Private Eye* can testify). It has been common practice for many rich and perhaps unscrupulous people to discourage public discussion of their doings, by making it known that they are extremely ready to sue. A particular notable example of this was the late Robert Maxwell. The underlying conclusion for a Producer must be this: do not assume that it is safe to say something derogatory about someone if it is true, as you may run out of money before you can prove it!

However, as can be seen from the uninhibited comments made about Robert Maxwell after his death, there can be no libel or slander of the dead, in that the heirs and/or estate of a dead person are not entitled to take action against someone who defames the deceased.

What kind of statement lowers the reputation of a person about whom it is made? The answer is often quite obvious. For example, it is defamatory to call someone 'a crook'. However, some examples are not so obvious. For instance, it may come as a surprise to some to learn that in this day and age it is probably still defamatory to say that someone is not heterosexual. In deciding what is not defamatory, a Producer really should check with a lawyer before making the statement. It is often not possible for those responsible for a production, who are very close to the material in question and may also be very liberal and broad-minded people, to see where the potential dangers lie. As a practical piece of advice, Producers who deal frequently in material which could lead to this sort of claim (such as news or current affairs, documentary and satirical programmes) need to be aware that lawyers are not usually in the business of guaranteeing that there is no risk. Lawyers will readily identify that there **is** a risk, and their advice will be to remove the offending material. The real art, in these situations, is to assess (as accurately as anyone can without the aid of a crystal ball) the **degree** of risk. Some lawyers are good at giving practical commercial advice about whether the risk is great or small, but at the end of the day it is the Producer/broadcaster who must make the decision as to whether the risk is worth taking – only those persons who are liable to be sued can decide whether they are prepared to take the chance. The risks are enormous. The cost of defending proceedings is immense. Defamation actions are heard by a jury which decides on the level of damages to be awarded, and this can result in very large awards being made (even though these tend to be reduced if the matter goes to appeal, when the amount is decided on by judges who are experienced in deciding what is proper compensation for the defamation in question).

Dangers of 'repeating' a libel

On the question of who is liable for defamation, the 'victim' can sue not only the persons responsible for the original statement, but anybody who repeats the libel by publishing it again. Thus it can be dangerous to report, by way of news, statements which have been made by the defendant to a libel action about the plaintiff.

Journalists seek to avoid this by making it clear that the statement about a person is something which has been 'alleged', thus making it clear that they themselves are not subscribing to the statement. However, the indiscriminate use of the word 'allegedly' might not be sufficient protection. In a satirical programme where the participants are in the habit of being offensive about public figures, if someone refers to a politician as 'allegedly' being an adulterer, this could well give the politician grounds for a defamation action, particularly if this is the first time that **anyone** has alleged that he has committed adultery.

Inadvertent libel

One particularly worrying aspect of this area of law is that it is perfectly possible for someone to sue even when he or she has been inadvertently referred to.

> For example, a fictional thriller depicts a young woman called Roberta Leigh, who is married to a doctor and who has three children. In the course of the story, she is shown to stifle one of her children with a pillow, but she claims that the death of the child is a 'cot death', and this is accepted by both the police and her family. Assume, however, that there exist several young married women called Roberta Leigh, who are all married to doctors, and who each have children. If one of those women has recently lost one of her children through cot death and, following the transmission of the thriller on television, she wakes up one morning to find the word 'murderess' spray-painted across her front door, she may well have the right to sue for defamation. This is so, despite the fact that the identification of her with the fictional character may have been purely inadvertent. It may be enough that she can show that a defamatory statement has been made, and that it has been understood by persons to whom it has been made (certain members of the viewing audience of the thriller) that the statement refers to her.

In this area, it is not just a problem if a real person's **name** is used. If the character in a fictional production is shown in circumstances from which a real person can still be identified, this can lead to a defamation action.

> For example, imagine a film set in modern Britain. The ruling monarch is shown as a King, whose name is George. He is depicted as a balding man with protruding ears and a slightly diffident manner, who is separated from his younger, glamorous and much more popular wife. He is also shown to have a strong interest in the environment, particularly in architecture. This character might seem familiar to some people, but if it were left at that, this would not necessarily present a legal problem. However, if the fictional 'King' were also shown to have

murdered his mother in order to succeed to the throne, and the production was shown not long after the Queen herself had sadly passed away in mysterious circumstances, the member of the Royal Family who succeeded her might well have some grounds for complaint!

This is a very extreme example. However, the principle remains the same even in examples less obvious than the one given above. Additionally, the identification between an unsavoury fictional character and a real person does not have to be one made by the general public at large. As long as it is reasonable to assume the persons knowing the 'victim' might make such an association, then the victim has the right to sue.

In this context, it is worth remarking that many people have relied on the fact that the Royal Family does not tend to sue in circumstances where their rights have been violated. This, however, is changing.

If defamation cannot be avoided in the production or a particular risk was simply overlooked, and a claim ensues, then there are defences (Chapter 15, pages 251–2). If all reasonable care has been taken, and the defamation was truly unintentional, then the Producer should be able to claim the cost of defending an action under the E&O insurance (Chapter 11, pages 196–200).

Additionally, the maker of the statement can reduce the damages to little or nothing if he is prepared to make an apology and offer to make amends in some suitable way. In this case, and certainly if the defamation was inadvertent and unintentional, the ultimate liability of the maker of the statement should be relatively small. Further comment on these aspects is contained in Chapter 15.

Privacy laws

At the time of writing, identification of a real person in a film or television production should only expose the Producer to legal action if it is defamatory (that is, if the character concerned is shown in an unfavourable light). However, there are moves afoot to introduce privacy laws into the UK and if these come into force, a situation similar to that which exists in other legal jurisdictions (most notably the US) may arise. In the US the mere **identification** of real people (whether deliberate or intentional) can lead to threatened or actual legal action for breach of rights of privacy and/or publicity.

AVOIDING LIABILITY

Negative checks

One of the ways to avoid any potential difficulties arising from the inadvertent identification of real people is to carry out so-called 'negative checks'. This is the process of checking available sources of information to establish whether people or companies shown in fictional material have names which resemble real life people or entities. One obvious source of information is telephone books. But problems can also arise with the use of telephone numbers and car licence plates. It may not be sufficient to establish the context in which the potentially identifying material appears is not defamatory. If the production has a potential sales abroad, particularly to the US, it is simply safer to avoid any possible identification with real people or their property. For more expensive productions, it may be worth spending part of the budget on the services of specialist checking agencies (like De Forest Research in Los Angeles) who can check all names and other potentially identifying references against a substantial number of information sources throughout the world.

Discussions with the writer of the script

In addition to reviewing material which has been written (or has even already been filmed) to ensure that there are no problems, the Producer should also have discussed with the writer (certainly in fictional productions) what sources he or she used for the script.

> For example W, a writer, writes a script about a small boy who has been taken into care, and who is then placed with foster parents. His real father kidnaps him and kills him rather than return the boy to his foster parents. W quite blithely signs an agreement for his services as scriptwriter which states that the script is **original** and is not based on any existing material. However, in fact he has written it based on a newspaper article which he read a few years before, although in the article it was the boy's mother who kidnapped and murdered the boy. The father of the real boy whose story was reported in the newspaper could claim to have been defamed, if he can establish that he could have been identified from the fictional depiction of the original events, and that this would lead to the assumption that it was he (and not the boy's mother) who was responsible for the boy's death.

Problems such as this could be avoided by early discussion with the writer, because if it is known what the writer has done, it may be possible to change the script in advance. With this particular example, that may not be feasible, since the real heart of the story would not be capable of being changed.

> As an alternative example, imagine that W has based his script on real life events, to the knowledge and at the request of the Producer, since the production is a so-called 'docu-drama'. However, to save time and trouble, instead of searching the original sources, W has used, for reference purposes, a book written about the real life events by a

journalist, J. W's script uses large chunks of the interviews printed in J's book as part of the dialogue in the script, and W has also written a voice narration for the script which follows, very nearly word for word, descriptions used in J's book. **This** is a very big problem indeed, because W has committed extensive infringements of J's copyright by using a substantial amount of J's work without permission. If the film or programme has already been made, the Producer would have no choice but to approach J, after the event, for a licence of the film/television rights in J's book. J is obviously entitled to refuse to grant a licence or, perhaps almost as bad for the Producer, may only be prepared to grant a licence in return for an extortionate sum of money.

On the other hand, if it is discovered in time what W has done, it may be possible to commission another script from another writer, making sure that the new writer works from the original research and has never read J's book. This, although still expensive (involving having to pay another writer a script fee), is considerably less expensive than the consequences where the truth is not discovered in time.

Of course, dealing with writers in this context is an extremely delicate business. In the second example given above, the end result of discussions with the writer might be to show that the writer is in breach of contract. This will result in considerable loss to the writer. In this example, even where the truth is discovered in time, W would probably be required to pay the fee payable to the second writer to be commissioned to produce an original script, because W would be in breach of the warranty that the material he wrote was original (except insofar as it was required to be based on materials supplied to him by P). In any case, the legal issues involved may not always be so clear-cut. Even where writers are not 'at fault', they are often extremely unhappy about compromising or adapting their work to alleviate risks which lawyers have identified. Writers also do not appreciate being 'interrogated' about how they have got their ideas.

There is no easy answer to the problem: all that needs to be said is that anyone who has been through the expense and misery of legal action in these circumstances would not hesitate to broach these issues with writers. Anything is acceptable if it will help to avoid ending up in court. Writers themselves should bear this in mind. If they are 'at fault' it is better to be found out early, when the damage is relatively small, than later, when their liability could lead to them losing everything they have.

Release forms

Lastly, where it is known that real life characters can be identified, particularly in a so-called 'docu-drama' which presents a dramatized account of actual events, the Producer should, if at all feasible, try to persuade the people concerned in the event to sign a form of 'release' if they are to be portrayed in the production.

This is a document not dissimilar to the sort of thing which performers or interviewees should be asked to sign (Chapter 9, pages 148–9, and Appendix H). However, for a larger scale drama production a more detailed agreement may be appropriate, and if there is any American involvement at the production stage, the Americans would certainly prefer a much more detailed document to cover the situation. In fact, the agreement will not be dissimilar to a rights agreement in an underlying copyright work, since the process is very much the same: the individual is granting to the Producer the right to film a production based on his or her life, agreeing to co-operate in that process and, most importantly, to refrain from exercising any of the rights he or she would otherwise have. As with the author of an underlying work, the individual may want rights of approval over how the story is developed in the script and on screen, and may wish to be credited in a consultative capacity. An example of a very simple release form which might be used in these circumstances is found in Appendix D.

Other legal danger areas

The main risks which have already been covered can arise in relation to any type of production. However, depending on the nature of the production, there are other laws for a Producer to steer round. The most obvious examples are:

- obscenity and indecency laws;
- the Official Secrets Act;
- contempt of court.

Obscenity

This expression is used to refer to two areas of law relevant to films and programmes, which are:

- obscenity (any film/programme will be obscene if it has a 'tendency to deprave and corrupt' viewers);
- indecency (in that the material is of a kind which ordinary people find sexually offensive).

To publish obscene material is a criminal offence under the Obscene Publications Act 1959. This act applies to feature films **and** television programmes (although it is unlikely that, given the burden on broadcasters to meet the standards imposed on them by the government or by the ITC, any material which could lead to prosecution would ever be broadcast or even commissioned in the first place) and 'publishing' means exploitation by any means, such as video distribution.

Feature films released in this country are censored by the British Board of Film Classification ('BBFC'). Thus, although this book considers what would be regarded under the 1959 Act as obscene, it also describes what kind of matters the BBFC takes into account in granting (or refusing to grant) a certificate.

What is obscene?

An article is treated as being **obscene** under the 1959 Act:

> If its effect is, taken as a whole, such as to tend to deprave and corrupt persons who are likely, in all the circumstances, to read, see or hear the matter contained or embodied in it.

Three points should be made.

- 'To deprave and corrupt' means very much more than simply offending or shocking.
- It must be shown that the material will tend to have this effect on persons **likely** to see it (not just people who **might** see it) and on a significant proportion of the likely audience (not just a susceptible few).

  For example, if a film is being shown in premises which make it clear that 'adults only' are allowed admission, the fact that someone who is technically still a child **might** be able to bluff their way on to the premises and see the material would not render the publishers of the material liable on an obscenity charge, if the usual habituees of the premises were not likely to be 'depraved and corrupted' by it.
- Lastly, the tendency to have the effect of depraving and corrupting **must** be the **dominant** effect of the article as a whole. A film will not necessarily be found to be obscene if any **parts** of it might have the effect complained of, if the film taken as a whole does not.

It is a defence to a charge of obscenity that the publication of the article (even if obscene by definition) is found to be 'for the public good'. In the case of films or television programmes, this defence would apply if they are shown to be 'in the interests of drama, opera, ballet or any other art, or for literature or learning'.

Prosecutions for obscenity against films or television programmes can only be brought with the consent of the Director of Public Prosecutions. However, for films, prosecution is not the only undesirable occurrence, since it is also open to local councils to refuse to licence screenings of films within their area (although they generally rely on the verdict of the BBFC and will show the film if a BBFC certificate has been granted).

Indecency

Offences of 'indecency' are committed by doing something which an ordinary decent man or woman would find shocking or revolting. Whether or not something is indecent is viewed by the courts in the light of generally prevailing public morals. For the reasons given above, 'indecent' material is unlikely to find its way into a television programme at all; and for feature films, indecent sections will not usually get past the BBFC.

In this last context, it is perhaps worth mentioning the offences of blasphemy, which are committed where the indecency applies to subjects of a religious nature. It is almost impossible to predict what will or will not be found to be blasphemous, particularly as the intention of the publisher in this respect is irrelevant. It can only be said with certainty that blasphemy can only be committed by indecency in relation to the Anglican religion. Therefore, persons of other religious persuasions have no criminal sanctions against those whom they feel have insulted their religion. Prosecutions for blasphemy are extremely rare.

The British Board of Film Classification

The BBFC is a body founded by the film and video industries which examines films and videos (in return for a fee) and certifies as to their suitability for viewing by particular parts of the public.

The BBFC is an independent, non-governmental body. Since it has no official status in relation to **films**, its certificates do not give immunity from prosecution. However, it **does** have official status in relation to **videos**, under the Video Recordings Act 1984, which requires that almost all videos are submitted for classification as being suitable for distribution, particularly with regard to people of particular ages.

Videos exempt from the classification requirements are those which, 'taken as a whole':

- are for information, education or instruction;
- deal with sport, music or religion;
- are video games.

However, the exemption does not apply if any of the following are shown:

- human sexual activity;
- torture of or gross violence towards humans or animals;
- human genital organs or excretory or urinary functions.

The maximum penalty for supplying non-exempt unclassified videos is very high, which is why distributors almost invariably submit their videos for classification. Additionally, video material which has been originally shown on television is not automatically exempt from having to be classified.

The classifications are:

- 'U' – UNIVERSAL: suitable for all;
- 'PG' – PARENTAL GUIDANCE: some scenes may be unsuitable for young children;
- '12' – suitable only for persons of 12 years and over (this category was introduced in 1989);
- '15' – suitable only for persons of 15 years and over;
- '18' – suitable only for persons of 18 years and over;
- 'R 18' – FOR RESTRICTED DISTRIBUTION ONLY (namely through specially licensed cinemas or sex shops to which no one under 18 is admitted).

The video industry has asked for an additional category, to be used for works to be stocked on the children's shelves at video shops, which is:

- 'Uc' – UNIVERSAL: particularly suitable for children.

As well as it being an offence to supply unclassified videos, it is also an offence to supply videos with the wrong labels, or to persons outside the classified age group. The penalty is restricted to a fine, but it can be up to £20 000. In addition, the police can seize videos if they have reasonable grounds to suspect an offence under the Video Recordings Act.

In relation to films, the BBFC may well require censorship in the case of:

- scenes where disturbing and/or explicit violence is depicted;
- scenes where drug taking is shown (if there is any suggestion that it is trivialized or glamorized);
- scenes where sex is shown in a violent context (if it is eroticized or endorsed or trivialized);
- indecent scenes involving the participation of children;
- scenes the showing of which has involved cruelty to animals;
- scenes demonstrating criminal techniques (such as breaking into cars).

The penalty for refusing to cut a film in accordance with the requirements of the BBFC is that a restrictive certificate may be imposed or no certificate at all may be given. The 'appeal' from this is, in theory, that the film company can submit the film to the local licensing authority to see if it takes a different view from the BBFC. This is unlikely to happen. Although it has been said that the BBFC has no official status in classifying films, it is undoubtedly true that submitting to the BBFC's censorship ensures that a film will have the widest possible distribution, because licensing bodies will regard prosecution and public outcry as unlikely. The BBFC also states that it is prepared to read scripts in advance (for British film makers) to advise on the probable category of classification 'and any other factors which may prove relevant', although this does not commit the BBFC, if the way the script is treated in the process of filming raises unforeseen difficulties.

The Official Secrets Act 1989

The Official Secrets Act makes it an offence:

- for those who have agreed to be bound by it to disclose information relating to national security and intelligence;
- for others to publish information which they know is protected by the Act, if it is also shown by the prosecution that those persons had reason to believe that the publication would be damaging to the security services or to the interests of the UK.

Information covered by the Act is that which relates to:

- security or intelligence;
- defence;
- international relations;
- crime (in the sense that information about it is likely to result in an offence being committed, or assisting the escape of a prisoner, or impeding the prevention or detection of offences).

For a Producer to be liable under the Act for publishing information, the information must originally have come from a servant of the Crown or a government contractor.

Contempt of court

The UK courts have the power to punish acts which amount to 'contempt of court', in that these acts might unfairly or unduly influence the course of pending or current litigation.

Thus, Producers of factual films/programmes must be careful to stay within the bounds of what is allowed, when reporting matters which are being considered by the courts.

Contempt, though never tried by a judge and jury (but only by a High Court Judge) is generally punishable as a crime. The penalty is a maximum of two years' imprisonment and/or a fine (of an unlimited amount). However, the judge may additionally order an injunction against films/ television programmes or publications which it is feared will be in contempt. Most aspects of contempt law are now covered by statute law: the Contempt of Court Act 1981.

A publisher of material (and this expression covers Producers **and** broadcasters of programmes) will be found to be in contempt if:

- the material creates a substantial risk that the course of justice in particular proceedings will be seriously impeded or prejudiced and, if this risk is then shown to exist, it is irrelevant that the publisher did not intend this effect; **or**
- the material is deliberately in contempt, in that the publisher actually intended to influence the proceedings; **or**
- the material contains an account of the deliberations of any jury coming to its verdict; **or**
- the publisher has disobeyed a court order.

The two most important of these situations are the first and the last. The last situation will arise usually when a court has placed restrictions on reporting the proceedings, and a Producer publishes material in defiance of the restrictions.

The first situation (often referred to as 'strict liability' contempt) is the one most likely to be a problem for Producers when considering whether certain material should be included in, for example, a current affairs programme. Note that it must be proved **beyond reasonable doubt** that the publication creates a **substantial risk** that proceedings will be **seriously prejudiced**.

This is quite a heavy burden of proof to discharge, so there is still a certain amount of latitude for journalists. Certainly where proceedings are being tried by a judge alone (as is the case for civil actions) a court considering whether contempt has been committed will not find very readily that the judge in the civil proceedings would be influenced by outside material. This is because judges are supposed to be conditioned to ignore everything except the evidence they hear in court when coming to a decision.

However, where a jury is concerned, it is generally assumed that they will be more easily influenced by media speculation, so great care has to be exercised when deciding what to report about cases to be tried by a jury. The same is true when the proceedings are being heard by lay magistrates (who are not lawyers).

Strict liability contempt can only be committed if the case is actually 'active' – in criminal cases, that is when (and after) the first official step in the process of prosecution has been taken. In civil cases, it is when a date has been fixed for the trial of the matter (even though that date may be many months away).

In criminal cases, it is also unwise to assume that the matter can be freely commented on after the verdict has been given, if the verdict was that the defendant was guilty. This is because there is often a delay between the verdict and the pronouncing of the sentence, during which adverse comment may be taken to have affected the decision of the sentencing body.

Certain acts should definitely be avoided. These are:

- publishing material which attacks witnesses; or (in serious cases) making payment to witness in a trial in return for a story or statement or interview;
- predicting the result of a trial;
- publishing the photograph or likeness of a defendant in a criminal case, where the identity of the defendant is a matter of dispute at the trial;
- publishing unfavourable information about the defendant's life or previous convictions.

Defences

The main defence is that the material was published 'as or as part of a discussion in good faith of public affairs or other matters of general public interest . . . if the risk of impediment or prejudice is merely incidental to the discussion.' This is known as the 'public interest' defence. For this defence to be available, the publisher/broadcaster must:

- have acted in good faith (namely, not improperly);
- have referred to the proceedings (or matters under consideration in those proceedings) in the context of wider issues.

It is also a defence if the publisher/broadcaster did not know and had no reason to believe that the case in question was actively proceeding. However, anyone claiming this defence must show that he took all reasonable care to find out the position.

Lastly, if the material is a fair and accurate report of the proceedings, publishing it cannot be in contempt even if it does prejudice the case.

Broadcasters' statutory duties

The responsibilities of broadcasters in this country (although differing in detail from one broadcaster to another) and the restrictions generally placed on broadcasters are fundamentally the same for all the main broadcasters.

The BBC has to abide by the requirements of the Licence and Agreement laid down by the government under which (in addition to the Royal Charter under which the BBC is incorporated) the BBC is authorized to operate as a public service broadcaster.

The ITV companies and Channel Four are required under the Broadcasting Act 1990 to observe the codes and standards devised by the Independent Television Commission ('ITC').

In addition, the Broadcasting Act 1990 established:

- the Broadcasting Complaints Commission ('BCC');

- the Broadcasting Standards Council ('BSC').

These bodies have jurisdiction over all broadcasters requiring a licence under the Broadcasting Act (ITV companies and Channel Four, as well as radio broadcasters) and the BBC.

The BCC's function is to consider and adjudicate on complaints of:

- unjust or unfair treatment in programmes;
- unwarranted infringement of privacy in or in connection with the obtaining of material included in programmes.

The BSC has the responsibility of drawing up a code giving guidance as to:

- practices to be followed in connection with the portrayal of **violence and sexual conduct** in programmes;
- standards of taste and decency for programmes generally.

The BSC monitors programme content and adjudicates on complaints where there has been an alleged breach of this code.

The effects of these codes as well as of the licences and other legal restrictions is that broadcasters have to take very great care in relation to areas such as:

- offences to good taste and decency;
- portrayal of sex and/or violence;
- impartiality, accuracy and straight dealings;
- party political and parliamentary broadcasting;
- national security;
- terrorism;
- crime, anti-social and imitative behaviour, defamation, contempt of court;
- Official Secrets Act;
- images of very brief duration;
- competition and reward shows;
- phone-ins and premium rate telephone services;
- charities;
- sponsorship;
- religion;
- communication with the public;
- commercial references and product placement.

The BBC publishes comprehensive Producers' guidelines for independent and in-house Producers to make them aware of the standards which the BBC must meet. The other broadcasters will generally issue somewhat similar material, and will always be very keen to give guidance and advice to Producers. It should be remembered, however, that it will be a warranty in the agreement between a Producer commissioned by a broadcaster, and the broadcaster, that the programme will comply with all codes and guidelines to which the broadcaster is subject. A prudent Producer should therefore require in the contract that the broadcaster will give full and accurate advice on those codes and guidelines from time to time as needed by the Producer, and that the Producer should not be liable for any failure to comply with the warranty, to the extent that the broadcaster has failed to give such advice.

The ultimate sanction to broadcasters if they breach a statutory responsibility would be the loss of their right to broadcast (by the termination of their licence), but lesser sanctions exist, which broadcasters are still very keen to avoid. It therefore behoves any Producer making programmes for broadcasters to get copies of the codes or guidelines by which those broadcasters operate and bear them in mind at all times.

<table>
<tr><td>**13**</td><td># Distribution agreements</td></tr>
</table>

ESSENTIAL ELEMENTS TO AN AGREEMENT WITH A DISTRIBUTOR

The exploitation (commonly referred to as 'distribution') of films and programmes is generally undertaken by companies which specialize in this activity. Thus the distributor will often be a separate entity from the original rights owner of the copyright in a film or television programme which has the potential to be exploited.

The owner of the rights in the production will therefore, in these circumstances, have to pass the necessary rights to the distributor to enable the distributor to exploit the film on the owner's behalf. This will be a **licence** or **assignment** of copyright. The difference between a licence and assignment has been discussed in Chapter 9, pages 138–41. The distributor should not normally require an **assignment** of copyright to it (unless the distributor has paid a suitable price to purchase all rights **outright**). If the deal is that a rights owner should receive, throughout the period during which the distributor is authorized to sell the production, a share of the profits realized from such sales, then the rights owner should only grant a licence. Furthermore, the owner should not give up the right to terminate that licence. The threat of termination not only gives the distributor an incentive to perform as agreed, but also gives the rights owner what may be its only protection if the distributor becomes insolvent and goes into liquidation or receivership.

The distributor will sometimes argue that it should take an assignment of the copyright, on the basis that this will enable the distributor to deal more effectively with copyright infringers and pirates. This is the argument proffered by the BBC when appointing BBC Enterprises Limited as distributor, in which case it prefers that Enterprises has an assignment of the rights.

This argument has **some** force when the production is being exploited internationally, in that in some countries only the copyright **owner** can sue if there has been an infringement of copyright. In this country **exclusive** licensees are entitled to sue as if they were the copyright owner, so they do not need to take an assignment to be able to protect their exclusive rights from third parties. However, the problem where only the owner can sue can usually be dealt with by the owner authorizing the distributor to take legal action in the name of and on behalf of the copyright owner (this can be done most conveniently in the agreement granting the distribution rights – 'the distribution agreement'). The owner may also like to take the additional precaution of reserving a right of final decision as to whether legal action should be taken as, although the distributor will initially pay the legal bill, the costs would eventually be recouped by the distributor from the exploitation revenues as 'a distribution expense' (page 228 below), thus potentially decreasing the profitability of the production. It is therefore the rights owner who will lose out, if legal action is taken when it cannot be commercially justified.

The rights, under copyright, which the distributor needs to distribute the production are:

- to make copies of the film/television programme;
- to distribute those copies to end users (cinemas, broadcasters etc.);
- to cut or edit the film/television programme;
- to authorize others where necessary to do the above three things (such authorization being technically referred to as 'sub-licensing').

The reason why the distributor may need to authorize others to exercise its rights are several – for example, where worldwide rights (or rights in territories beyond those where the distributor is capable of operating personally) are granted, the distributor may have to appoint a 'sub-distributor' in another territory. The sub-distributor will usually be a local company with the right expertise and connections to get better deals in that territory. Alternatively, a distributor may be granting rights to a home video distributor (who will therefore need to make copies and/or edit the production for censorship purposes. When granting rights to a broadcaster, the distributor may have to authorize the broadcaster to make copies so that the original material can be used in a broadcast format, or to cut or edit the programme so that it fits both scheduling requirements of the broadcaster and the legal standards which the broadcaster has to meet.

As to the extent of rights which will be granted to the distributor, this will differ depending on the expertise of the distributor. It may be authorized to sell **primary rights** alone, or primary and **secondary rights**.

Primary rights are the **audio-visual** exhibition and transmission rights in the production itself. This will include extract rights and video rights. The term 'primary rights' is therefore fairly self-explanatory – it is the main way in which one would expect to exploit a film or television production.

Secondary rights (sometimes called ancillary rights) are rights exercisable independently of the film's or television's physical material. They include the right to:

- sell merchandise using the production's name/logo/characters or other identifying material;
- to publish novelizations of a screenplay;
- to sell the format and changed format rights.

It is often the case that primary and secondary rights will not be granted to one and the same distributor, as the expertise required for exploitation of secondary rights is quite different to that needed to make the film and television sales. However, where the distributor is very large and experienced, this may not be a concern. Further details on the exploitation of secondary rights is contained in Chapter 14.

It may be helpful to comment in more detail on the separate rights granted to the distributor under copyright.

Making copies

The more copies there are in existence, the greater the chances of them getting into the wrong hands and enabling people to make unauthorized use of them. Any distribution/licence agreement should therefore restrict the right to make copies to the extent absolutely necessary for the proper exploitation of the rights granted; and the agreement should also require the return or destruction of all copies made when the rights granted come to an end.

For example, D, a distributor, grants to B, a foreign broadcaster, the right to transmit a television programme up to twice in B's territory during a period of three years commencing:

- on the date of the agreement between B and D;
- on the date of actual delivery to B of the production (whichever is later).

The material which D delivers to B might not be in the format which B needs to enable it to broadcast, so naturally B must be authorized to make copies of the material. B should be required by D:

- to make copies only as strictly necessary for broadcast (i.e. only a certain number and no more, unless one of the copies B needs is lost or damaged);
- to return the material to D after a time period just long enough to enable B to make the necessary copies;
- not to part with copies in B's possession to any third party;
- either to return to D or (more probably) to destroy B's copies when B's rights come to an end. The choice will usually be D's and if it

chooses destruction, D will generally require some evidence that B has actually done this (such as a signed certificate attesting to the destruction, the signatory being either an officer/director of B, or if D is particularly suspicious of B, an independent third party).

Cutting/editing rights

A distributor will need the right to cut or edit the production, and more usually to allow others to do so, because end users may be subject to certain requirements which, if they cannot be met, mean that the production cannot be exploited.

For example, a broadcaster has scheduling requirements. It may have to insert advertisements at regular intervals and it will broadcast within regular 'slots', such as by the hour. The production must be made to fit within those slots, and must be cut to allow commercials to be inserted. Equally, the end user will be under certain legal constraints as to the nature of the material which can be exhibited/broadcast in that end user's territory (Chapter 12, *Script and content clearance*). However, the rights owner may find it prudent to restrict the distributor's rights to cut, or to authorize others to cut the production, to these particular reasons, rather than giving unlimited permission. Perhaps in addition, the rights owner should require that cuts for censorship or legal reasons can only be made if backed up by the advice of independent lawyers; and that cuts for any other reason (where permitted in the first place) should be subject to specific consultation or even approval with the rights owner, where the cuts are more than minor, or result in more than a set amount of minutes in length being taken out of the production.

The obligations of a distributor

The obligations which a distributor generally assumes are:

- to sell the film/production;
- to collect revenue from the sales;
- to account for that revenue to the rights owner;
- to pay use fees and residuals which become payable as a result of the sales made by D;
- to publicize and advertise the film/production, to maximize its chances of being exploited;
- to see that the credit obligations which the rights owner has, in relation to contributors of the production, are respected.

Some further comment on each of these is necessary.

Obligation to sell

Distributors will not, if they are sensible, generally undertake an unquali-fied obligation to try to realize the maximum income from the exploitation of the film. After all, no distributor can guarantee sales – it depends on the production, as well as the current requirements of potential buyers. Distributors will not usually even agree to use **best endeavours** to sell it. The kind of thing which normally appears in distribution agreements is an obligation to use 'reasonable endeavours consistent with generally accepted sound commercial practice' to sell the production and to seek to make money from it.

Obligation to collect revenue

It would be sensible of the rights owner to insist that any sales made by the distributor must be at 'arm's length'. This means that the sales must be to end users with whom the distributor has no close connection, such as being part of the same group of companies and therefore owned by the same person. It also means that the terms of the sale must be those which would be obtainable in the open market. Alternatively, if the rights owner **does** permit the distributor to contract with a connected company, this should be on condition that the terms are equivalent to 'arm's length'.

> For example D, a distributor, is granted all rights of exploitation in the film in the UK by the producer, P. D happens to be part of a group of companies in the same group as another company, V, a home video distribution company. If D is itself not equipped to operate in its own right as a distributor of home videos, it makes sense for D to grant these rights to someone who is. However, while D has a natural incentive to grant these rights to V, D must be discouraged from 'improving' the situation for its parent company, by doing a deal with V which will involve V paying less for the rights than any normal video distributor would do. In the distribution agreement with D, therefore, P will want to ensure that D is prevented from granting these rights to V except on terms acceptable to P. This can be done by stating that no rights may be granted to an 'associated' company without P's prior consent, both as to the actual identity of the company and the financial and other terms on which that company is authorized to exploit the rights.

Inclusive commissions

Another sensible precaution when granting distribution rights is to state that if an associated company is appointed as a sub-distributor in another territory, that sub-distributor's commission has to come out of the head distributor's commission. If this were not the case, then the distributor could maximize income within the group of companies to which it belongs by granting rights to a foreign distributor which is still part of the same group. If the foreign distributor takes a commission before sending money back to the head distributor, who then takes a further commission, the income paid to the rights owner is considerably less than it ought to be. (This, incidentally, was the ruse operated by Elton John's original music publisher – music publishers being to music what distributors are to film and television programmes. This led to Elton John bringing and winning a celebrated court case, on the grounds that he had been deceived out of his profit share of income from the overseas exploitation of his songs, since commission had been effectively charged twice by what amounted to the same entity.)

It is actually quite common, in any case, to require international distributors to agree that their commission rates are all-inclusive, so that if they appoint sub-distributors in any other territory, then the commission payable for the sub-distributor is payable out of the head distributor's commission.

Foreign exchange controls

On the subject of overseas income, the distribution agreement should contain a so-called 'blocked currency clause'. This deals with the situation where the money paid by a foreign end user cannot actually be removed from the country where it has been paid, owing to local exchange control regulations (such as in South Africa and other African countries). A blocked currency clause usually states that income which would normally be payable to the rights owner, but which cannot be paid for any governmental or legal reason, should be paid by the distributor into a bank account at a bank in the territory where the money is situated, the account having been opened by the distributor in the name of the rights owner. Having paid the money into the account, the distributor's responsibility to make payment of that sum would then cease. At least then, the money will belong to the rights owner, so that he can either claim it if the relevant exchange controls were ever to be relaxed, or draw on the bank account to spend the money when he is actually present in the relevant country.

Distributor's power to take legal proceedings to enforce payments by end users

The distributor may or may not be authorized under the distribution agreement to take legal action if:

• an end user fails to pay the agreed price for the rights granted;

- the film or programme is 'pirated' by an authorized person (i.e. the copyright is infringed).

In either case, if the rights owner wanted to try to put the distributor under an **obligation** to sue anybody, the owner would have to agree that the costs of the litigation come out of distribution income (as a distribution expense). The rights owner must also agree to meet any part of the cost which cannot be recovered from sales income. In normal practice, it is probably better to leave the question of what action should be taken until the circumstances actually arise. The costs and uncertainty of litigation being what they are, it is commercially reckless to take legal action without giving thought beforehand both as to the likely chances of winning and, more practically, as to the chances of getting any money out of the losing side, even if the case is won. However, in the distribution agreement, the distributor should at least be required to inform the rights owner as soon as it becomes aware of any infringement (or any other fact which might cause the rights owner to take legal action) and to give all necessary help and assistance in relation to any action which the rights owner may want to take. Being informed of infringement immediately will enable the owner to take a sensible decision without potentially harmful delay. In infringement actions, speed can make all the difference between success and failure.

Protection against potential insolvency

The rights owner runs a risk, where the distributor is collecting distribution income and is allowed to mix it with all the distributor's other income before having to account, that the distributor may become insolvent before it **does** account to the rights owner. As explained in Chapter 6, page 99, the rights owner, as an unsecured creditor, may not be able to recover everything which the distributor owes to it (although it should naturally exercise any rights of termination it may have as soon as possible, to put an end to the distributor's right to receive further money). One possible way of trying to protect the rights owner's share of money due to it from income received by the distributor is to require the distributor to open a separate account, in the name of the distributor **and** the rights owner, for the income received from sales of the rights owner's production, and into which no other income can be paid. The distributor would of course be entitled to take out its commission and expenses, but if it became insolvent at any time, the rights owner could claim that it was entitled, as a beneficiary to the trust account, to its share of the income, and not as an ordinary creditor (Chapter 7, page 112). This is not a foolproof suggestion – for a start, not all distributors would agree to it, because it would involve them losing part of their cash-flow (as they would not be entitled to use the rights owner's share of income before they were due to account for it).

Secondly, liquidators or receivers appointed over the assets of an insolvent distributor who had set up such an account would naturally try to argue that the trust was not effective. Where there are any concerns about the financial strength of a distributor, it is worthwhile for the rights owner to take legal advice, before entering into the distribution agreement, on what precautions can and should be taken against the distributor's insolvency.

OBLIGATION TO ACCOUNT

Accounting periods

It is impractical for a large distributor to pay over money to a rights owner as soon as it is received. This is because money is generally being received from very many sources, expenses are being incurred at the same time, and there needs to be time to allow the distributor to sort out its accounts. The distributor will certainly not wish to part with the money it receives from the exploitation of the production until it has had ample opportunity to deduct its distribution expenses. It is therefore common practice for the distributor to account (namely, to pay the rights owner's share) at regular intervals; usually these intervals are at every three months during the first two years after the production has been made available to the distributor, and then every six months (because it is assumed that after the first two years the flow of income will have slowed down). The account will be in respect of sums actually received during the relevant time period (for example, three months) which is often referred to in contracts as 'the accounting period', as well as expenses incurred during that period. In addition, since the distributor needs some time to work out at the end of the accounting period what has been received and what has been paid out, it is normal for the rights owners to be paid after a short delay following the end of the accounting period. This 'waiting period' can be between thirty and ninety days after the accounting period has ended. Ninety days (which is another three months) is really excessive in this day and age, when computers have considerably eased and speeded the process of accounting and accounting for income. Sixty days is probably still too long, but it is quite common for rights owners and distributors to compromise on forty-five days.

Statement of account

The distributor should also be required to supply a written statement of account setting out all information which the rights owner will require to see how the sums payable to it have been calculated. The distributor will have deducted both its commission and its expenses, but sometimes the rate of commission differs (for instance, there may be a higher rate of commission on sales to US syndicated television than there is on sales to US network television). In such cases, the sources of the income have to be differentiated in the statement of account.

Distribution expenses

Distribution expenses should also be stated in the account, although they may not be set out in fully itemized detail. The distribution agreement, when dealing with expenses, may actually specify in great detail what type of expenditure will qualify as a distribution expense (and a typical example is set out in Appendix I). In shorter distribution agreements, it is usually stated that deductible expenses must be those which have been 'properly and reasonably' spent in exploiting the production. This wording theoretically gives the rights owner the opportunity to protest if excessive money is spent. The distributor may often be selling the production in conjunction with other films which do not belong to the rights owner (and this will be the case at a major film and television festival or sales market). The distribution agreement should therefore set out some fair basis for sharing out or apportioning the distributor's expenses in relation to the rights owner's production. In the absence of some kind of apportionment process, there will be nothing to stop the distributor, if it has only succeeded in selling the rights owner's production (and not the other films or programmes which it was seeking to sell on the same occasion) from setting its entire expenditure against the income realized from the sale.

Cross-collateralization

When recouping its expenses from income, the distributor will naturally wish to recoup **all** its expenditure from **all** income, even though the expenditure may largely have resulted from trying to make one kind of sale (perhaps unsuccessfully) whereas the income which has come from another sale may have involved the distributor in very little expense.

However, where the types of sales are very different (for example, primary rights as opposed to secondary rights if all these rights have been granted to the same distributor) the rights owner may wish to stipulate that the expenses incurred in one kind of exploitation cannot be deducted from income resulting from another kind of exploitation. In other words the rights owner will be prohibiting 'cross-collateralization' of distribution expenses. The rights owner may or may not be able to achieve this. However, where it grants rights in more than one **production** to a distributor, it should certainly try to prohibit cross-collateralization of expenses from selling one film against income from the sale of another film. In this instance, the distributor should be obliged to keep separate accounts for each film (although with some kind of apportionment mechanism for expenses incurred in trying to sell two or more of the rights owner's films on the same occasion, such as at a festival or sales market).

Withholding tax

Another deduction which the distributor may have to make before paying income to the rights owner (if the rights owner is in another country) is 'withholding tax'. This is a tax usually required to be deducted (in this country, at the basic rate) under the law of most territories, from payments being made to copyright owners abroad, in return for the use of the copyright. The payor pays over the amount deducted to the local tax authority and presents the rights owner (the payee) with a certificate of the amount deducted. The payee can then give the certificate to his own tax authority, to set against his tax bill, so that in theory the rights owner does not have to pay tax twice on the same income. However, most countries have entered into 'double taxation treaties' with other countries of the world (for example, there is such a treaty in force between the UK and the USA). Under these treaties, each of the two countries agree that if one of its nationals pays income to someone in the other territory on which withholding tax is payable, the rate of withholding tax is reduced (usually to a rate as low as 10%). Distributors and rights owners can only take advantage of a double taxation treaty (assuming that there is one in force between their respective territories) if the distributor applies for clearance to pay at the reduced rate from its own tax authority. Clearance will only be given if that tax authority receives a clean bill of health from the tax authority in the country where the payee is resident, to the effect that the payee is a good and honest taxpayer.

Rights to query the statement of account

The rights owner should not put itself in the position where it has no choice but to accept the information contained on the statement of account. First of all, the rights owner should require the distributor, under the terms of the distribution agreement, to keep proper, accurate books and records of account relating to all transactions on the production. These books and records should be maintained separately from the distributor's other accounts. Additionally, the rights owner should take the right to inspect those books and records and to take copies of the records if necessary. The distributor should be required to pay up the amount of any shortfall found by any such inspection, together with interest calculated from the date when it should have been paid at an interest rate of two or three per cent above one of the clearing bank's minimum rate. Additionally the distributor should pay the cost of the inspection if the shortfall is found to be more than a certain percentage of what should have been paid (between 5% and 10%).

In these circumstances, the distributor in turn will want:

- the number of inspections to be limited to one or at most two in any year;
- the inspection to be carried out by reputable independent accountants and to be limited purely to books and records relating to the film/ television programme in question;
- its obligation to have to pay the cost of inspection to be limited to circumstances where the shortfall is 10% or more of what should have been paid;
- a 'limitation period' on the right to inspect. For example, the rights owner should not have the right to question any statement of account rendered more than a specified period of time previously (say, two years before the date on which a request for inspection is made). If the opportunity for inspection is not limited, the distributor would never be able to dispose of its accounting records, which any business prefers to do after their records have reached a certain age.

Obligation to pay use fees/residuals

As will be apparent from Chapter 9, the sales of productions (certainly television productions) can lead to further 'use fees', also known as residuals, becoming payable to contributors to the production, and in particular to actors and writers. It is usual to require the distributor to pay these fees as and when they become due (which is when the relevant sale of the production is made). However, the rights owner will be required in turn to provide full information as to what further use fees will become payable and when. The cost of these use fees will be deductible by the distributor as a distribution expense.

In this context, it is particularly important for the rights owner to require an **indemnity** from the distributor, if residuals are not paid when they should be. If the rights owner is the Producer, it will be liable for the failure to pay, and the disgruntled distributor will therefore sue the Producer. The Producer will have no defence to such an action and will therefore probably have to pay both the amount of the residuals **and** the contributor's legal costs. If the Producer does not have an indemnity from the distributor it may not be able to recover the costs from the distributor, even if it can sue for the amount of the residuals which it has had to pay. (Chapter 4 contains further details on how indemnities work.)

Obligation to advertise/publicize

Again, the cost to the distributor of doing this will be deductible as a distribution expense.

Obligation to accord credits

The rights owner will have incurred obligations to third parties that certain persons will be accorded credits on screen, and possibly also (depending on the importance of the contributor to the production) in major paid advertising. The distributor must therefore be placed under an obligation to honour the rights owner's duties in this respect, by:

- not cutting credits which appear on screen, or authorizing any end user to do so;
- ensuring that in major advertising issued by the distributor, credits are accorded to those who are entitled to a major paid advertising credit.

In relation to paid advertising, the distributor will naturally require full details of what credits must be accorded and in what manner (for example what size, what prominence, what position – whether above or below the title of the production, or wherever the director is mentioned etc.).

The distributor will also exclude its obligation to see that credits are accorded in relation to types of advertising such as:

- group, list or teaser advertising, publicity or exploitation;
- special advertising, publicity or exploitation specially relating to any of the other personnel who were involved in the production;
- any exploitation, publication or fictionalization of the story, screenplay or other literary or musical material on which the production has been based, or by-products (such as records) or commercial tie-ups;
- advertising relating to the television exhibition of the production (where it is a feature film);
- trailer or other advertising on the cinema screen, radio or television;
- institutional or other advertising or publicity not relating primarily to the production;
- so-called 'award ads' (including references to consideration, nomination or congratulation for an award being made) relating to any person involved with the production;
- advertising of eight column inches in size or less.

Additionally, if there are requirements in relation to a particular credit that it be a certain size (for example, 80% of the size of the title of the production), the distributor will exclude itself from having to comply with this in advertising which is in a narrative form. Equally, in relation to the size of credit by reference to the title, obligations should be limited to 'normal' use as opposed to 'artwork' use (for instance where the title appears in very large print as part of the main visual image used on publicity posters).

The distributor will also exclude liability for 'casual or inadvertent' failure to accord any credit, and will require that any **deliberate failure** will not entitle the rights owner to restrain exploitation of the production, but only to damages for loss actually suffered by the absence of the credit.

As mentioned above (Chapter 8, page 130), the rights owner should have passed on these restrictions by making it clear, when taking on an obligation to accord credits, that this will be subject to the standard industry exclusions adopted by distributors and other end users in the film and television industries.

SALES AGENTS

In the context of distribution rights, it is worth mentioning the role of sales agents who are appointed under contracts which can look very much like distribution agreements. However, the function of a sales agent is actually to find distributors throughout the world – the agent is therefore a kind of 'broker' who sets up distribution deals on behalf of the owner.

A Producer who does not have the necessary contacts or resources to seek out the best distributors for a film will usually appoint a sales agent. The sales agent will take a commission (between 10% or 15% of income realized from the distribution deals which it makes) and may also act as a collecting agent for that income, which it will naturally prefer to do, because that makes it easier for the agent to deduct its commission. If the agent is collecting income, Chapter 4, pages 38–9, should be consulted as to the potential dangers to the rights owner if the recipient of income becomes insolvent. It has to be said that the best collecting agent for distribution income is a major bank, which is never likely to suffer insolvency problems (BCCI apart!).

Thus, because the sales agent is selling rights and accounting for income, many features of the agreement between the rights owner and the sales agent will be similar to a distribution agreement.

The major role of the sales agent will be in setting up pre-sales, namely the sale of rights in a production to a distributor or broadcaster before the production is actually made (Chapter 6, pages 90–94).

Secondary exploitation | 14

SECONDARY RIGHTS

The previous chapter covered the legal arrangements generally made for exploitation of the 'primary rights'. This chapter considers the legal implications of exploiting what are known as the secondary rights. The most important of the secondary rights are:

- format/changed format rights;
- book publishing;
- character merchandising.

Before going on to consider each of these aspects in turn, it is worth remembering that whatever the Producer makes out of exploiting the secondary rights will be shared with the owner/creator of the underlying rights. The secondary rights will involve exploitation of a mixture of the elements involved in the original work on which the film or programme is based, and the way in which a film or programme has turned out on screen. The form and content of an agreement with the owner of a pre-existing underlying work was considered in Chapter 5. However, it often happens that a film script is entirely the original creation of the screenwriter, or a project has been specially created for television by a television writer. The writer's ability to share in the exploitation of the primary rights is covered under the PACT/WGGB Agreement, which sets out schedules of use fees and residuals payable to the writer whenever different forms of exploitation take place (Chapters 5 and 9). However, the PACT/WGGB Agreement does not cover what happens to the secondary rights, and how the writer is to share in those when the underlying format of the work has been created by the writer. The Agreement simply leaves these matters for negotiation between the parties at the time. It may therefore help to explain the kind of deal which, by custom and practice, has developed between writers and Producers, enabling the writer to share in the success of secondary exploitation.

The deal with the writer

Where the writer has created the original format on which a film, television programme or series is to be based and that film, programme or series has potential secondary exploitation, the writer and the producer should agree in advance on how the writer is to share in the proceeds of exploiting secondary rights. The major secondary rights will be as outlined in Chapter 13, page 222. Frequently the writer's share of income derived from exploiting these rights will be a straight percentage of 'net receipts' of the Producer.

'Net receipts' should be defined as the sum or sums which are actually received by the Producer and **retainable for its own benefit** derived from the exploitation of the relevant rights.

The significance of the emphasized words is that, in exploiting these rights, the Producer may well have had to incur some extra expenditure, and it would not be fair for the writer to share in the Producer's gross income from these sources, but only in the income after the deduction of the Producer's expenses.

> For example if P, a producer, decides that a 'book of the series' should be written based on the plot and development of a dramatic television series, P will have to pay someone to write the book. The writer of the **book** will no doubt demand a lump sum fee, and possibly also a share of the royalties which P will be getting from the publisher of the **book** (page 245 below). It is then only right that the original writer of the **series** should **not** be entitled to receive a share of any money which P has to pay to the writer of the **book**. Additionally, in negotiating the agreement with the publisher, P may have incurred legal and other administrative expenses, and these should also be deductible from gross income before 'net receipts' are reached.

Where the Producer is exploiting secondary rights this will, more often than not, be done by appointing a third party specialist distributor/agent. However, if the Producer has the expertise and the contacts to sell some or all of the secondary rights itself, it should also require that the calculation of 'net receipts' will exclude a suitable commission figure (equivalent to what the Producer would have had to pay to a third party distributor) which the Producer can retain for its own benefit.

However, the deal with the writer of the underlying format may be slightly more complicated in relation to potential exploitation of book publishing rights and format/changed format rights.

Format/Changed Format Rights

Future series produced by the Producer

It is common practice that in relation to a UK television series created by a writer, the parties should provide as to what is to happen if a second and any future series is commissioned (assuming that the programmes are a success in the first place). The writer will usually have written all of the scripts for the first series, and may therefore want some kind of guarantee that he or she will be engaged to write scripts for a second and subsequent series based on his or her format. This may be some (for example, not less than 50%) or all of the scripts for a second or subsequent series. The Producer may have different views about the number of scripts it is prepared to guarantee that the writer will be offered to write. Whatever the position, the Producer must be careful to make it clear that the obligation to offer the scripts to the writer depends upon (and is subject to) the writer's **availability** at the relevant time, and the writer's **capacity**. 'Capacity' is used in the legal sense of whether or not the writer is mentally and physically capable of doing the work, which he or she would not be, for instance, if afflicted by some form of serious illness. The Producer does not want any question that it is in breach of its obligations to the writer, by not offering the writer the opportunity to write the scripts when it is patently obvious that the writer is incapable of doing so.

The parties may agree in advance on what fee would be payable to the writer for each script. They may also agree that all other terms of the agreement will be on the same terms as the PACT/WGGB Agreement. In that case, the 'option' of the writer to write the script for subsequent series is enforceable. All the necessary terms are present and ascertainable, and once the engagement has been offered to and accepted by the writer, the parties have a binding agreement (Chapter 4, *The deal*). However, if the deal is that the writer will be offered the opportunity to write scripts on terms **to be agreed**, this is not a binding option – the Producer is under an obligation to offer the scripts to the writer, but if the writer does not agree to the financial or other terms offered by the Producer, there is no obligation on the part of the Producer to engage the writer. To protect both parties, it is common to say that the parties will negotiate 'acting reasonably and in good faith'. This is probably meaningless, as a court will not enforce any suggested 'obligations' of any party not to negotiate in its own commercial best interests. However, from the point of view of the Producer, it should be made clear that there should be a specific time period for negotiation on the terms (perhaps 30 or 45 days after the Producer's first offer to the writer), and then if the parties have still not reached agreement by the end of that period, the Producer will be free to engage another writer to write the relevant script.

Format royalties

In recognition of the fact that the writer may not write all of the scripts for all subsequent series, it is therefore commonly agreed that the writer should receive a 'format royalty' on all scripts not written by the writer. (In fact, some deals envisage that a writer who has created a format should get a format royalty on all future episodes based on that format, whether or not he or she has written that script – this is usually not acceptable to the BBC or Channel 4 and therefore not usually agreed to by independent Producers.) A format royalty is a fee paid in respect of each relevant episode. It is usually calculated as a percentage of either:

- the highest fee paid to any writer on the series;
- the fee paid to the actual writer of the episode in respect of which the format royalty is being paid.

The former calculation is obviously more favourable to the writer, particularly if he or she is an experienced and popular writer and is also writing some of the scripts for that series!

The actual percentage will be something between 10% and 15% of the relevant base figure; 15% is high, and it is not normal to agree to a percentage this high, if the base figure is the highest fee paid to any writer on the series.

In addition, the writer's agent may negotiate that the writer should, if the series is sold, receive the equivalent of use fees or residuals calculated on the format royalty (as if it were a script fee).

Foreign sales of the format

Foreign sales of the format will involve a sale of the right to produce a foreign version of the series. This is often referred to as the 'changed format' right, because the sale to a foreign broadcaster/producer usually requires the format to be adapted to reflect local conditions. On making such a sale either the Producer will agree to pay the original writer a share of the Producer's 'net receipts' from making sales of these rights or, alternatively, the writer may insist that he or she be paid an actual specific figure per episode of any foreign series. The latter may well apply in relation to changed format sales to the US. The figure per episode will differ according to whether the sale was made to US network television, to syndicated television, and whether the series is going to be 'stripped' (i.e. shown at the same time on a number of days in the same week).

It is worth mentioning here that writer's agents in these circumstances also like to negotiate for what the writer will receive if there is any 'spin-off' series. A 'spin-off' is, effectively, a sequel. One example on British television was the series *In Sickness and in Health*, which followed on (rather a long time) after *Till Death Us Do Part*. Another, less recent, example was *Robin's Nest*, which was a spin-off from *Man About the House*. There are normally two definitions of spin-off: either 'generic' or 'planted'. The fee payable to the writer in relation to 'planted' spin-offs will generally be less than that applicable to 'generic' spin-offs. In either case, however, the fee will again be assessed in a similar way to the format royalty payable on future episodes based on the original format. Namely, it will be a percentage of the script fee payable to the writer who writes the script of that episode, or the highest paid writer on the relevant series in which the episode appears.

'Generic' spin-off series are television series which are based on the original series and which present as a central continuing character one which was contained in the original format and the series based on that format.

A **'planted' spin-off** is a series which is based on the original format but which presents as its central continuing character one which was neither contained in the original format nor in the original series based on that format.

Book publishing

In situations where a book is contemplated, the writer of the original film/programme may also wish to be offered the first opportunity to write the book. The same comments, made in relation to the writer being offered first opportunity to write future scripts, will apply here. However, if the deal with the writer, in writing the book, is that he or she is paid a lump sum fee, plus a royalty on sales of the book, the writer should obviously not receive a separate share of the Producer's net receipts from the publication of the book.

Net profits shares

The deal with the writer may include a share of 'net profits' from exploitation of the production as a whole, particularly if the deal relates to a feature film, rather than a television series. In this case, the Producer should remember that if the writer has negotiated for a different share of secondary rights income, all income from these sources should be **excluded** from the definition of net profits. Otherwise, the writer stands to get a share (albeit different shares) on two occasions, from the same income.

EXPLOITATION OF CHARACTER MERCHANDISING RIGHTS

Character merchandising is the licensing of names/logos/characters/ situations in relation to products and services. A notable example of successful character merchandising is *Thomas the Tank Engine and*

Friends. There can be few parents in this country who do not have some form of merchandise (whether it be toy trains, fluffy slippers or T-shirts) which do not have the face of *Thomas the Tank Engine* appearing on them.

Character merchandising can be extremely profitable, if a successful property is found. A producer who wishes to make money out of merchandising needs to be sure that it has tangible rights and benefits to offer potential licensees, such as:

- material which is protected by copyright;
- material which is protected by other legal rights (such as trade marks).

It cannot be over-stressed that, in merchandising, if the property being merchandised is not protectible then it is not really licensable. Manufacturers of products are not happy to take the risk of paying large sums of money for the right to attach a particular name or character to their products, if there is nothing to stop other people from using that name without having to make payment.

The way in which copyright operates was covered in Chapter 3. In the context of merchandising, copyright can be used to protect the **appearance** of a character in graphic form (which would be an artistic work). It can also sometimes be used to protect a name, in that while copyright does not subsist in a name as such (page 23) if the name is produced in some sort of stylized design, such as a logo, it too can be protected as an artistic work of copyright. However, the characteristics of a fictional character, apart from its appearance, are not protected.

If the merchandisable property consists more or less of names only (with very little other copyright material), the Producer should seriously consider using the protection of trade mark law for that name.

Trade mark law

Registered trade marks

Registered trade marks are the result of statute law. The Trade Marks Act 1938 (soon to be replaced) enables the registration of trade marks and service marks by persons who use or license them.

A trade mark is something which operates as a means of identification linking its owner with a product or a service in the course of a trade. This enables the consumer to distinguish the product from other goods of the same kind, or the services from those provided by others. A trade mark can take various forms – it can be a symbol, a signature or a logo. The trade mark right will subsist not only in the word or words of a brand name, but also in the design of the symbol or the stylization of the signature or logo, so that use of the symbol alone would constitute a trade mark infringement. Where a trade mark involves a symbol, signature or logo, this will appear on the Trade Mark Register (an example is mentioned in Chapter 12, page 202). It is not a condition of trade mark protection that the trade mark should be accompanied by the letters 'TM' or 'R', but it is good practice for the trade mark owner to do this, as it gives notice of the owner's rights.

Unregistered trade marks

There are also unregistered trade marks, so-called 'common law' trade marks, in the sense that they are protected only under principles of common law, not under the Trade Mark Act. The most widely used method of protection for these is the action for 'passing-off'. This gives a remedy to a trader in the following circumstances, namely where:

- the trader has developed a reputation (or goodwill) in respect of a particular product or service in the course of trade;
- another trader makes a representation to potential consumers of his goods or services by 'passing-off' his goods or services as those of the first trader; **and**
- passing-off by the other trader is calculated to injure the business of the first trader.

On this basis, one can see how a person who uses a particular brand name or other form of product or service identification which is not registered as a trade mark can still seek to prevent others from using a similar 'mark' on their goods to try to confuse consumers into buying those goods (Chapter 12, page 203).

The availability of the passing-off action depends on whether the 'owner' of the trade mark can prove that he has developed a sufficient reputation or goodwill for the public to distinguish his goods or services from others in the same market, when marketed under that trade mark.

Two points should be made.

- The use of the action of passing-off is one example of how to protect a title or a name (notwithstanding the fact that copyright protection will not be available – Chapter 12, page 203).
- However, the action is only available when a reputation has **already** been established. It is therefore of no use to someone who is starting business under or in relation to a new name.
- There is also a doubt as to whether passing-off is available to someone in the position of a Producer, who is not actually producing goods or providing services under a particular name, but is licensing other people (such as manufacturers of T-shirts or toys) to do so. In those cases, the reputation on which the action is based will belong in reality to the

manufacturer of the goods, not the Producer.

Thus, if the trade mark can be registered, registration is always a better option.

Application for registration

Registered trade mark protection is given to 34 separate classes of goods (each class containing a greater or lesser variety of products) and 8 classes of services. In most cases, it is not possible to make a general application against all classes, because it is obvious that the applicant will not be trading in all of the possible goods or services. The applicant for a trade mark must therefore prepare a **specification** which accurately describes all the goods/services in respect of which he is confident the mark will be likely to be used. If this covers more than one class of goods, a separate application has to be made in each class. If the mark is not used in respect of any specific product for which application was made, the owner might subsequently lose the registration for that product; equally if the owner uses the mark for a product which is not covered by the application and the registration itself, there will be no protection for it.

Examples of the most popular classes (particularly relevant to character merchandising) are:

- Class 3 – cosmetics;
- Class 16 – stationery;
- Class 25 – clothing;
- Class 28 – games and playthings.

Problems for character merchandisers

Under the Trade Mark Act 1938, use of the trade mark by someone else would generally not count to save the registration if the proprietor of the mark was not himself using it (even use by a licensee of the owner, such as a manufacturer of products who has been licensed) unless the proprietor and the licensee applied to register the licensee under the Trade Marks Act as a 'registered user'. In that case, the Act stated that use by the registered user would be treated as used by the proprietor.

However, this was a particular problem for character merchandisers, who do not manufacture or deal in goods but license the use of the name or image to others who manufacture or deal in the goods in question. In most character merchandising situations, given the delays and inconvenience of applying to register licensees as 'registered users', this was not a practical way of operating, and it made it very difficult for character merchandisers to register trade marks and ensure that the trade marks are not open to attack. However, under the new Trade Marks Act which is expected shortly to replace the 1938 Act, it will be possible for character merchandisers to own trade marks in classes of goods which the merchandisers do not themselves manufacture (such as toys or stationery) simply licensing them to third parties.

To give an example, P produces a children's animation series called *The Yesterday People*, which centres on the adventures of a group of children who are able to travel back in time. The children are a set of clearly delineated characters with unusual names, such as 'Spig' and 'Blurt'. They also use catch-phrases, which become very popular with children. P decides that the project has potential for being licensed to toy and games manufacturers. What P can license the use of are:

- the title;
- the names of the characters;
- their physical appearance;
- their catch-phrases.

The appearance of the characters will be automatically provided by copyright.

However, as for the title and the names and sayings of the characters, if P wants to license them, it should seek to register them as trade marks in Class 9 (to cover films and videos); Class 16 (to cover printed material and stationery); Class 25 (to cover clothing); and Class 28 (for toys and games). This means, if registration of the mark is granted, that they will be protectible property in relation to all the types of product on which they might possibly be used; they will therefore be of greater potential value to licensees. If they are not registered, P may not be able to stop unauthorized third parties from using them on 'pirate' merchandise – much to the annoyance of P's legitimate licensees. This is because, until the products featuring the names/phrases have been on the market for a sufficient time, **no one** will have established the reputation in them which is required before an action for passing-off can be taken. Equally, even when sufficient time has passed, it might be argued that it is not P who has established the reputation, but P's licensees, and therefore only they could sue. That is a state of affairs which neither P nor the licensees will like.

Merchandising licences

Having discussed the ways of ensuring that the Producer has a protectible property which can be licensed to manufacturers of goods, the typical contents of such a licence are as follows.

- The licence will provide for the licensor to receive a royalty on each product sold which bears the name/logo/design which has been licensed.

There need to be restrictions preventing the licensee from giving away free products, or from selling products at a low price to associated companies, thereby reducing the base figure on which the licensor's royalty is calculated.

- Since there is a payment on **sales**, there have to be accounting provisions which enable the licensor to be provided with a **statement of account** on a regular basis, together with payment of sums shown to be due to the licensor. It is common practice for accounting to take place every three months (Chapter 13, pages 227–8, contains further details on accounting provisions).

- Since the value of the property licensed lies in its **reputation** with the public, the licensor should be keen to preserve it as a symbol of quality. The licensor will therefore usually require rights of **approval** of the product from design stage to the point of final manufacture (giving itself the power to prevent the products from being sold without such approval being given). Additionally, the licensor should also contractually require the licensee to comply with the highest standards of product safety which are applicable (whether or not they are compulsory, or voluntary such as British Standards).

- The licensor should naturally protect itself and its property against the possible insolvency of the licensee. The licensor will therefore want to be able to **terminate the licence** quickly and retrieve the rights to the property (hopefully, licensing it elsewhere) if the licensee becomes insolvent and is no longer able to pay the royalty. It is common to provide that any particular **symptom or sign of insolvency** will trigger an **automatic termination** of the licence – the licence should state that, as from the date of termination, the licensee is not entitled to sell any more of the products bearing the name/design which has been licensed. This means that the liquidator/receiver of the licensee will have to come to some kind of arrangement with the licensor to be able to sell the remaining stock of products, because selling them without making such an arrangement might be in breach of copyright or infringement of a trade mark.

- It is also normal to allow a **sell-off period**, when the licence expires in the normal course of events (for example, if it was granted for a three year period and the three years have now finished). Naturally, there should be no 'sell-off period' if the licence is **terminated** because of the licensee's breach or insolvency. During the 'sell-off period', the licensee can continue to sell remaining stock, on the basis that it continues to account for and pay to the licensor royalties on that stock. However, at the end of the sell-off period, all remaining stock must be destroyed (or the licensor may take an option to purchase it at cost price).

Since piracy is rife in this area, the licensor needs to take very strict controls over how the licensee can use the name/design which has been licensed. For instance, to save costs, toy-making licensees often arrange for the manufacture of goods outside this country, more often than not in the Far East. The Far East is a 'hot bed' of manufacturers of counterfeit goods, and therefore allowing companies in those jurisdictions to have access to the designs increases the risks of pirate goods being produced, particularly once the arrangement between the Far Eastern manufacturer and the licensee comes to an end. Companies for whom character merchandising is big business usually require the right to approve whether or not a product can be manufactured outside this country, and also require some form of direct relationship with the foreign sub-contracting manufacturer, so that they can take action if the manufacturer continues to make products featuring the licensed property, when its right to do so has ended.

Where counterfeit goods are concerned, as well as taking action for trade mark/copyright infringement, character merchandisers should also consider reporting matters to the Trading Standards Office, which has a duty to protect the public from 'fake' goods and will therefore investigate and take action in cases where 'counterfeiting' appears to have occurred.

Merchandising agents

For most Producers, their primary business will not be the exploitation of merchandising rights. It is therefore common to take on the services of a merchandising agent, who operates very much in the same way as a sales agent (Chapter 13, page 232) by publicizing the property to be licensed to a network of potential licensees (clothes manufacturers, toy manufacturers etc.) and concluding licensing deals with those licensees on behalf of the owner of the property. As with sales agents, merchandising agents operate by taking a commission and their expenses from the income realized from licensing.

FORMAT SALES/CHANGED FORMAT SALES

A Producer who wishes to exploit the underlying format of a television series or a film is in fact contemplating the licensing of an underlying right to third parties whom they wish to make television programmes or films based on that underlying work (in this case the format). Chapter 5, *Development*, considers in detail the contents of an agreement requiring rights in underlying works. An added detail here, however, is that because the format may well have potential to be sold separately in different countries of the world, the rights granted by the owner of the format may well be restricted to a particular country. For example, the rights may be granted to a French producer to produce a French version of the programme, in the French language only, and for transmission only in France. The grant of rights may not, in those circumstances, include any secondary rights, as the owner of the format may wish to retain the right to exploit merchandising and publication rights in that territory. In this kind of deal, the licensor of the format will be receiving a straight payment per episode of the series.

If, however, any other rights are licensed (such as the rights to exploit the programme made based on the format in territories abroad, or the right to exploit any secondary rights), the licensor should also require a share of the 'net profits' derived from the exploitation of these other rights. In addition, if the licensor of the format is also the Producer of the original series made from the format, the Producer may contract to give consultancy advice or even co-produce the new series with the licensee. This could result in further consultancy fees to the Producer, or perhaps in a share of the production fee, and any other fees payable to the foreign licensee out of the production budget.

Another way in which licences of format/changed format rights will differ from the normal assignment of a licence of underlying works is that, in relation to television series, it is usual for the owner to provide that the rights will last only for a certain period after the completion of the **last** programme to be made based on the format. Thus, if a new programme or series of programmes has not commenced production within that period, the rights will lapse. However, if a new series/programme is started, the rights will continue for that series and again, for a certain period after that, to see if another series will be made.

In Chapter 3, the ephemeral nature of formats was discussed – they are so often, in themselves, not capable of qualifying for copyright protection, since they consist of mere ideas. However, for the Producer who is licensing a format of this nature, such as for a games show or an action adventure show, various means of enhancing the format are available. Essentially, the Producer should seek to add elements which **are** capable of protection. For instance, if the format involves the use of a very stylized set, the set itself will be protected as an artistic work; the title and any catch-phrases used in the show may well be registrable as trade marks; the show may also use a distinctive logo, capable of being protected by copyright, but also registrable as a trade mark. The more these elements are used to hedge round the underlying format, the more likely it is that anybody wishing to benefit from the success of the underlying format will also want to use the surrounding identifying elements, which **are** protected. This makes it more likely that third parties will ask for a licence to use the format, rather than simply going ahead and using it without permission. Equally, those who do not ask for a licence are more likely to make the mistake of using a protected element (such as the copyright design of the set; or a catch phrase which is registered as a trade mark), without realizing what they have done, and this gives the owner of the original format the opportunity to sue.

BOOK PUBLICATION RIGHTS

If a Producer wishes either to exploit a novelized version of a film/ television series, or even to publish the original screenplays, this will involve reaching agreement with a book publisher to print and publish the book or the screenplay.

Book publishers operate by paying a royalty on sales of books in which the rights are licensed to them – thus, they account and pay at regular intervals (six months or twelve months, depending on the publisher). The comments in Chapter 13, pages 227–8, apply equally in this case.

If a publisher takes rights in the book for a long period, it is wise for the Producer to require that the rights will revert if the book goes out of print for more than a certain period. However, the publisher will usually require to be given written notice to put the book back in print, and will return the rights only if it has failed to re-publish the book within a specified period (for example, six months) after receiving such a notice.

In relation to the payment of royalties, book publishers commonly give themselves the right to establish a 'reserve' against returns. Since books are sold to booksellers on a sale or return basis, the publisher cannot guarantee that, once a book has been ordered by a bookseller, it will not be returned. Therefore, in relation to any accounting period when a publisher can report that a number of books have left its warehouse to go to a bookseller, it would be wise to assume that a royalty will not ultimately be payable on all those books – the publisher therefore keeps back some of the money which would otherwise appear to be due to the Producer, to cover it against books being returned. If the figure reserved is not required to meet returns, it will be paid to the Producer within a certain period (and this should not be more than two accounting periods after the period in respect of which the reserve was made).

15	**Legal proceedings**

AVOIDING BEING SUED OR PROSECUTED

In producing and exploiting films and television programmes, there are a number of situations in which those involved either want to sue, or are being sued by others. These are:

- copyright infringement and the infringement of other 'intellectual property rights' (such as trade marks);
- actions for breach of confidence;
- actions for breach of contract;
- defamation actions;
- actions for breach of some other legal right, such as a right of privacy or publicity, or trespass on to private property.

In addition, there are laws which can lead to criminal liability, such as:

- obscenity and indecency laws;
- contempt of court;
- breaches of the Official Secrets Act.

Previous chapters have already covered, at least in outline, what dangers to bear in mind to avoid being sued or prosecuted. This chapter therefore concentrates on:

- what happens to a person who is sued ('the defendant');
- what a person who wishes to take legal action ('the plaintiff') should bear in mind.

'Remedies' in a legal action

In a legal action, the plaintiff will normally be seeking any one of a number of possible benefits (depending on the nature of the cause of the action) – referred to in legal terms as 'remedies'. These can be:

- damages (namely, monetary compensation for loss suffered);

- an injunction (namely, an order to prevent the defendant repeating whatever it was which caused the plaintiff to sue in the first place, or an order requiring the defendant to do something which should have been done and was not);
- an account and payment to the plaintiff of profits (where the defendant has encroached without permission on the property rights of the plaintiff and made money out of doing so – for example, by selling 'pirate' videos, in breach of the copyright in the film which is featured on the videos).

Some discussion of the assessment of damages (in relation to breach of contract which, apart from copyright infringement actions, is the form of action most likely to be relevant to those involved in film and television production) has been included in Chapter 4, pages 41. However, the topic of injunctions should be considered further.

INJUNCTIONS

Final injunctions

Put very simplistically, there are two types of injunction – **final** or **interim**. The **final injunction** comes at the end of a case, when the court has decided the matter in, say, the plaintiff's favour and finds it necessary to make an order against the defendant requiring it:

- to do something which it should have done;
- to stop doing something which it should not be doing.

This order may be necessary to bring about the state of affairs which the plaintiff is entitled to expect, his or her rights having been vindicated by the decision of the court.

To take the example already mentioned, the pirate video distributor will be ordered, at the end of the trial, when he has lost:

- to destroy all infringing videos;
- not to repeat the infringement.

Interim injunctions

An **interim** (or interlocutory) injunction is, as its name suggests, a temporary measure which is aimed at reducing the potential damage of the defendant's **allegedly** unlawful behaviour at the very outset of proceedings, when of course the matter has not yet been decided. The availability of interim injunctions is particularly important because the courts are very slow – an action can take a year or two (sometimes more) to come to final trial. If the defendant is doing something which strikes right at the heart of the plaintiff's welfare or business, the plaintiff may suffer irreparable loss if the defendant carries on with this behaviour, unchecked, until trial.

Thus, for example, it is open to a film distributor who discovers that a 'pirate' is selling unauthorized videos of one of its films to apply for an interim injunction against the pirate. This will stop those videos being sold until a court can decide if the distributor truly owns the rights, which the 'pirate' is actually exploiting **and** that the 'pirate' has not actually been given permission to sell the videos.

Another example is if an individual is aware that a programme which is due to be broadcast may infringe some right of that individual. For instance, an injunction might be available to a prominent public figure who finds out that unpleasant (and defamatory) things are going to be said about him in a current affairs programme about to be broadcast on television.

A real life example occurred in the *Clockwork Orange* case mentioned in Chapter 9, page 142, where the distributors of the film applied for an injunction to stop Channel Four showing a programme featuring clips from the film, which had been incorporated in the programme without the distributor's permission.

It is a serious thing for a film or programme maker to be threatened with an injunction which will prevent or delay the exhibition of the production – the very purpose for which it has been made. A final and perpetual injunction is of course disastrous, as it means that all the money invested in the making of the production will go to waste with no chance of recoupment. However, even a temporary delay can cause great loss.

Obtaining an interim injunction – what the plaintiff needs to establish

It is therefore a great comfort to know that a court will not automatically grant an interim injunction to anybody who asks for one. While the court will not (at least in theory) decide who is right or wrong at this stage, it has to take into account the following in deciding whether to issue an interim injunction.

- The plaintiff may or may not have a **serious case to be tried** – if the plaintiff cannot show that there is some evidence that his or her rights might have been or may be going to be violated, the matter will end there. However, this 'barrier' is not very hard to surmount, because the plaintiff does not have to prove his or her case, just to show that there is one.
- The damage to the plaintiff, if the injunction were not granted, must be

evaluated as opposed to the damage to the defendant if it **is** granted, supposing in each case that the party which was **unsuccessful** at the injunction stage were to be shown to be **in the right** when the case has been tried. The court will decide the injunction proceedings in favour of the person who can show that they would suffer **most** damage in these circumstances. But damage in this context does not usually mean **monetary damage** alone – it has to be the kind of damage which **cannot** be compensated adequately by money, for example:

- damage to the plaintiff's reputation in a libel case;
- proof that the plaintiff would go out of business before trial of the matter, if the injunction is not granted or, on the contrary, that the defendant will go out of business if the injunction **is** granted.

- If the damage feared by the plaintiff is one that can be fully compensated by money at the end of the trial, it will not be taken into account by the court.
- The plaintiff may have **delayed** in bringing in a claim for an injunction. A certain amount of delay after the plaintiff has found out what the defendant has been doing may be explicable – but if it is too long a period, this may lead the court to refuse an injunction almost automatically on the basis that the grant of interim injunction is a great privilege to the plaintiff (as well as being a great imposition on the party against whom it is made) and a duty is owed to the court to act without delay.

Costs of interim injunction proceedings

One further barrier of protection for those who fear interim injunction proceedings against them (or, to put it another way, for those who are considering taking such proceedings) is that they are horrifically expensive. Legal and other costs of around £10 000 can be run up in a matter of a few days, unless the matter involves a very simple issue. This can be a major deterrent to anyone who might otherwise want to apply for an injunction. However, it is a major headache for anyone on the receiving end of the injunction proceedings, because it will cost just as much to **resist** the claim as it does to make it. The defendant to injunction proceedings also faces the risk that he or she may never get his or her costs back even if the injunction is not granted. This is because the court does not usually decide who (as between the plaintiff or the defendant) should bear the costs at this stage because, of course, it does not decide who is right or wrong. That, and therefore the costs bill, are left to be decided at trial. If the plaintiff drops the action before the matter goes to trial, the defendant has no chance of recovering the expenditure of having had to defend himself against the injunction.

When interim injunctions can decide the matter

The decision in interim injunction proceedings can often decide the whole action, because one party or the other may not find it tactically wise or economically possible to go on to a full-blown legal action. This is most frequently demonstrated in claims for infringement of copyright. If the plaintiff alleges that the defendant is infringing his copyright, the plaintiff will have to show that there is a serious case by:

- producing basic evidence of copyright ownership in the work of copyright;
- showing that the defendant is doing something in relation to the work which is restricted by the copyright.

Once these are established, an injunction will probably be granted, because it is generally assumed in infringement of copyright cases that infringement causes damage going beyond purely financial loss. The injunction will often cover (and exceed) the time period during which the defendant actually wanted to do what he has now been prevented from doing.

For example, a theatre workshop adapts a story by a well-known children's author into a play for performance over the Christmas period. The copyright owner of the story has not given permission for his work to be either **adapted** or **performed in public**. This means that, for a start, there are two copyright infringements being contemplated by the theatre workshop. The owner therefore goes to court to get an injunction to stop the performances going ahead. He can prove his ownership and he tells the judge that he has not given permission for the adaptation or the performance of his work. The representatives of the theatre workshop may well not be present at this stage to give evidence, because interim injunctions can be applied for (in very urgent cases) without the applicant having to give notice to the other side, as long as the applicant promises to the court to commence formal legal action as soon as possible. However, the owner in this case has brought to the court a publicity poster making it clear that a play, with a very similar title to that of his story, is going to be performed between 10 December and the following 25 January. If the injunction is granted, the performances cannot go ahead. Even if the theatre workshop could conceivably have won the trial – for instance, if they could prove that the play had only the same **title** as the owner's story but had not been adapted from it, and was written by someone who had never even read the story –

there is no point going on with the defence of the action.

It has been mentioned at several points, that when concluding contracts with any person contributing to or involved with film or television production, while it is not possible necessarily to restrict their right to take legal action if the contract is breached, it is certainly possible to get them to agree that if there is a breach, their remedies are limited to damages, and that they cannot seek an injunction (either interim or permanent) which would then interfere with the successful exploitation and publishing of the final production. Chapter 8, page 133 demonstrates suitable wording.

DEFAMATION

The damages potentially payable by a losing defendant, if sued for defamation, can be enormous, as a line of well-publicized cases demonstrates. However, there are a number of matters which normally discourage people from taking defamation actions lightly, these being:

- the enormous expense of doing so (as there is no legal aid for defamation proceedings);
- the potential distress and disruption of the plaintiff's life while the action is going on;
- the fact that legal proceedings can make the original allegedly defamatory statement much more widely known than it was in the first place (so that it may be less distressing simply to forget about it);
- the fact that the usual defendants to defamation actions (newspapers, broadcasters and the like) have access to experienced lawyers and relatively large funds, with which to fight the action.

However if, despite these discouragements, defamation action is taken, the defendant does have a number of avenues to follow, either by putting up a defence (of which there are a number to choose from) or by admitting liability and offering an apology. Many types of defamation are effectively answered by an apology in the same place and of more or less the same prominence as the original defamatory statement (for example, if the defamation took place during the course of a programme broadcast at 9pm, the feelings of the plaintiff may well be satisfied if an apology is broadcast at the same time on the same channel).

The **defences** to defamation claims are:

- **justification**: namely, proving that the defamatory statement was true;
- **consent**: namely, showing that the plaintiff actually consented to the statement being published;
- **fair comment** on a matter of public interest; but this defence is not

effective if it can be shown that the comment was made for **malicious** or **improper** purposes;

- **privilege**: namely, that the defendant was entitled, owing to his or her status or by reason of the occasion on which the statement was made, to absolute or qualified immunity from liability for having made the statement. **Absolute** privilege (such as that available to MPs speaking in the House of Commons) is still effective, even if the motives behind the statement were malicious or improper. However, qualified privilege can be removed if malice can be shown in the intentions of the person making the statement.

The most relevant of these defences to Producers, distributors and broadcasters is likely to be 'justification', closely followed by 'fair comment'.

Another tactic for defendants in defamation proceedings is to pay a specific sum into court. The plaintiff is notified that this sum has been lodged with the court, and has a certain amount of time in which to accept it in full settlement of his or her claim. If he or she does not accept it, the matter proceeds. However, neither the jury nor the judge knows about the payment. Even if the plaintiff wins, if he or she fails to be awarded damages of a **greater** amount than the amount of the payment into court, he or she will have to pay both his or her costs **and** the defendant's costs from the date of the payment into court. This is a great disincentive to plaintiffs to go on with legal proceedings after a reasonable offer of settlement has been made.

SUMMARY

In case the point has not already been adequately made, both taking and defending litigation is extremely expensive, time-consuming and uses up the energy and creative ability which most people could effectively use for more positive purposes. It is therefore not a pastime for anybody who is not rich, and no one should take legal action unless he is certain that he is going to feel exactly the same way about the matter two years down the line.

The potential loss (in terms of time and money and in other ways) of having to defend a legal action is enormous. Thus, those involved in television and film production should make it a matter of priority to ensure that, wherever possible, they comply with the law and do nothing which can be said to violate the rights of any person. This is a situation where consulting a lawyer at the right time can be a very effective use of money in a production budget.

Appendix A: Professional bodies and useful contacts

UNIONS

Writers' Guild of Great Britain (WGGB)
> 430 Edgware Road,
> London W2 1EH
> 071 723 8074

Musicians Union (MU)
> 60 Clapham Road,
> London SW9 0JJ
> 071 582 5566

British Actors' Equity Association (Equity)
> Guild House,
> Upper St Martins Lane,
> London WC2H 9EJ
> 071 379 6000

Broadcasting, Entertainment, Cinematographic
and Theatre Union (BECTU)
> 111 Wardour Street,
> London W1V 4AY
> 071 437 8506

COLLECTING SOCIETIES

Performing Right Society Limited (PRS)
> 29–33 Berners Street,
> London W1P 4AA
> 071 580 5544

Phonographic Performance Limited (PPL)
> 14–22 Ganton Street,
> London W1V 1LB
> 071 437 0311

Mechanical Copyright Protection Society (MCPS)
    41 Streatham High Road,
    London SW16
    081 769 4400

Design and Artistic Copyright Society (DACS)
    St Mary's Clergy House,
    2 Whitechurch Lane,
    London E1 7QR
    071 247 1650

Authors' Licensing and Collecting Society (ACLS)
    33–34 Alfred Place,
    London WC1E 7DP

TRADE BODIES

Producers' Alliance for Cinema and Television (PACT)
    10 Gordon House,
    Greencoat Place,
    London SW1P 1PH
    071 233 6000

Industrial Relations Service (IRS)
    18–20 Highbury Place,
    London N5 1QP
    071 354 5858

OTHERS

Thomson & Thomson (copyright searches etc.)
    1750 K Street, NW, Suite 200,
    Washington DC 20006
    USA
    0101 202 835 0240

Independent Television Commission (ITC)
    33 Foley Street,
    London W1P 7LB
    071 255 3000

Department of National Heritage (DNH)
    2–4 Cockspur Street,
    London SW1Y 5DH
    071 211 6000

Network Centre/ITVA
200 Grays Inn Road,
London WC1X 8HF
071 843 8000

British Screen/European Co-Production Fund
14–17 Wells Mews,
London W1P 3FL
071 323 9080

British Film Institute (BFI)
21 Stephen Street,
London W1P 1PL
071 255 1444

Foreign Entertainers Unit (FEU)
5th Floor, City House,
140 Edmund Street,
Birmingham B3 2JE
021 200 2616

British Film Commission
70 Baker Street,
London W1M 1DJ
071 224 5000

Appendix B: Recommended reference materials

Producer's Guidelines – published by the BBC

Agreed Structure of Working Practices and Procedures for Independent Productions Commissioned by the BBC – made available by the BBC

Tripartite Contract published by the Network Centre (for ITV Network commissions from independent producers)

Agreement between the Writers' Guild of Great Britain and the Producers' Alliance for Cinema and Television

The Screenwriting Credits Agreement between the Film Production Association of Great Britain and the Writers' Guild of Great Britain (effective from 1 May 1974)

Agreement between British Equity and Producers' Alliance for Cinema and Television

Agreement between Producers' Alliance for Cinema and Television and the Film Artistes Association

Freelance Production Agreement between BECTU and Producers' Alliance for Cinema and Television

Agreement between the Musicians Union and Producers' Alliance for Cinema and Television

Appendix C: Recommended reference books

Blackstone's Guide to the Copyright, Designs and Patents Act 1988 by Gerald Dworkin and Richard D Taylor

Media Law by Geoffrey Robertson and Andrew Nicol

Discipline at Work published by ACAS

Running a Limited Company by David Impey and Nicholas Montague

Appendix D: Release to be signed by individuals permitting fictionalization

FROM: (Name of Individual)
TO: (Name of Production Company)

                                        Dated   19

Dear Sirs

(Name of Production) ('the [Film/Programme'])

In consideration of the payment by you to me of the sum of [   ]
(the receipt of which I acknowledge) I warrant, confirm and agree with you
as follows:

1   You have the irrevocable right to portray me and the events ('the Events') [relating to (specify)] [described in (specify)] in the [Film/Programme].

2   You shall have the right to edit and delete material relating to the Events and/or to change the sequence of the Events in the [Film/Programme] and/or of any questions or answers relating to the Events in the [Film/Programme] and/or to fictionalize any person including myself in the [Film/Programme] and/or to make any changes that you wish in your entire discretion, including using the material from the [Film/Programme] with any other material.

3   I have read and approved the screenplay for [Film/Programme] [and my portrayal in it].

4   I waive and release you from any claim, action or demand arising out of or in connection with the [Film/Programme].

5   The confirmation, waiver and release contained in this document are irrevocable and may be transferred by you freely to your successors, licensees and assignees and you and they shall have the right to

exploit the [Film/Programme] and any subsidiary or ancillary material relating to the [Film/Programme], whether or not the same contains my name or likeness or biographical material relating to me, in any and all media by any and all manner or means, whether now known or in the future invented throughout the world.

Yours faithfully

. . . .
for and on behalf of
[Individual   ]

                          ACCEPTED AND AGREED

                          . . . .
                          [Production Company]

Appendix E: Analysis of typical provisions in production and financing agreements

Appendix E:
Analysis of typical provisions in
production and financing agreements

Provision	100% Commission	Co-production	Pre-purchase	Acquired material
1. Approvals (see also other headings)	The commissioner has approval over: (a) essential elements: (i) script (ii) cast (iii) key personnel (e.g. director, Producer) (iv) selection of other personnel and replacements (b) budget (c) cashflow (d) production schedule (e) production contracts: (i) credit (ii) publicity (iii) consents (iv) waivers of moral rights.	The co-producers have joint approval over: (a) screenplay/script (b) underlying rights and third party material (c) principal artists (d) principal personnel (e) technical specification (f) budget/cashflow.	The licensee has the right of approval over: (a) leading artists (b) director (and/or replacement) (c) Producer (and/or replacement) (d) shooting script (e) budget (f) technical specifications. Extent of approvals will depend on whether any part of the licence fee is payable **before** delivery.	None.

Provision	100% Commission	Co-production	Pre-purchase	Acquired material
2. *Production*	The Producer agrees: (a) to make the programme in accordance with the essential elements and the agreed programme or technical specification. (b) that all production contracts will be in the Producer's name. (c) that production of the programme will be first class in technical and pictorial quality, and fully synchronized as to music and dialogue. (d) that the programme must be technically suitable for television transmission. (e) to use the services of persons within the licence area of the commissioner. (f) to report on a regular basis to the commissioner as to the	Each co-producer agrees to produce specified material in accordance with the agreed production schedule. The co-producers agree that: (a) the screenplay/shooting script will be written by those persons approved to do so. (b) the programme will not depart from the shooting script and will be first class quality, technically, artistically, and in all other respects. (c) the film will be originally recorded in the [English] language. Production contracts may be in the name of one of the co-producers only and must contain all necessary waivers of moral rights and consents. The other co-producer agrees not to rescind or vary	See licensor's warranties.	No reference.

Provision	100% Commission	Co-production	Pre-purchase	Acquired material
2. *Production* (continued)	financial and other aspects of the production. (g) to keep true and accurate books of account.	the terms of the production contracts and to abide by them. Each co-producer agrees to keep full accurate and proper records and books of account.		
3. *Finance/ consideration*	Subject to the Producer complying with its obligations the commissioner agrees to advance the amount of the budget for the programme into a separate trust bank account set up by the Producer in accordance with a mandate approved by the commissioner. The budget generally includes a production fee payable in instalments as set out in the approved cashflow. The last instalment is held by commissioner until final delivery of the programme.	Each party is responsible for a proportion of the budget (to be specified by the co-producers). The production account is a trust account set up in the joint names of the co-producers. Underspend and over cost is shared in or contributed to in the proportions to which each party has contributed to the budget.	The licensee pays an advance to the budget of the programme as consideration for the rights granted to it (described below). This may be payable on delivery, but if payable in earlier instalments, approval rights are more important.	The licensee pays the licensor a licence fee in respect of the rights granted (which may be non-returnable).

Provision	100% Commission	Co-production	Pre-purchase	Acquired material
3. *Finance* (continued)	The Producer may be required to have the final cost of the programme certified by an accountant.			
	Underspend is shared by the Producer and commissioner in such proportions as the commissioner may decide but underspend is often shared equally by the parties (subject to a maximum limit on the Producer's share).			
	If there is overspend which has been incurred as a result of the Producer's negligence, the commissioner is usually entitled to retain the unpaid part of the production fee and sometimes to require repayment of the part already paid.			

Provision	100% Commission	Co-production	Pre-purchase	Acquired material
4. Warranties	The Producer warrants that: (a) it has the power and authority to enter into the agreement. (b) it will be the sole owner of the copyright in the programme. (c) it will acquire all necessary rights in the underlying rights material to enable the programme to be fully exploited. (d) the programme will not infringe the rights of third parties. (e) nothing in the programme will be defamatory or obscene, in breach of contract, contempt of court or in breach of statute. (f) there will be on delivery no liens, claims, or encumbrances affecting the programme.	The co-producers warrant to each other that: (a) each party is free to enter into the agreement. (b) each party shall consult with the other at all stages of production. (c) production contracts shall be for the amount specified in the budget. (d) the programme will not be obscene, defamatory or infringe the copyright privacy or any other third party rights. (e) the programme will be produced in accordance with the relevant union agreements. (f) the programme will be of first class condition and of first class technical quality. (g) all delivery material shall be cleared for full exploitation.	The licensor warrants that: (a) the programme will be fully synchronized as to music, effects and dialogue and will be of first class technical quality. (b) the licensor has the right to make the grant of rights to the licensee. (c) the rights granted to the licensee have not previously been transferred to a third party in any way to derogate from the grant of rights to the licensee. (d) subject to the rights of the PRS, all music will be cleared. (e) the licensor will obtain all necessary consents, grants and rights in order for the licensee to exploit the programme. (f) on delivery there will be	The licensor warrants as for pre-purchase. The licensee warrants: (a) not to assign the rights granted to it without the consent of the licensor. (b) the programme will not be broadcast by the licensee outside the transmission area or on pay cable, satellite or close circuit medium. (c) that it has no rights to exploit the audio track on its own. (d) not to make copies and to return all copies supplied to it after the expiry of the licence period. (e) it has the right to enter into the agreement. (f) it will not cut or edit the programme and it will show the credits in their complete form.

Provision	100% Commission	Co-production	Pre-purchase	Acquired material
4. *Warranties* (continued)	(g) it will obtain from all persons participating in the programme the non-exclusive right to issue publicity material featuring their name and likeness. (h) it will comply with ITC programme guidelines. (i) the production agreements will conform with the relevant union agreements. (j) if E&O insurance is required, the Producer will effect all necessary clearances. (k) the programme will not be exhibited or distributed prior to its exhibition by the commissioner. (l) the Producer agrees to indemnify the commissioner.	(h) each party agrees to indemnify the other.	no claims, liens or encumbrances affecting the programme. (g) the licensor will obtain from those participating in the programme the non-exclusive right for the licensee to issue publicity featuring those persons. (h) the licensor indemnifies the licensee. The licensee warrants as for acquired material.	(g) it will not make censorship cuts without the licensor's consent. (h) it will observe all credit obligations (on screen and/or paid advertising). (i) it will keep the programme and delivery materials secure and insured and to make good any damage to the delivery materials. (j) to be responsible for obtaining licences and permission for the public performance broadcast and transmission of the programme. (k) not to impair or prejudice the copyright in the programme. (l) not to impose subtitles without the licensor's consent.

Provision	100% Commission	Co-production	Pre-purchase	Acquired material
4. Warranties (continued)				(m) to punctually make all payments due to licensor. (n) to indemnify the licensor.
5. Rights	All copyright and other rights in the programme are usually assigned to the commissioner (in certain cases, format and changed format rights are reserved to the Producer).	All rights (including copyright) in the programme are assigned to the co-producers (in agreed shares as tenants in common).	The licensee is granted a license to exercise certain specified rights in the programme in a specified territory for a specified period of time.	The licensee is granted a licence to exercise certain specified rights in the programme in a specified territory for a specified period of time.
6. Repeat Fees/residuals	The Producer must try to clear as many repeat fees and residuals from the budget as possible. In any event, the agreement specifies the minimum the Producer is expected to clear. The Producer must notify the commissioner of any such fees not cleared as delivery item.	The co-producers specify territories in respect of which rights have been bought out. Any residuals or repeat fees which are not bought out will be treated as a distribution expense.	Repeat fees and residuals are payable by the licensor (NB this is often a point decided by strength of bargaining power).	Repeat fees and residuals are payable by the licensee.
7. Delivery	The Producer agrees to deliver specified materials by an agreed date, and time is of the essence. The commissioner will have a	Each co-producer agrees to produce and deliver to each other a duplicate of specified material by a specified date and thereafter to deliver the	The licensor (at its own cost) agrees to deliver specified delivery material to the licensee by a certain date.	The licensor will supply specified delivery material to the licensee who bears the cost of duplicating that material.

Provision	100% Commission	Co-production	Pre-purchase	Acquired material
7. *Delivery* (continued)	certain period within which to approve the delivery materials and to require the Producer to make changes to the materials if required. The cost of doing so must be borne by the Producer if the delivery materials are not in accordance with the programme or technical specifications, otherwise the commissioner agrees to pay for any alterations it requires.	whole programme to an agreed laboratory and distributor.		The licensee will be deemed to have accepted the delivery material if it does not notify the licensor of any defect within a specified period.
8. *Credits/ sponsorship*	The Producer is entitled to a credit on the programme (which will include a logo and in some cases may be an animated logo). The commissioner is usually entitled to approve all credits of participants (NB approval may be deemed to be given in the case of collective bargaining agreement credits e.g. Equity).	Each co-producer is entitled to a screen and paid advertising credit. Each co-producer agrees that the third parties it contracts will receive a screen credit but not paid advertising and also the co-producer will be liable for any inadvertent failure to accord credit.	The licensee is generally entitled to receive an 'in association with' credit on all copies of the programme under the licensor's control and in major paid advertising. The licensee agrees to honour all on screen credits and (possibly) other credits notified to it.	The licensee usually has no right to a credit. The licensee agrees to honour all contractual credits notified to it.

Provision	100% Commission	Co-production	Pre-purchase	Acquired material
8. *Credits* (continued)	In some cases the commissioner will not agree to accord credits in paid advertising.			
	The commissioner agrees to honour credits approved by it and to require others to do so but will not be liable for any inadvertent failure to accord credit to any third party.			
	For Channel 3 companies credits for sponsors have to be in accordance with ITC guidelines and approved by the commissioner.			
9. *Exploitation*	All rights of exploitation are assigned to the commissioner who may license certain rights back to the Producer.	The exploitation rights may be transferred either to one of the co-producers or to both of them for various territories or to a separate distributor/agent.	Not applicable.	Not applicable.
		Co-producers share (equally) in profits.		

Provision	100% Commission	Co-production	Pre-purchase	Acquired material
10. *Insurance*	The Producer has to effect and maintain all usual production insurances (including Errors and Omissions if required by the commissioner). The commissioner must be noted as an insured party on all the policies.	Each co-producer is responsible for effecting and maintaining certain production insurances and the other co-producer is named on the policies taken out by that party.	The licensor effects and maintains Errors and Omissions insurance for a period of not less than three years from the delivery date, the licensee is named as an additional insured on such policy.	The licensee must insure all delivery material but generally has no other obligations.
11. *Editing*	The commissioner has the final right of approval over the editing of the programme. The Producer must carry out such re-editing as the commissioner may request – this will be at the Producer's cost if the programme is not in accordance with the programme and technical specification or if the programme has to be edited to comply with legal advice received by the	Each co-producer has the right to see the other party's rushes. No cutting can be made to the negative but either co-producer can edit a positive copy to comply with relevant territorial regulations of the co-producer country etc. All other editing decisions are to be made jointly.	The licensee may generally only cut or edit the programme for the purpose of making the programme suitable for broadcast by television.	Any cuts or editing can only be made by the licensee with prior consent of the licensor (sometimes including even editing for insertion of commercials).

Provision	100% Commission	Co-production	Pre-purchase	Acquired material
11. *Editing* (continued)	commissioner or if it does not comply with ITC guidelines. In all other cases the commissioner generally agrees to pay for the cost of re-editing.			
12. *Take-over/ abandonment/ termination*	The Commissioner may (but is not obliged to) take over and (if appropriate) abandon production if: (a) the Producer commits a material breach of the agreement which is either not capable of remedy or not remedied within [7] days of the Producer receiving notice of the breach. (b) the Producer becomes insolvent. (c) there is an event of *force majeure* (described below).		Either party may terminate: (a) for material breach by the other. (b) insolvency of the other. The licensee's rights must be strengthened if any payments have been made before delivery (with provision for repayment). If delivery to the licensee is delayed due to an event of *force majeure*, the licence period will be deemed to be extended by the period of delay.	The licensor may terminate if: (a) the licensee fails to make payment when due. (b) the licensee is in material breach which is either not capable of remedy or not remedied within [7] days. (c) the licensee's representations prove to have become materially incorrect or the licensee disposes or threatens to dispose of its assets.

Provision	100% Commission	Co-production	Pre-purchase	Acquired material
12. *Take-over* (continued)				(d) the licensee becomes insolvent or ceases to be in the business of broadcasting programmes.
13. *Force majeure*	If an event of *force majeure* occurs the commissioner may either suspend production, or take over and/or abandon production.			If delivery to the licensee is delayed due to an event of *force majeure*, the licence period will be deemed to be extended by the period of delay.
14. *Assignment*	The Producer may not assign its rights under the agreement without consent but the commissioner may generally assign its rights without requiring the consent of the Producer.	The co-producers may assign their rights within their respective territories.	This will depend on respective bargaining powers of either party and the nature of the deal.	The licensee may not assign or sub-license any of the rights granted to it.

Appendix F: Summary of the Broadcasting (Independent Productions) Order 1991 ('the Order')

The Broadcasting (Independent Productions) Order 1991 defines the expressions 'qualifying programmes' and 'independent productions' used in the Broadcasting Act 1990 ('the 1990 Act'). This provides for the requirements to be met by an ITV broadcaster, one of which is the stipulation that at least 25% of 'qualifying programmes' broadcast must be made up of 'independent productions' (The BBC is also under a statutory requirement to commission at least 25% of its output from independent producers).

QUALIFYING PROGRAMMES

Qualifying programmes are all programmes which fall within these categories:

- programmes made by the broadcaster or by a person commissioned by it;
- co-productions (defined as programmes made by the broadcaster with another person, or by a person commissioned by the broadcaster with some other person) where the broadcaster has contributed not less than 25% of the production cost;
- programmes which contain pictures or sound and pictures provided by someone who has not been commissioned by the broadcaster) where:

  - the pictures consist of live coverage of events;
  - they do not exceed 75% of the duration of the programme;

- the broadcaster or person commissioned by him provides the remainder of the programme.

It is clear that advertising, repeats, news coverage (which is live and usually shown at least four days a week), Open University or Open College programmes, party political broadcasts and Ministerial statements are not 'qualifying programmes'.

The fact that a programme was initially intended to be first shown commercially in cinemas does not prevent it from being a qualifying programme so long as the other conditions are met.

INDEPENDENT PRODUCTIONS

An independent production is any production which:

- fulfils the requirement of a 'qualifying programme';
- in the case of programmes falling within the first two categories in the previous section, has been made by an independent producer or where, in the case of the third category, the remainder of the programme has been made by an independent producer;
- has been made under a contract which contains any contractual obligations between a broadcaster and a producer which concern, directly or indirectly, the **making** of programmes (but not their exploitation) and which are capable of remaining in force for longer than five years, states that either party has the right to terminate those obligations at intervals of not more than five years (but without prejudice to any rights relating to obligations that have not been discharged at the date of termination);
- has not been made subject to the broadcaster's requirement that the producer uses the 'production facilities' (i.e. premises, equipment or employees) of that broadcaster or does **not** use the production facilities of some other broadcaster.

INDEPENDENT PRODUCER

A producer is the person 'by whom the arrangements necessary for the making of the programme are made'. 'Independent producer' means a producer:

- who is not an employee (whether or not on temporary leave of absence) of a broadcaster;
- who does not have a shareholding (either in number of shares or in terms of voting power) greater than 15% in a broadcaster;

- which is not a company in which a broadcaster has a shareholding greater than 15%.

References to 'broadcasters' or 'producers' will include persons 'connected with' them. A person will be 'connected with' a broadcaster or producer if he or it controls the broadcaster/producer or is an 'associate' of the broadcaster/producer (or even an associate of a person who controls the broadcaster/producer), or a body which is controlled by the broadcaster/producer or by an associate of the broadcaster/producer.

'Associate' is defined as follows – in relation to a company, it means a director of that company, or a company in the same group; in relation to an individual it means his spouse or relatives (by blood or marriage); a company of which he is a director; the trustee of any trust he has set up; his partners in a partnership and the partner's spouse and relatives; or anyone with whom he is acting in concert to secure control of a company/ association/enterprise or any assets.

'Control' is also defined, and essentially 'control' is treated as being possessed by a person who or which owns more than 50% of a company or even if he/it does not, can bring about the performance of his wishes by that company.

Appendix G: Inducement letter

From: CONTRIBUTOR

To: PRODUCER

Dated   19

Dear Sirs

I refer to the agreement ('the Agreement') into which you are about to enter with [   ] LIMITED ('the Lender') for the assignment and provision by the Lender of certain rights and services otherwise vesting in me as [an actor in]/[the Director/Producer of]/[a writer of the screenplay(s) for] the [film/television series/programme] ('the Film/the Series/the Programme') to be produced by you and provisionally entitled '   ', a copy of which has been supplied to and read by me.

In order to induce you to enter into the Agreement I hereby:

1   Irrevocably consent and agree to the execution and delivery of the Agreement by the Lender and to the assignment and provision by the Lender of all rights and services aforesaid under the Agreement

2   Warrant that there is subsisting and will throughout the relevant period subsist an agreement between me and the Lender entitling the Lender to assign such rights and to provide such services for all purposes necessary to enable you to produce and deliver the [Film/Series/Programme] without let or hindrance

3   Guarantee and warrant to you as a principal and not merely as a surety the truth and binding agreement of the Lender of and to all matters as to which any agreement representation or warranty on the part of the Lender is contained in the terms of the Agreement

4   Subject to all the terms and conditions of the Agreement hereby agree to render all of the services therein required of me and to be bound by and duly to perform and observe each and all of the terms

and conditions of the Agreement requiring performance or compliance on my part

5   Agree that if the Lender should be dissolved or should otherwise cease to exist or for any reason whatsoever should fail be unable neglect or refuse duly to perform and observe each and all of the terms and conditions of the Agreement requiring performance and compliance on the part of the Lender I shall at your sole discretion be deemed substituted for the Lender as a party to the Agreement in place and stead of the Lender provided that in the event that you exercise such discretion you will from the date of such exercise make payment to me personally of all moneys that would otherwise be payable to the Lender under the terms of the Agreement and in such event I shall (save where the Lender has been dissolved or has otherwise ceased to exist) procure that the Lender shall acknowledge that any such payments shall discharge you from all liability to make further payments to the Lender under the Agreement

6   Agree that in the event of a breach or threatened breach of the Agreement by the Lender or by myself of my obligations hereunder you shall be entitled to legal and equitable relief by way of injunction or otherwise against the Lender and/or myself at your discretion in any event without the necessity of first resorting to or exhausting any rights or remedies which you may have against the Lender and/or myself [and in this connection I hereby submit to the non-exclusive jurisdiction of the English Courts]

7   Agree to indemnify you fully from and against any breach by the Lender of any of its obligations representations warranties and undertakings under the Agreement or by myself under the terms of this letter

8   As beneficial owner assign to you to the extent of my interest therein if any the entire copyright in the products of my services pursuant to the Agreement (and where such services are as yet unperformed as at the date of this agreement by way of present assignment of future copyright) and hereunder and acknowledge that all rights whatsoever throughout the world in the [Film/Series/Programme] and in all photographs and sound recordings taken and made pursuant to the Agreement including all rights of copyright therein and in any written or other material contributed by the Lender or myself shall belong absolutely to you throughout all periods for which such rights may be conferred or created by the law in force in any part of the world and that subject as provided in the Agreement you may make or authorize the use of the same and may exploit the same in any manner and in this connection (recognizing the requirements of film and television production) I hereby waive the benefits of any provision of law known as the 'droit moral' or any similar law in any

territory throughout the world whether now or hereafter brought into force and hereby agree not to institute, support, maintain or permit any action or proceedings on the ground that any use of the products of my services pursuant to the Agreement in any way constitutes an infringement of any 'droit morale' or similar rights or is in any way a defamation or mutilation of the products of my services pursuant to the Agreement or contains unauthorized variations, alterations, adaptations, modifications, changes or translations

9   Agree:

(a) to look solely to the Lender for all compensation for my services to be rendered under the Agreement and not in any event to look to you for such compensation or any part thereof save as provided in paragraph 5

(b) that if you in your sole discretion elect or give notice to withhold any part of the remuneration payable pursuant to the Agreement by virtue of any ruling or determination of the Inland Revenue, neither I nor the Lender shall challenge the same, but shall cause the Lender to provide to you forthwith all such documentation and assistance as you may properly request in order to comply properly with any such ruling or determination

(c) that if at any time during the term of the Agreement or after the expiry thereof you shall be obliged to make payment of any additional sum to any statutory authority in connection with any payments made to the Lender thereunder, I shall repay the same to you forthwith upon request

10   Undertake that no breach by the Lender of any of its obligations to me shall constitute or be deemed to constitute a breach by you under the Agreement and accordingly notwithstanding such breach I undertake to continue to fulfil all my obligations hereunder if and so long as you fulfil your obligations to the Lender

11   Warrant that I am a Director of the Lender and that such company is incorporated in and validly existing under the laws of [England] and that throughout the term of the Agreement I will not without your consent voluntarily transfer charge or dispose of any interest in the Lender or resign any office therewith or take any other steps which might diminish my ability to procure the Lender to observe and perform all terms of the Agreement

Yours faithfully

CONTRIBUTOR

Appendix H: Release form

FROM: [PRODUCER]
          [Address]

TO: [PARTICIPANT]
          [Address]

                               DATED   199

Dear [Participant]

'   ' ('the [Film/Programme]')

We are producing the [Film/Programme]. This letter when signed by you shall constitute the terms of your participation in the [Film/Programme], as follows:

1   In consideration of the fee payable to you as set out in paragraph 2 below you hereby irrevocably:

   (a) agree and consent to participate in the [Film/Programme];

   (b) agree and consent to the filming and recording of you and your voice and performance and that such film and recording may be incorporated in the [Film/Programme] in whole or in part at our discretion (but you acknowledge that we are under no obligation to use such film and recording);

   (c) consent to the exploitation of the [Film/Programme] or any part(s) of the [Film/Programme] (including your performance) by all means and in all media and formats whether now or hereafter invented throughout the world in perpetuity;

   (d) consent to the use and reproduction of your performance and film and recordings of your performance or any part thereof by all means and in all media throughout the world in perpetuity for the purposes of advertising, publicity and otherwise exploiting the [Film/Programme];

   (e) waive and release us from any claim, action or demand arising out of or in connection with the [Film/Programme].

2   In consideration of your participation in the [Film/Programme] and your agreements and consents, we shall pay you the total sum of £   payable as to [half] on signature (receipt of which you acknowledge) and as to the balance on completion of the filming and recording of your participation.

3   We shall be entitled to assign or license the whole or any part of the benefit of this letter to any third party.

4   This letter shall be governed by and construed in accordance with English Law.

Please signify your acceptance of the foregoing by signing and returning to us the attached duplicate of this letter.

Yours sincerely

. . . .
for and on behalf of
[PRODUCER]

Agreed and Accepted

. . . .

[PRINT NAME OF PARTICIPANT]

Appendix I: Definition of distribution expenses

'Distribution Expenses' means and includes all sums directly incurred expended or suffered by the Distributor in connection with the exploitation of the [Film] in respect of:

(a) all prints and all other laboratory charges and other costs for dubbing titling sub-titling and editorial work and the cost of despatching and examining prints
(b) censorship fees and costs of editing to meet censorship requirements trade shows films and television festival attendances premieres and screening charges
(c) freight and carriage customs duties and charges in connection with the importation of the Film into any country or countries of the Territory including but not limited to dubbing and similar taxes and any and all costs incurred in the physical delivery of the Film or related material including (but not limited to) permits necessary to secure the entry of the Film into any part of the Territory
(d) insurance of negative duplicating material and prints and all other physical properties of the Film
(e) advertising marketing and publicity
(f) registration of the Film
(g) copyright registration and protection
(h) checking percentage film engagements
(i) commission charged by the Distributor's Licensees
(j) repeat fees, residuals or any other use fee which may become payable to any third party as a result of the exploitation of the Film
(k) collecting or suing for sums due from the Distributor's Licensees
(l) reasonable legal fees and expenses incurred by the Distributor in connection with the Film

(m) all taxes however denominated imposed or levied against the Distributor relating to the Film or the Film or the rights granted to the Distributor

(n) any other expense which is reasonably incurred and is fairly to be regarded as a direct distribution expense of the Film.

Index